Walter W. Wymer, Jr.
Sridhar Samu
Editors

WITHDRAWN

Nonprofit and Business Sector Collaboration: Social Enterprises, Cause-Related Marketing, Sponsorships, and Other Corporate-Nonprofit Dealings

Nonprofit and Business Sector Collaboration: Social Enterprises, Cause-Related Marketing, Sponsorships, and Other Corporate-Nonprofit Dealings has been co-published simultaneously as *Journal of Nonprofit & Public Sector Marketing*, Volume 11, Number 1 2003.

Pre-publication
REVIEWS,
COMMENTARIES,
EVALUATIONS . . .

BEST BUSINESS BOOKS

Best Business Books
An Imprint of The Haworth Press, Inc.

Nonprofit and Business Sector Collaboration: Social Enterprises, Cause-Related Marketing, Sponsorships, and Other Corporate-Nonprofit Dealings

Nonprofit and Business Sector Collaboration: Social Enterprises, Cause-Related Marketing, Sponsorships, and Other Corporate-Nonprofit Dealings has been co-published simultaneously as *Journal of Nonprofit & Public Sector Marketing*, Volume 11, Number 1 2003.

The *Journal of Nonprofit & Public Sector Marketing* Monographic "Separates"

Below is a list of " separates," which in serials librarianship means a special issue simultaneously published as a special journal issue or double-issue *and* as a "separate" hardbound monograph. (This is a format which we also call a "DocuSerial.")

"Separates" are published because specialized libraries or professionals may wish to purchase a specific thematic issue by itself in a format which can be separately cataloged and shelved, as opposed to purchasing the journal on an on-going basis. Faculty members may also more easily consider a "separate" for classroom adoption.

"Separates" are carefully classified separately with the major book jobbers so that the journal tie-in can be noted on new book order slips to avoid duplicate purchasing.

You may wish to visit Haworth's Website at . . .

http://www.HaworthPress.com

. . . to search our online catalog for complete tables of contents of these separates and related publications.

You may also call 1-800-HAWORTH (outside US/Canada: 607-722-5857), or Fax 1-800-895-0582 (outside US/Canada: 607-771-0012), or e-mail at:

getinfo@haworthpressinc.com

Nonprofit and Business Sector Collaboration: Social Enterprises, Cause-Related Marketing, Sponsorships, and Other Corporate-Nonprofit Dealings, edited by Walter W. Wymer, Jr., DBA and Sridhar Samu, PhD (Vol. 11, No. 1, 2003). *"Well organized, interesting, and highly readable . . . The most expert and comprehensive analysis of the subject to have appeared to date . . ." (Roger Bennett, PhD, Professor of Marketing, London Metropolitan University)*

Social Marketing, edited by Michael T. Ewing, PhD (Vol. 9, No. 4, 2001). *"STIMULATING. . . . EXTREMELY TIMELY . . . With contributions from eminent academics from diverse parts of the world, this book covers a wide range of ideas, research methods, and philosophical concepts." (Barry Howcroft, ACIB, MSc, BA, Professor of Retail Banking, Banking Centre, Loughborough University, United Kingdom)*

Marketing Communications for Local Nonprofit Organizations: Targets and Tools, edited by Donald R. Self, DBA, Walter W. Wymer, Jr., DBA, and Teri Kline Henley, MBA (Vol. 9, No. 1/2, 2001). *"Excellent . . . a text that is of great relevance to practitioners and academics alike. The authors have successfully produced a comprehensive review of the marketing needs of nonprofit professionals/organizations and offer relevant sets of tools." (Ram Cnaan, PhD, Associate Professor, School of Social Work, University of Pennsylvania, Philadelphia)*

Volunteerism Marketing: New Vistas for Nonprofit and Public Sector Management, edited by Donald R. Self, DBA, and Walter W. Wymer, Jr., DBA (Vol. 6, No. 2/3, 1999). *"Offers the volunteer coordinator in these organizations the information needed to better understand where, and how, to effectively recruit and mobilize these increasingly important 'customers'." (Michael J. Tullier, East Alabama Community Blood Bank, LifeSouth Community Blood Centers)*

Marketing University Outreach Programs, edited by Ralph S. Foster, Jr., BS, William I. Sauser, Jr., PhD, and Donald R. Self, DBA (Vol. 2, No. 2/3, 1995). *"Should be required reading . . . The authors not only know marketing but they also reflect a deep understanding of outreach and its place in the 21st century university." (James C. Vortruba, Vice Provost for University Outreach, Michigan State University)*

Public Mental Health Marketing: Developing a Consumer Attitude, edited by Donald R. Self, DBA (Vol. 1, No. 2/3, 1993). *"Provides a balance of theoretical and practical information on marketing local, state, and national mental health agencies." (Reference and Research Book News)*

Nonprofit and Business Sector Collaboration: Social Enterprises, Cause-Related Marketing, Sponsorships, and Other Corporate-Nonprofit Dealings

Walter W. Wymer, Jr., DBA
Sridhar Samu, PhD
Editors

Nonprofit and Business Sector Collaboration: Social Enterprises, Cause-Related Marketing, Sponsorships, and Other Corporate-Nonprofit Dealings has been co-published simultaneously as *Journal of Nonprofit & Public Sector Marketing*, Volume 11, Number 1 2003.

Best Business Books
An Imprint of
The Haworth Press, Inc.
New York • London • Oxford

Published by

Best Business Books®, 10 Alice Street, Binghamton, NY 13904-1580 USA

Best Business Books® is an imprint of The Haworth Press, Inc., 10 Alice Street, Binghamton, NY 13904-1580 USA.

Nonprofit and Business Sector Collaboration: Social Enterprises, Cause-Related Marketing, Sponsorships, and Other Corporate-Nonprofit Dealings has been co-published simultaneously as *Journal of Nonprofit & Public Sector Marketing*, Volume 11, Number 1 2003.

Cover design by Lora Wiggins

Library of Congress Cataloging-in-Publication Data

Nonprofit and business sector collaboration: social enterprises, cause-related marketing, sponsorships, and other corporate-nonprofit dealings / Walter W. Wymer, Jr., Sridhar Samu, editors.
        p. cm.
"Co-published simultaneously as Journal of nonprofit & public sector marketing, volume 11, number 1, 2003."
Includes bibliographical references and index.
        ISBN 0-7890-1992-2 (hard : alk. paper) – ISBN 0-7890-1993-0 (pbk :
alk. paper)
1. Social marketing. 2. Nonprofit organizations–Marketing. 3. Corporate sponsorship. 4. Social responsibility of business. 5. Partnership. I. Wymer, Walter W. II. Samu, Sridhar. III. Journal of nonprofit & public sector marketing.

HF5414 .N66 2003
658.8–dc21

2002010556

Indexing, Abstracting & Website/Internet Coverage

This section provides you with a list of major indexing & abstracting services. That is to say, each service began covering this periodical during the year noted in the right column. Most Websites which are listed below have indicated that they will either post, disseminate, compile, archive, cite or alert their own Website users with research-based content from this work. (This list is as current as the copyright date of this publication.)

(continued)

Special Bibliographic Notes related to special journal issues (separates) and indexing/abstracting:

- indexing/abstracting services in this list will also cover material in any "separate" that is co-published simultaneously with Haworth's special thematic journal issue or DocuSerial. Indexing/abstracting usually covers material at the article/chapter level.
- monographic co-editions are intended for either non-subscribers or libraries which intend to purchase a second copy for their circulating collections.
- monographic co-editions are reported to all jobbers/wholesalers/approval plans. The source journal is listed as the "series" to assist the prevention of duplicate purchasing in the same manner utilized for books-in-series.
- to facilitate user/access services all indexing/abstracting services are encouraged to utilize the co-indexing entry note indicated at the bottom of the first page of each article/chapter/contribution.
- this is intended to assist a library user of any reference tool (whether print, electronic, online, or CD-ROM) to locate the monographic version if the library has purchased this version but not a subscription to the source journal.
- individual articles/chapters in any Haworth publication are also available through the Haworth Document Delivery Service (HDDS).

Nonprofit and Business Sector Collaboration: Social Enterprises, Cause-Related Marketing, Sponsorships, and Other Corporate-Nonprofit Dealings

CONTENTS

ABOUT THE EDITORS

Walter W. Wymer, Jr., DBA, is Associate Professor of Marketing at Christopher Newport University in Newport News, Virginia. Dr. Wymer's research has focused on marketing in nonprofit organizations. His work has been published in several academic journals and presented at numerous academic conferences. Dr. Wymer is the editor of the *Journal of Nonprofit & Public Sector Marketing*. He also serves on the editorial boards of the *International Journal of Nonprofit & Voluntary Sector Marketing, Health Marketing Quarterly*, and the *Journal of Ministry Marketing & Management*.

Dr. Sridhar Samu, Guest Editor, is Assistant Professor of Marketing in the Faculty of Business at Memorial University of Newfoundland, St. John's, Canada. Dr. Samu has published in the *Journal of Marketing*, the *International Journal of Purchasing & Materials Management*, and the *Journal of Nonprofit & Public Sector Marketing*. He has presented papers at a number of international conferences. Dr. Samu's current research interests involve brand management and nonprofit-business collaboration and advertising.

Introduction

One topic that uniquely bridges the divide between nonprofit marketing and marketing activities of the business sector is cause-related marketing and other collaborative associations between businesses and nonprofit organizations. Nonprofits are turning to the business sector to attract resources and publicity. As the government sector continues to reduce support for the nonprofit sector, nonprofits increasingly look toward the corporate world for help. Businesses look for nonprofit organizations which they can support while improving their images and identifying with their target markets. The relationship between the business and nonprofit sectors is evolving from one of beneficence, as in traditional corporate philanthropy, to one of market exchange in which partners mutually benefit from their collaborative relationship.

Business involvement with nonprofits has increased greatly during the prior decade and is expected to continue to grow. This volume brings together important work on this topic. Conceptual and empirical articles from leading scholars in this field provide a vital perspective that will enhance our current knowledge of the field and provide direction for future research.

Walter W. Wymer, Jr.
Sridhar Samu

Walter W. Wymer, Jr., DBA, is Associate Professor of Marketing, Christopher Newport University, Management and Marketing Department, Newport News, VA 23606 (E-mail: wwymer@cnu.edu).

Sridhar Samu, PhD, is Assistant Professor of Marketing, Asper School of Business, University of Manitoba, 181 Freedman Crescent, Winnipeg MB R3T 5V4, Canada (E-mail: ssamu@ms.umanitoba.ca).

[Haworth co-indexing entry note]: "Introduction." Co-published simultaneously in *Journal of Nonprofit & Public Sector Marketing* (Best Business Books, an imprint of The Haworth Press, Inc.) Vol. 11, No. 1, 2003, p. 1; and: *Nonprofit and Business Sector Collaboration: Social Enterprises, Cause-Related Marketing, Sponsorships, and Other Corporate-Nonprofit Dealings* (ed: Walter W. Wymer, Jr. and Sridhar Samu) Best Business Books, an imprint of The Haworth Press, Inc., 2003, p. 1. Single or multiple copies of this article are available for a fee from The Haworth Document Delivery Service [1-800-HAWORTH, 9:00 a.m. - 5:00 p.m. (EST). E-mail address: getinfo@haworthpressinc.com].

Dimensions of Business and Nonprofit Collaborative Relationships

Walter W. Wymer, Jr.
Sridhar Samu

SUMMARY. Collaborative relationships between businesses and nonprofits have grown tremendously in the last few years. These cross-sector alliances are different from within-sector alliances (business-business alliances) which has been examined in prior research, and include corporate philanthropy, corporate foundations, licensing agreements, sponsorships, transaction based promotions, joint issue promotions, and joint ventures. This paper discusses the growth, size, and scope of various business and nonprofit collaborative relationships and develops a typology of these relationships. Motivations for business-nonprofit collaborations and expected outcomes are presented as well as fruitful topics for further investigation. *[Article copies available for a fee from The Haworth Document Delivery Service: 1-800-HAWORTH. E-mail address: <getinfo@ haworthpressinc.com> Website: <http://www.HaworthPress. com> © 2003 by The Haworth Press, Inc. All rights reserved.]*

Walter W. Wymer, Jr., DBA, is Associate Professor of Marketing, Christopher Newport University, Management and Marketing Department, Newport News, VA 23606 (E-mail: wwymer@cnu.edu).

Sridhar Samu, PhD, is Assistant Professor of Marketing, Asper School of Business, University of Manitoba, 181 Freedman Crescent, Winnipeg MB R3T 5V4, Canada (E-mail: ssamu@ms.umanitoba.ca).

[Haworth co-indexing entry note]: "Dimensions of Business and Nonprofit Collaborative Relationships." Wymer, Walter W., Jr., and Sridhar Samu. Co-published simultaneously in *Journal of Nonprofit & Public Sector Marketing* (Best Business Books, an imprint of The Haworth Press, Inc.) Vol. 11, No. 1, 2003, pp. 3-22; and: *Nonprofit and Business Sector Collaboration: Social Enterprises, Cause-Related Marketing, Sponsorships, and Other Corporate-Nonprofit Dealings* (ed: Walter W. Wymer, Jr. and Sridhar Samu) Best Business Books, an imprint of The Haworth Press, Inc., 2003, pp. 3-22. Single or multiple copies of this article are available for a fee from The Haworth Document Delivery Service [1-800-HAWORTH, 9:00 a.m. - 5:00 p.m. (EST). E-mail address: getinfo@haworthpressinc.com].

KEYWORDS. Cross-sector alliances, nonprofit, social alliances, cause related marketing, sponsorship, philanthropy, social enterprise

Collaborative relationships between businesses and nonprofits have grown in recent years as businesses have shown a great deal of interest in working with organizations from the nonprofit sector (Berlinger 1997). In general, businesses can develop collaborative relationships with organizations in the same sector (within-sector alliances) or with organizations in different sectors (cross-sector alliances). While within sector relationships have received growing research attention (Das and Teng 1999), marketing researchers have given substantially less attention to cross-sector relationships. This is unfortunate for two reasons. First, cross-sector relationships, particularly between businesses and nonprofit organizations, are increasing in number (Berger, Cunningham, and Drumwright 1999). Second, the dynamics of cross-sector relationships differ from those of within-sector ones. For example, nonprofit organizations have different objectives, cultures, and operating styles compared to businesses (Sagawa and Segal 2000).

Prior research has focused on specific types of cross sector relationships without identifying common themes and connections between the various types of relationships (Andreasen 1996, Drumwright 1996, Milne, Iyer, and Gooding-Williams 1996, Varadarajan and Menon 1988). There have been calls for developing a comprehensive model to examine cross-sector relationships and this paper responds by presenting a typology of business-nonprofit organization relationships which complements prior research.

The utility of generalizing prior research on business-to-business relationships to business-nonprofit relationships is questionable. Previous research on business-to-business relationships has portrayed alliance formation as being motivated by the need to develop new markets, products, or technologies (Cunningham and Varadarajan 1995, Webster 1992). Business-to-business relationships tend to be long-term in their focus, needing trust and commitment to succeed (Das and Teng 1999, Dwyer, Schurr, and Oh 1987, Morgan and Hunt 1994), with organizational compatibility and equal power being crucial to their success (Bucklin and Sengupta 1993). Conversely, business-nonprofit relationships consist of fundamentally different types of organizations with different motivations (Andreasen 1996). The nonprofit organization could be interested in reaching a broader market and increasing awareness, while the business could be more interested in either a promotion/public relations objective or in being socially responsible. While some business and nonprofit relationships may share characteristics of business-to-business relationships, there are sufficient differences to warrant a closer examination of business-nonprofit relationships (Himmelstein 1997).

A second purpose of this article is to develop a framework to explain the factors influencing the formation and outcomes of business-nonprofit relationships identified in the typology. The article proposes that partner motives and expectations for establishing relationships will influence the type of alliance created and that the type of relationship will influence the outcomes experienced by alliance partners.

A TYPOLOGY OF BUSINESS-NONPROFIT RELATIONSHIPS

Corporate Philanthropy

Some businesses make monetary or nonmonetary (i.e., in kind) contributions to nonprofit organizations on an episodic, informal basis. Other companies allocate funds to a corporate philanthropy budget, have a manager oversee the disbursement of funds, and earmark these funds as charitable contributions for tax deductions. Corporate philanthropy also includes allowing employees to volunteer for local nonprofit organizations while the volunteers receive compensation from their companies (this is contrasted with those companies who encourage employees to volunteer without compensation). Examples of corporate philanthropy are provided in Table 1.

In corporate philanthropy the business's interest in the relationship is on supporting the nonprofit organization and its mission (see Table 2). Since the business is disbursing funds where it wishes, it maintains a good measure of power over the collaborative relationship. Compared to other types of business-nonprofit relationships, corporate philanthropy requires the least commitment in terms of business resources and managerial involvement. In addition to supporting a worthy cause, a business may also wish to help its target markets and its employees identify with it by supporting causes they care about. The primary benefit to the participating business is favorable publicity, enhanced public goodwill, and greater public awareness of the business or its brand. Any subsequent increase in sales would be an indirect effect of the relationship, because the link between the product and the sale is mediated by

TABLE 1. Examples of Business-Nonprofit Alliances

Alliance Type	Business Partner	Nonprofit Partner	Description
Corp Philanthropy	Walt Disney Co.	Habitat for Humanity	Walt Disney donated $70,000 for construction of a townhouse in Burbank, California.
Corp Philanthropy	Mentadent	Imus Ranch	Mentadent donated $250,000 to Imus Ranch (which provides recreational experiences for children with cancer).
Corp Foundation	Ford Foundation	Consortium for North American Higher Education Collaboration	The Ford Foundation, among others, provides CONAHEC with substantial funding.
Corp Foundation	Delta Air Lines Foundation	Atlanta Symphony Orchestra	In 1998, donated $500,000 to the symphony.
Licensing Agreement	SmithKline Beecham	American Cancer Society	SmithKline uses American Cancer Society's logo to help promote its nicotine patch.
Licensing Agreement	Florida Dept of Citrus	American Cancer Society	American Cancer Society's logo used to promote the role of orange products in preventing cancer.
Licensing Agreement	MBNA America	National Education Association (NEA)	Affinity card (mastercard) targeted at NEA members. Percentage of sales goes to NEA.
Sponsorship	Honda Motor Company, Acura, Saucony, Tylenol, Gas Company, and Adhor Farms	13th Annual Los Angeles Marathon	This event attracted 40,000 participants and 1 million spectators. Sponsors helped to promote the event. For example, Adohr Farms printed event ads on millions of milk cartons.
Sponsorship	Insight.com, Blue Cross Blue Shield of Arizona, MicroAge	Fiesta Bowl	Fiesta Bowl National Band Championship, MicroAge Fiesta Bowl Parade, Insight.com Tucson Fiesta Bowl Football Classic
Transaction-Based Promotion	Nabisco	American Zoo Aquarium Association	(1995) Nabisco produced a special edition of its Barnum's Animal Crackers. Five cents of each box, up to $100,000.
Transaction-Based Promotion	SC Johnson Wax	15th Annual Night Out Against Crime	In 1998, agreed to pledge up to $200,000 based on consumers coupon redemptions for various products (Glade, Ziplock, Shout).

Alliance Type	Business Partner	Nonprofit Partner	Description
Transaction-Based Promotion	Borders Bookstores	National Literacy Nonprofit Organization, Reading Is Fundamental (RIF), and local libraries	At the checkout, Borders asks each customers to donate $1. Each quarter, Border matches customer donations and gives money to target nonprofits.
Joint Issue Promotion	Wunderman Cato Johnson, Young & Rubicam, Globix, Grey Entertainment, and others	Partnership for a Drug Free America	Partnership for a Drug Free America, reaching the American population with strong anti-drug, drug education, and prevention messages.
Joint Issue Promotion	Kellogg	America's Promise—The Alliance for Youth	Kellogg advertised America's Promise on 30 million boxes of its Corn Flakes and Rice Krispies cereal products.
Joint Venture	Unilever	World Wildlife Fund	Unilever, a large British-Dutch food corporation which supplies 20 percent of the frozen fish market in the U.S. and Europe, partnered with the World Wildlife Fund (WWF) to develop a certification system that would identify fish products being harvested on a sustainable basis.
Joint Venture	LightOS Internet Guide, and others	Trust Assure	The TrustAssure Internet Business Reliance Bureau © program certifies participating web site compliance with the specified privacy, security, and reliability principles stipulated within the organization's code of ethics.

the effects of customer recognition of the business-nonprofit relationship.

A primary motivation for recipient nonprofit organizations is the additional funding (see Table 3). In some instances, announcing large funding from major corporations is prestigious, publicly demonstrating the worthiness of one's cause, and may improve the ability of the nonprofit to raise funds from other sources in the future.

All the business-nonprofit relationships described in this article have a degree of risk associated with them. A chief risk is that a partner will behave in a scandalous manner, sullying (by association) the reputation/image of the innocent partner(s). Another potential risk for the business partner is that its philanthropy may be resented by employees

TABLE 2. Risks of Nonprofit and Business Relationships

Business Partner Perspective

Type	Management	Motivations[1]	Commitment	Risks[2]
Corporate Philanthropy	Philanthropy	1, 3, 2, 4	Lowest	a, c
Corporate Foundation	Separate Management Team	1, 3, 2, 4		a
Licensing Agreements	Marketing	5, 2, 3, 1		a, b
Sponsorships	Marketing Public Relations	2, 3, 2, 1, 5		a, b
Transaction-Based Promotions	Marketing Public Relations	2, 5, 1, 3, 4		a, b
Joint Issue Promotion	Marketing Public Relations	1, 2, 3, 4		a, b
Joint Ventures	Separate Management Team	3, 2, 1, 4	Highest	a, b

[1]Motivations: (1) supporting cause, (2) target market relations, (3) public relations, (4) human resource enhancement, (5) sales.
[2]Risks: (a) corporate/brand reputation/image, (b) sales/market share, and (c) shareholder/employee resentment.

or shareholders who may resent corporate giving during periods of declining valuation of the corporation's stock. Similarly, employees may also resent corporate giving during periods of declining business cycles which result in pay freezes or layoffs (Himmelstein 1997).

For nonprofit partners, the potential risk of collaborating with businesses may be even greater than for the business partner. For example, the ability of the nonprofit to raise funds from private donors (usually a nonprofit's major source of funding) may be greatly reduced as a result of damage to its reputation, threatening the nonprofit's survival. Another potential risk faced by the nonprofit is an unexpected withdrawal or reduction of funding from its corporate partner (Himmelstein 1997).

Corporate Foundations

The corporate foundation is a nonprofit entity created by a company to manage its philanthropy objectives.[1] As in corporate philanthropy, this type of corporate involvement with the nonprofit sector emphasizes

TABLE 3. Risks of Nonprofit and Business Relationships

Nonprofit Partner Perspective

Type	Motivations[1]	Risk Level	Risks[2]
Corporate Philanthropy	1, 3	Lowest	a, c
Corporate Foundation	1, 3		a, c
Licensing Agreements	1, 3		a, b, c
Sponsorships	1, 3		a, b, c
Transaction-Based Promotions	1, 3		a, b, c
Joint Issue Promotion	4, 2, 1, 3		a, c
Joint Ventures	4, 2, 1, 3	Highest	a, b, c

[1]Motivations: (1) funding, (2) other business resources, (3) publicity, (4) operational support.
[2]Risks: (a) reputation/image damage, (b) reduced funding, (c) withdrawal of corporate support.

the nonprofit's mission/cause. The business partner maintains control through its surrogate, the foundation. The foundation is responsible to trustees who are usually corporate officers (Himmelstein 1997). In most cases, the foundation establishes a directive which specifies the types of causes the foundation is seeking to fund. Potential grantees submit competitive grant proposals to the foundation, which awards grants based on the merits of the proposals and available funds.

While supporting worthy causes is the primary motivation of corporate foundations, they may also wish their good works to be noticed by their target markets and their employees. While the risks and motivations of foundations are similar to those of corporate philanthropic programs (see Tables 2 and 3), the creation of a foundation reduces the risk of shareholder and employee resentment during periods of business down-cycles. A corporate foundation, compared to corporate philanthropy, allows a company to put away more money than it donates in good times and donate more than it puts aside in bad times. It is possible for a foundation to establish an endowment that serves as a disbursement regulator in which companies can regulate their giving to the foundation to correlate with fluctuations in business cycles. This would reduce stockholder/employee resentment of corporate giving during periods when stockholders' stock values were not increasing and employees were experiencing austerity measures.

For nonprofits, funding and publicity would be key motivations while they would run the risks of reputation/image damage and possible withdrawal of corporate support. This is very similar to the motivations and risks associated with corporate philanthropy and illustrates the similarities between the two types of business organizations.

Licensing Agreements

In this type of business-nonprofit relationship, nonprofit organizations allow corporations to use their names and logos in return for a flat fee and/or a royalty (The Alliance Analyst 1996). Businesses look for nonprofit organizations with strong, favorable images (e.g., names, brands) in the minds of important market segments (Sexton 1998).

A typical company is primarily interested in generating sales from its licensing agreements with nonprofits (see Table 2). Frequently, a partnering business is seeking increases in sales in addition to the favorable publicity common in business-nonprofit relationships. Therefore, the business's focus is primarily on itself, secondarily on the nonprofit or its cause. It is unlikely, however, that a business would enter into a relationship with a nonprofit that it is opposed to, leading to the conclusion that the business views supporting the nonprofit favorably.

A business will typically have a great deal of operational control in this type of relationship. The business must perform the marketing activities necessary to generate sales from the licensing agreement. A nonprofit organization's control is generally limited to how its name is presented (see Table 1 for examples).

Affinity cards are an example of a licensing agreement. They generally take the form of a major credit card printed with the identity of an institution of particular interest to a target group. For example, a university would enter into an agreement with a credit card company to produce credit cards printed with the university's image. The university would receive a nominal percentage of sales charged with the card (e.g., 1%). The university would provide the credit card issuer with a list of alumni or students and endorse the association. Then the card issuer would solicit customers using direct marketing tactics.

Benefits to participating organizations are publicity, public relations, customer/employee goodwill, and increased sales. However, businesses are using the nonprofit's favorable image to attract new customers by leveraging the loyalty that exists within the nonprofit's sphere of influence. Businesses place more emphasis on the marketing aspects of this nonprofit-business relationship. Nonprofits are using the licensing agreement as a revenue source and benefit in terms of increased funding, greater publicity, and recognition.

The risks for nonprofits (see Table 3) in licensing agreements are possible damage to reputation and image, reduced funding, and withdrawal of corporate support. The licensing partnership does expose the nonprofit to a higher level of risk as such an agreement implies that the nonprofit *endorses* the product, in addition to benefitting from sales. When a product has been linked to a nonprofit, the public believes the nonprofit has evaluated the product (Sagawa and Segal 2000). If the product happens to be of poor quality, or even harmful to consumers, the nonprofit's reputation can be especially tarnished.

For the business partner, a licensing agreement, in addition to the expenses associated with the formation of the agreement, represents a possible investment in merchandise, and marketing, distribution and other expenses associated with promoting the licensed items. A nonprofit scandal may lead to a loss of sales in addition to harm to the company's reputation.

Sponsorships

In licensing agreements, a business pays a nonprofit for using the nonprofit's images in their advertisements, packaging, and so forth. In sponsorships, the business pays the nonprofit a sponsorship fee for using the business's brand in the nonprofit's advertisements or other external communications. There are two components of sponsorships: (1) the sponsor pays the sponsee a fee for the right to associate itself with the activity sponsored, and (2) the marketing of the association by the sponsor. Both activities are necessary if the sponsorship is to be a meaningful investment (Cornwell and Maignan 1998, p. 11).

A business participating in sponsorships is primarily interested in promoting its brand or company name, although sponsors also want to fund/promote the event (see Table 2). Nonprofits are concerned about protecting their favorable public images and will generally have preponderance of control about how the sponsors advertise their association. Sponsors, however, have paid for the right to associate their name with the event and will exercise some power in the alliance as well (examples are provided in Table 1).

There are several types of business-nonprofit sponsorships. Abratt, Clayton, and Pitt (1987) present eight types of sponsorships. There are sports sponsorships (five types of sports sponsorships), book sponsorships, exhibitions, education sponsorships, expeditions, cultural activities, local events, and documentary films.

Sponsorships between businesses and nonprofits have experienced a sharp rise in corporate marketing budgets (Smith 1994). Marketing dollars allocated to sponsorships in the U.S. increased from $2.1 billion in 1989 to $4.25 billion in 1995. This amount just covers the amount paid for sponsorship rights while the total sponsorship expenditures would be much higher as they would include the promotion of such sponsorships.

While businesses are motivated primarily by the opportunities to associate name/brand before its target markets and the public in a favorable manner, nonprofits are motivated to enter into sponsorship agreements to generate funding. The desired funding may be generated to support the event (e.g., Special Olympics), or the sponsored event may be a fund raiser for the nonprofit (e.g., Race for a Cure).

The partners' face certain risks (see Tables 2 and 3). Business partners risk being associated with negative publicity generated by the nonprofit and the nonprofit partners face similar concerns. The nonprofit faces an additional risk. Should something go wrong which creates a publicity scandal, it may be difficult for the nonprofit to attract future sponsors.

Transaction-Based Promotions

In the Transaction-Based Promotion, " . . . a corporation donates a specific amount of cash, food, or equipment in direct proportion to sales revenue–often up to some limit–to one or more nonprofit firms" (The Alliance Analyst 1996, p. 4). Transaction-Based Promotions (TBPs) are also known as cause-related marketing (Varadarajan and Menon 1988), defined as, "the process of formulating and implementing marketing activities characterized by an offer from the firm to contribute a specified amount to a designated cause when customers engage in revenue-providing exchanges that satisfy organizational and individual objectives."

A key characteristic of TBPs is that a business's contribution to the nonprofit is linked and proportional to sales. TBPs became popular in 1983 when funds were being solicited to restore the Statue of Liberty. American Express created a campaign and contributed a few cents each time its customers used their American Express cards in a transaction (see Table 1 for more examples).

TBPs are characterized as being primarily controlled by the business partners. Besides contributing money to the nonprofit, businesses also promote their association with the cause through promotional/advertising activities. Businesses may spend much more on advertising their association with a favorable cause than they actually contribute to the cause. Businesses that participate in TBPs are interested in supporting the cause. However, they are also interested in exposing market segments to favorable images of the company and its brands (Sexton 1998).

The benefits of TBPs to the participating businesses are publicity, public relations, customer/employee goodwill, and increased sales (Table 2). The benefits to nonprofit organizations are increased funding, greater publicity and recognition (see Table 3). Either the business or the nonprofit can create the idea for the TBP. Some businesses are proactive, while many nonprofits are also becoming more assertive by identifying prospective businesses, developing TBPs which would appeal to the prospect, and then presenting the idea to the target business (Aschermann 1988).

Partner risks include possibility of corporate/brand reputation damage, reduced funding and possible withdrawal of corporate support (nonprofit organizations), and loss of brand reputation and sales or market share (business).

Joint Issue Promotions

In joint issue promotions, nonprofit organizations and businesses work together to support a cause. Instead of a business giving money to a nonprofit to support its activities, businesses engage in activities to further the cause. A characteristic of joint issue promotions is that the business and nonprofit partners are jointly advertising for the purpose of furthering the nonprofit's cause. The contribution of participating businesses is generally promotional and operational. Business partners are often involved in the nonprofit's programmatic operations (The Alliance Analyst 1996). This following example should clarify this point.

Hand in Hand was a program created to better educate women about breast cancer. The American College of Obstetricians, the American Health Foundation, and the National Cancer Institute were the nonprofit partners and *Glamour* magazine and Hanes Hosiery were the corporate partners. The educational objectives of *Hand in Hand* were achieved through the distribution and advertisement of educational materials. While *Glamour* and Hanes wanted to support a worthy cause, they also wanted to place their name before their target markets in a meaningful and positive manner. (Other examples are provided in Table 1.)

In this type of nonprofit and business relationship, nonprofits have a preponderance of control. However, business partners can exercise varying levels of power themselves, depending upon the agreement forming the Joint Issue Promotion. Businesses may contribute resources and expertise which allow for substantial power in the relationship.

Joint Issue Promotions can be prominent when the partnering organizations are well known, the business's mission and its nonprofit partner's cause have some linkage, and the publicity is performed over mass media. While supporting a worthy cause is the business's primary motive for entering into this relationship (see Table 2), a secondary motive is generating favorable publicity directed toward a desirable market segment (Sagawa and Segal 2000). The publicity is more strategically directed than other types of nonprofit-business relationships. By participating in Joint Issue Promotions, businesses are hoping to be perceived as champions of a cause which is important to their customers. In the *Hand in Hand* example, *Glamour* magazine and Hanes Hosiery's customers are females who are most concerned and most affected by breast cancer. Obviously, partnering businesses may use a Joint Issue Promotion to target desirable market segments which are not current customers.

Nonprofits are motivated to join this relationship because it is directed at achieving their goals and objectives. By tapping into the resources and capabilities of companies, nonprofits are able to bring much greater awareness to their cause than would otherwise be possible. Control and coordination among participating organizations is not great, but it is greater than in other types of nonprofit-business relationships simply because partnering organizations are all operationally involved in the promotion.

The potential risks for partners are similar to those in the previous examples. A partner's scandal can bring negative publicity to one's own organization. Corporations are better suited to recover from the negative effects of partnering with an unscrupulous nonprofit than vice versa. Companies are more likely to have public relations expertise or to have the resources to hire publicists. Furthermore, a company's customers are likely to make purchase decisions based on a product's benefits and value, and would only refrain from buying a superior product in the most egregious cases (Smith and Stodghill 1994). The vast majority of funding for nonprofits comes from individual donors. If the nonprofit's reputation is damaged, its ability to acquire funds can be weakened. Another risk for nonprofits is the potential for relational dissolutions. A nonprofit's ability to fulfill its mission can be restricted if business partners withdraw from the relationship in which they were providing marketing, creative, and other support.

Joint Ventures

A business-nonprofit joint venture is a new nonprofit entity created by the partnering organizations to achieve mutually desirable objectives. For example, environmental groups educate the public about environmental hazards and socially irresponsible business practices. Environmental groups seek policy remedies from the government in the form of new restrictions, regulations, and laws. In the past, business viewed environmental groups as adversaries. Now, some businesses are finding that cooperating with advocacy nonprofits by forming joint ventures produces more favorable results than opposing them (Bendell and Murphy 1997, Hartman and Stafford 1997).

Some businesses are forming joint ventures with former nonprofit adversaries. The purpose is to evaluate certain aspects of the businesses' operations formerly criticized by the watchdog organization. This trend has been most prevalent between manufacturers and environmental groups. Typically, the joint venture is responsible for developing standards, for monitoring business compliance, and for the management of a certification program. Responsible businesses, that operate in compliance with standards, are given the right to place certification logos on their product packaging to signal to the public their social responsibility and goodwill (Marx 1998). (See Table 1 for examples.)

Businesses generally enter into these agreements as a policy shift from opposing the watchdog's efforts to cooperating. Their motivations for changing their tactics are to establish more favorable relations with their target markets and the public at large (which influences legislators). Human resource benefits may also accrue as the company develops a more favorable public image. Companies may see these cooperative arrangements as a means to differentiate themselves from competition. The risks to partnering businesses are similar to those previously discussed, namely being associated with a partner that misbehaves and attracts negative publicity.

Nonprofits enter into these agreements as a means to accomplish their mission or goals. In cases in which advocacy groups find it impractical to garner public or government support to accomplish its goals, negotiating with the targeted industry/corporation may be an attractive means to achieve progress. Austin (2000) provides a case study of The Nature Conservancy (TNC) and Georgia Pacific's joint venture. TNC was able to preserve valuable forest land owned by Georgia Pacific, which would have been very difficult to preserve through normal advocacy methods. Furthermore, TNC, through its relationship with Georgia Pacific, has access to many more resources than it would have otherwise.

Nonprofit partners of joint ventures with businesses face a unique risk. It is possible for the watchdog group to alienate itself from part of its constituency as well as other advocacy groups agitating for similar causes. Some members of advocacy groups may be idealistic or hold extreme positions, viewing pragmatic cooperation with business as a total defeat instead of a partial victory. Other advocacy groups may feel the partnering nonprofit is compromising its values and integrity. Joint venturing nonprofits, therefore, may risk losing support of some of its membership and being ostracized by other advocacy groups. To ameliorate these risks, they will have to heavily promote the potential benefits of cooperation to its community and then continue to communicate the successes achieved through cooperation instead of agitation.

Derived Typology of Business-Nonprofit Relationships

In general, businesses would prefer to deal with nonprofit organizations that they view favorably and want to support. Also, businesses want to benefit from their relationships with nonprofits (Weeden 1998). A key characteristic of business-nonprofit relationships involves the degree to which the business is seeking its own benefit versus furthering the nonprofit's cause. The horizontal dimension in Figure 1 illustrates this characteristic.

A second key characteristic of business-nonprofit relationships involves the proportion of power in the business's relationship with the nonprofit organization. In some types of relationships, businesses exercise more power than in other types of relationships. The vertical axis of Figure 1 illustrates this characteristic.

In addition to demonstrating how the various types of business-nonprofit relationships differ along two dimensions, the typology also guides managers in selecting the type of relationship appropriate for its objectives. It is assumed that businesses will only develop relationships with nonprofits for which they have positive evaluations. Therefore,

FIGURE 1. Typology of NBA's

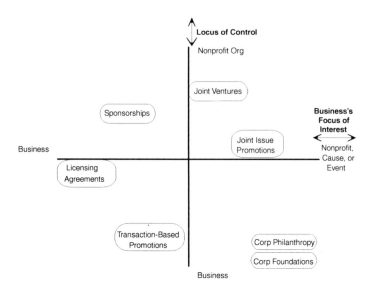

managers can formulate their objectives for entering into a collaborative relationship with a nonprofit, and then determine the level of business returns they wish to achieve. Once managers acknowledge the relative proportion of business returns they desire from the collaboration, they can determine the level of control they want to maintain. Should managers not find a corresponding relationship, they may have to adjust their expectations along one of the dimensions. This is most likely due to the fact that nonprofits also have objectives which must be considered.

Partner Selection

Selecting a partner is an important decision. There are two concerns here. First, where does one find a cross sector partner? Second, what does one look for in a potential partner? In terms of locating a partner, there are several common means of finding one. Business and nonprofit managers may go through social networks. There are numerous examples in which leaders of nonprofits and businesses meet socially, the business manager learns of the good cause of the nonprofit, and searches for ways to support the cause (Austin 2000, Sagawa and Segal

2000). Consultants are available that offer to find a collaborative partner. These consultants have contacts in both sectors, maintain databases of organizations, and offer to locate a partner for a client. Sagawa and Segal (2000) suggest that consultants be used to locate potential partners, but not to develop the relationship or program. Finally, managers can purposively search for a partner. Whichever method of partner identification is chosen, potential partners must also be screened for suitable characteristics.

Nonprofits and businesses should look for partners that appear to be a good fit for a relationship. Drumwright, Cunningham, and Berger (2000) identify various types of business-nonprofit fit. They describe mission fit, management fit, workforce fit, target market fit, product/cause fit, cycle fit, and cultural fit. Based on the several case studies in Austin (2000) and Sagawa and Segal (2000), management fit appears to be crucial. If organizational leaders fail to establish supportive, respectful relational bonds, then the organizational relationship is unlikely to flourish. As organizational leaders are discovering more about their cultures and expectations, mission fit, workforce fit, target market fit, and cultural fit are naturally assessed as a consequence of active exploration of forming a collaborative relationship. Managerial enthusiasm will encourage more favorable assessment of the various fit dimensions.

Relational Characteristics Leading to Successful Outcomes

Appropriate partner selection is not the only prerequisite for a successful business-nonprofit relationship. The relationship must be managed. Misconceptions about partners may shipwreck the collaboration. Therefore, it is essential that partners are open about the objectives of the association, and about their expectations of their own and their partner's performance (Drumwright, Cunningham, and Berger 2000).

Some business-nonprofit collaborations are discrete events, like sponsorships or cause-related marketing promotions. These collaborations have natural ending points. At the conclusion of these relationships, managers should determine whether their goals were achieved, and what other outcomes resulted. This can help managers learn what aspects of the program worked well to aid their learning which can be applied to future collaborations.

Open, clear, and frequent communication between organizations from different levels of the organizations can help to prevent resentment at perceptions of manipulation or unfairness. Also, distributing the communications beyond the organizational leaders can help the relationship survive executive turnover. Over time supporting a cause may become part of the business's identity, establishing an impetus for long term success (Austin 2000, Drumwright, Cunningham, and Berger 2000, and Sagawa and Segal 2000).

NOTE

1. Although technically the Foundation to nonprofit relationship is non-profit-to-nonprofit, it is included in this typology because the foundation is the means through which a corporate is associating with the nonprofit sector.

REFERENCES

Abratt, Russell, Brian C. Clayton, and Oeyland F. Pitt (1987), "Corporate Objectives in Sports Sponsorship," *International Journal of Advertising*, 6 (4), 299-311.

Andreasen, Alan (1996), "Profits for Nonprofits–Find a Corporate Partner," Harvard Business Review, Nov-Dec, 47-59.

Andreasen, Alan (1995), *Marketing Social Change: Changing Behavior to Promote Health, Social Development, and the Environment.* San Francisco: Jossey-Bass.

Andreasen, Alan R. (1996), "Profits for Nonprofits: Find a Corporate Partner," *Harvard Business Review* 74 (6), 47-59.

Anheier, Helmut and Wolfgang Seibel, eds. (1990), *The Third Sector: Comparative Studies of Nonprofit Organizations.* New York: Walter de Gruyter.

Aschermann, Kurt (1998), "Ten Commandments of Cause-Related Marketing," *Causes & Effects*, June, p. 1.

Austin, James E. (1999), "Strategic Collaboration between Nonprofits and Businesses," *Nonprofit & Voluntary Sector Quarterly* 29 (supplemental).

Austin, James E. (2000). *The Collaborative Challenge: How Nonprofits and Businesses Succeed Through Strategic Alliances*, San Francisco: Jossey-Bass.

Becker-Olsen, Karen L. (1998), "Corporate Sponsorship: A Look at the Moderating Effects of Fit and Reach on Image and Purchase Intentions." Dissertation, Lehigh University.

Bendell, Jem and David Murphy (1997), "Strange Bedfellows: Business and Environmental Groups," *Business and Society Review*, issue 98, 40-44.

Berger, Ida E., Peggy H. Cunningham, & Minette E. Drumwright (1999), "Social Alliances: Company/Nonprofit Collaboration," *Social Marketing Quarterly* 5 (3), 49-53.

Berlinger, Lisa R. (1997), "Assessing the Effectiveness of Cross-Sector Programs in an Age of Devolution: A Call for Cross-Discipline Research and Action," Proceedings of 1997 Annual Conference of the Association for Research on Nonprofit Organizations and Voluntary Action.

Bucklin, Louis P. and Sanjit Sengupta (1993), "Organizing Successful Co-Marketing Alliances," *Journal of Marketing*, 57 (April), 32-46.

Burlingame, Dwight F. and Dennis R. Young, eds. (1996), *Corporate Philanthropy at the Crossroads*. Bloomington, Indiana: Indiana University Press. (1998a), August.

_____ (1998b), "Charity Sponsorship: Who's Doing What," June, p. 7.

Cause-Related Marketing (1998). Available online at http://www.crm.org.uk/step1/index.html

Cornwell, T. Bettina and Isabelle Maignan (1998), "An International Review of Sponsorship Research," *Journal of Advertising*, 27 (1), 1-22.

Cunningham, Margaret H. and P. Rajan Varadarajan (1995), "Strategic Alliances: A Synthesis of Conceptual Foundations," *Journal of the Academy of Marketing Science* 23 (4), 282-296.

Das, T.K. and Bing-Sheng Teng (1999), "Managing Risks in Strategic Alliances," *Academy of Management Executive*, 13(4), 50-62.

Drumwright, Minette E. (1996), "Company Advertising With a Social Dimension: The Role of Noneconomic Criteria," *Journal of Marketing*, 60 (Oct), 71-87.

Drumwright, Minette E., Peggy H. Cunningham, and Ida E. Berger (2000), "Social Alliances: Company/Nonprofit Collaboration," Marketing Science Institute Working Paper Series, Report Summary #00-101.

Dwyer, F. Robert, Paul Schurr, and Sejo Oh (1987), "Developing Suyer-Seller Relationships," *Journal of Marketing*, 51 (April), 11-27.

Gidron, Benjamin, Ralph Kramer, and Lester Salamon, eds. (1992), *Government and the Third Sector: Emerging Relationships in Welfare States*. San Fransico: Jossey-Bass Publishers.

Greco, Susan (1994), "Cause-Related Marketing: What Works," *Inc.*, August, p. 102.

File, Karen Maru and Russ Alan Prince (1998), "Cause Related Marketing and Corporate Philanthropy in the Privately Held Enterprise," *Journal of Business Ethics*, 17 (4), 1529+.

Harbison, John R. and Peter Pekar, Jr. (1998). *Smart Alliances: A Practical Guide to Repeatable Success*. San Francisco: Jossey-Bass.

Harbison, John R. and Peter Pekar, Jr. (1993), *A Practical Guide to Alliances: Leapfrogging the Learning Curve*. Los Angeles: Booz-Allen and Hamilton.

Hartman, Cathy L. and Edwin R. Stafford (1997), "Green Alliances: Building New Business with Environmental Groups," *Long Range Planning*, 30 (2), 184-196.

Herman, Valli (1998), "A Market For Charity: Companies Trumpet Virtues of Causes in Selling Products," *The Dallas Morning News*, Feb 15, 1J.

Himmelstein, Jerome L. (1997), *Looking Good and Doing Good: Corporate Philanthropy and Corporate Power*, Indianapolis, IN: Indiana University Press.

Marks, Mitchell Lee and Philip H. Mirvis (1997), *Making One Plus One Equal Three in Mergers, Alliances and Acquisitions*, Macmillan Library Reference.

Marx, Wesley (1998), "Who's Watching Over the Global Fish Market," *California Coast & Ocean*, winter, available online at http://www.coastalconservancy.ca.gov/win98/A02.htm

Mescon, Timothy S. and Donn J. Tilson (1987), "Corporate Philanthropy: A Strategic Approach to the Bottom-Line," *California Management Review*, 29 (2), 49-61.

Milne, George R., Easwar S. Iyer, and Sara Gooding-Williams (1996), "Environmental Organization Alliance Relationships Within and Across Nonprofit, Business, and Government Sectors," *Journal of Public Policy & Marketing*, 15 (2), 203-215.

Morgan, Robert and Shelby Hunt (1994), "The Commitment-Trust Theory of Relationship Marketing," *Journal of Marketing*, 58 9 July), 20-38.

Nowak, Linda I. and Judith H. Washburn (2000), "Marketing Alliances Between Non-Profits and Businesses: Changing the Public's Attitudes and Intentions Towards the Cause," *Journal of Nonprofit & Public Sector Marketing*, 7 (4).

Pekar, Peter, Jr. and Robert Allio (1994), "Making Alliances Work–Guidelines for Success," *Long Range Planning*, 27(4), 54-65.

Sagawa, Shirley & Eli Segal (2000). *Common Interest, Common Good: Creating Value Through Business and Social Sector Partnerships*. Boston: Harvard Business School Press.

Salamon, Lester (1990), "The Nonprofit Sector and Government: The American Experience in Theory and Practice," in *The Third Sector: Comparative Studies of Nonprofit Organizations*, Helmut Anheier and Wolfgang Seibel, eds. New York: Walter de Gruyter, 219-240.

Saxton, M. Kim (1998), "Where do Reputations Come From?" *Corporate Reputation Review*, 1 (4), 393-399.

Segal, Larraine (1996), *Intelligent Business Alliances: How to Profit Using Today's Most Important Strategic Tool*. New York: Times Books.

Sagawa, Shirley and Eli Segal (2000). *Common Interest, Common Good: Creating Value Through Business and Social Sector Partnerships*. Boston: Harvard Business School Press.

Sexton, Ruth (1998), "Q & A on Corporate Philanthropy and CRM Today," *Causes & Effects*, December, p. 4.

Smith, Craig (1994), "The New Corporate Philanthropy," *Harvard Business Review*, 72 (May-June), 105-116.

Spethmann, Betsy (2000), "Charity Begins at the Home Page," *Promo Magazine*, available online 7 Feb2000 at *http://promomagazine.com/Content/Features, 2000/2000020101.htm.*

Stafford, Edwin R. (1994), "Using Co-operative Strategies to Make Alliances Work," *Long Range Planning*, 27(3), 64-74.

Stafford, Edwin R. & Cathy L. Hartman (2000), "Environmentalist-Business Collaborations: Social Responsibility, Green Alliances, and Beyond," in *Advertising Research: The Internet, Consumer Behavior and Strategy*, George Zinkhan (ed.). Chicago: American Marketing Association.

Stafford, Edwin R., Michael Jay Polonsky, & Cathy L. Hartman (2000), "Environmental NGO-Business Collaboration and Strategic Bridging: A Case Analysis of the Greenpeace-Foron Alliance, *Business Strategy and the Environment*, 9, 122-135.

Smith, Geoffrey & Ron Stodghill II (1994), "Are Good Causes Good Marketing?" *Business Week* (March 21), 64-65.

The Alliance Analyst (1996), "Peter Drucker: Nonprofit Prophet," Nov 11, available online at *http://www.allianceanalyst.com/Drucker.html*

Varadarajan, P. Rajan and Anil Menon (1988), "Cause-Related Marketing: A Coalignment of Marketing Strategy and Corporate Philanthropy," *Journal of Marketing*, 52 (July), 58-74.

Webster, Frederick W., Jr. (1992), "The Changing Role of Marketing in the Corporation," *Journal of Marketing*, 56 (Oct), 1-17.

Weeden, Curt (1998), *Corporate Social Investing: The Breakthrough Strategy for Giving and Getting Corporate Contributions*, San Francisco: Berrett-Koehler Publishers.

Yoshino, Michael Y. & U. Srinivasa Rangan (1995), *Strategic Alliances: An Entrepreneurial Approach to Globalization*. Boston: Harvard Business School Press.

Marketing's Role
in Cross-Sector Collaboration

James E. Austin

SUMMARY. Collaborations between businesses and nonprofit organizations are becoming more prevalent, important, and complicated. Marketing plays an increasingly significant role in these cross-sector relationships. This article will first set forth a framework for understanding alliances between companies and nonprofits. It will then examime how such cross-sector collaborations relate to four strategic and interrelated marketing areas: institutional marketing, cause-related marketing, market development, and internal organizational marketing. *[Article copies available for a fee from The Haworth Document Delivery Service: 1-800-HAWORTH. E-mail address: <getinfo@haworthpressinc.com> Website: <http://www.HaworthPress.com> © 2003 by The Haworth Press, Inc. All rights reserved.]*

KEYWORDS. Cross-sector collaborations, institutional marketing, cause-related marketing, market development, internal organizational marketing

UNDERSTANDING CROSS-SECTOR COLLABORATION

My field-based research on collaborations between businesses and nonprofits, encompassing a wide range of industries and social sectors, revealed a distinctive pattern in the types and evolution of relationships

James E. Austin, DBA, is Snider Professor of Business Administration, Harvard Business School, Boston, MA 02163 (E-mail: jaustin@ hbs.edu).

[Haworth co-indexing entry note]: "Marketing's Role in Cross-Sector Collaboration." Austin, James E. Co-published simultaneously in *Journal of Nonprofit & Public Sector Marketing* (Best Business Books, an imprint of The Haworth Press, Inc.) Vol. 11, No. 1, 2003, pp. 23-39; and: *Nonprofit and Business Sector Collaboration: Social Enterprises, Cause-Related Marketing, Sponsorships, and Other Corporate-Nonprofit Dealings* (ed: Walter W. Wymer, Jr. and Sridhar Samu) Best Business Books, an imprint of The Haworth Press, Inc., 2003, pp. 23-39. Single or multiple copies of this article are available for a fee from The Haworth Document Delivery Service [1-800-HAWORTH, 9:00 a.m. - 5:00 p.m. (EST). E-mail address: getinfo@haworthpressinc. com].

(Austin 2000a). As an analytical framework I conceptualize these as the Cross-Sector Collaboration Continuum along which there are three types and stages of relationships (see Figure 1):

- *Philanthropic Stage.* This is the most common type of relationship between businesses and nonprofits. It largely consists of annual corporate donations of money or goods made in response to requests from nonprofits. The level of engagement and resources is relatively low, infrequent, simple, and nonstrategic. It is basically a check-writing relationship. The giver has a charity mindset and the recipient a grateful attitude. The relationship is valuable as part of an effort to market the company as a caring, responsible institution and even to market the nonprofit as a credible organization meriting support.
- *Transactional Stage.* Significant numbers of firms and nonprofits are migrating into this second stage, in which the interaction tends to focus on more specific activities in which there is a significant two-way value exchange. The organizations' core capabilities begin to be deployed and the partnership is more important to each other's missions and strategies. It is no longer simply a transfer of funds. This stage would encompass such activities as cause-related marketing programs, event sponsorships, special projects, and employee volunteer services.
- *Integrative Stage.* A smaller but growing number of collaborations evolve into strategic alliances that involve deep mission mesh, strategy synchronization, and values compatibility. People begin to interact with greater frequency and many more kinds of joint activities are undertaken. The types and levels of institutional resources used multiply. Core competencies are not simply deployed but combined to create unique and high value combinations. The degree of organizational integration begins to take on the appearance of a joint venture, and in some instances the partners have actually created new, jointly governed entities to carry out their collaboration. This stage of collaboration sometimes involves market development and also internal organizational marketing.

As depicted in Figure 1, as one moves along the Continuum the level of engagement deepens, mission relevance becomes more central, resource deployment expands, activities broaden, interaction intensifies, and managerial complexity magnifies, but so, too, does the strategic value.

It is important to note that progression along the continuum is not automatic; it is the result of explicit decisions and actions by the partners.

FIGURE 1. Cross-Sector Collaboration Continuum

	Stage I	Stage II	Stage III
NATURE OF RELATIONSHIP	*Philanthropic>>>>Transactional>>>>Integrative*		
• *Level of Engagement*	*Low>>>>>>>>>>>>>>>>>>>>>>>>>>>>>High*		
• *Importance to Mission*	*Peripheral>>>>>>>>>>>>>>>>>>>>>>>Central*		
• *Magnitude of Resources*	*Small>>>>>>>>>>>>>>>>>>>>>>>>>>>Big*		
• *Scope of Activities*	*Narrow>>>>>>>>>>>>>>>>>>>>>>>>>Broad*		
• *Interaction Level*	*Infrequent>>>>>>>>>>>>>>>>>>>>>>Intensive*		
• *Managerial Complexity*	*Simple>>>>>>>>>>>>>>>>>>>>>>>>>>Complex*		
• *Strategic Value*	*Minor>>>>>>>>>>>>>>>>>>>>>>>>>>>Major*		

Source: J. Austin, The Collaboration Challenge (San Francisco:Jossey-Bass, 2000)

And regression and exit are always possible. The Collaboration Continuum is particularly useful in mapping the type of relationships a business or a nonprofit has in terms of the stages. Generally, businesses and nonprofits have multiple relationships, so the Continuum can be used as an instrument for managing their "Partnering Portfolios." Not only can one ascertain the current nature of the existing relationships, but also begin to strategize as to the ideal mix of relationship types one might want to have and assess the organizational and strategic implications for attaining that. For example, within their portfolios, businesses and nonprofits might wish to continue to have several philanthropic relationships as relatively low maintenance engagements that serve useful albeit not critical functions. For another set of relationships there may be opportunities to enter into higher engagement and higher value transactional collaborations. And, for a smaller, highly selective set, the partners might create the more intensive and demanding but higher pay-off strategic integrative alliances.

Collaborative relationships are multifaceted. Figure 2 provides additional characteristics of the relationships in each of the three stages. The evolution of these various dimensions does not necessarily take place simultaneously. Consequently, a particular relationship might have some aspects that fall into one stage and others that are in another, thus creating hybrids of different stages.

My research reveals that the more effective collaborations are characterized by clear purpose, mission congruency, high and mutually balanced value creation, effective communication, and deep reciprocal commitment. Using these "drivers" and the Cross-Sector Collaboration Continuum as a basic framework for analyzing the interactions between

FIGURE 2. Collaboration Continuum

	Philanthropic	Transactional	Integrative
Collaboration Mindset	• Gratefulness and charity syndromes	• Partnering mindset • Increased understanding and trust	• "We" mentality replaces "us versus them"
Strategic Alignment	• Minimal fit required, beyond a shared interest in a particular issue area	• Overlap in mission and values	• Relationship as strategic tool • High "mission mesh" • Shared values
Collaboration Value	• Generic resource transfer • Typically unequal exchange of resources	• Core competency transfer • More equal exchange of resources	• Joint value creation • Need for value renewal
Relationship Management	• Corporate contact usually in community affairs or foundation; nonprofit contact usually in development • Minimal personal connection to cause • Project progress typically communicated via paper status report	• Expanded personal relationships throughout the organization • Strong personal connection at leadership level • Emerging infrastructure, including relationship managers, communication channels/vehicles	• Expanded opportunities for direct employee involvement in relationship • Deep personal relationships across organization • Culture of each organization influenced by the other • Partner Relationship Managers • Explicit internal and external communication strategies and processes
Collaboration Definition and Performance	• Minimal collaboration in defining activities • Foundation guidelines often determine types of projects or corporations respond to specific requests from nonprofits • Minimal performance expectations	• Shared visioning at top of organization • Projects of limited scope and risk that demonstrate success • Explicit performance expectations • Informal learning	• Projects identified and developed at all levels within the organization, with leadership support • Broad scope of activities of strategic significance • Organizational integration in execution, including shared resources • Incentive systems encourage partnerships • Active learning process • High mutual expectations and accountability

Source: J. Austin, The Collaboration Challenge (San Francisco: Jossey-Bass, 2000)

businesses and nonprofits, let us now examine the role of marketing in these collaborations. Institutional marketing has traditionally been a prominent factor in the Philanthropic Stage of collaboration and is evolving into the other stages. Cause-related marketing is a salient and important form of collaboration in the Transactional Stage. Market development and internal organizational marketing appear to be particularly relevant in the Integrative Stage of collaboration.

INSTITUTIONAL MARKETING
AND PHILANTHROPIC STAGE COLLABORATIONS

For corporations, traditional philanthropy has generally been perceived as contributing to the company's image as a responsible citizen. It has been a standard component of institutional marketing programs. Nearly two-thirds of U.S. consumers express greater trust in companies that support social issues (Austin 2000b). A survey of over 25,000 consumers in 23 countries revealed that they expect companies to contribute to society beyond being profitable and law-abiding (Weiser 2000). Given the growing importance of companies' involvement with their communities, most corporations are beginning to conceive of and manage this engagement as a more integral part of their overall strategies.

Citicorp, for example, made community service one of its six key strategy areas worldwide because its goal is to become an "embedded" part of each community's institutional fabric. A senior manager stated their rationale: "We do this because it is the right thing to do and ... because we want a positive and trusted image with customers, potential customers, regulators, legislators, and community groups, all of which supports our global image as a trusted brand name. We are talking here about how we run our business, not just about contributions, volunteerism and PR . . . It has moved from 'nice to do' to 'need to do' as part of our business strategy."

This shift in thinking led the company to change its philanthropic orientation from donating to a multitude of nonprofits involved in a wide range of social activities to a focused strategy that concentrated its resources in two key areas, public education and microfinance. To implement this strategy it formed alliances with selected nonprofits specializing in these areas. This shift toward strategic philanthropy propelled movement along the Cross-Sector Collaboration Continuum. Citicorp's alliances moved from the philanthropic stage into the transactional and even integrative stage. They were more central to the company's and nonprofits' missions, employed and fused the organizations' core competencies in a set of activities in the strategically focused areas. The traditional focus of institutional marketing on relatively simple, check-writing philanthropic relationships is evolving into the more sophisticated and complex forms of cross-sector collaboration.

Georgia-Pacific, a global forest resources company, entered into what would appear to be an improbable alliance with The Nature Conservancy, a major land conservation organization. The organizations shifted from their historically adversarial roles into a partnership to manage jointly company-owned land in a way that was more environmentally friendly. This involved setting aside some ecologically critical land areas and using lower impact timbering techniques for the lumber removal from the rest of the land. One of the motivating factors for the company was the belief that this collaboration would reinforce the creation of its new image as a good steward of natural resources. This, in turn, would be perceived positively by government regulators of the timber industry as well as by environmentally conscious consumers. The collaboration was one important element in the company's institutional marketing strategy and it clearly went beyond traditional check writing philanthropy.

For nonprofits, too, institutional marketing is extremely important. In fact, because many have nonpaying consumers of their services, marketing their organization effectively to their donors is vital to financial survival. Collaborations with companies can often be seen as enhancing the nonprofit's credibility with other funders because they have passed the corporation's acceptability screen.

Partnering with one corporation can create access to others. For example, City Year, a youth-based community service organization, started a relationship with Timberland, the international boot and outdoor apparel company by asking for and receiving a donation of 50 pairs of boots. This was simple philanthropy contributing to the company's image. Over time it developed into a deep integrative alliance in which the company completely outfitted City Year's youth corps from head to foot and supported the organization to the tune of $1 million dollars annually over a five-year period. But beyond this, Timberland helped City Year recruit other major corporate sponsors. Access often works both ways. City Year was the model that motivated the creation of the national service program, Americorps. Consequently, City Year was featured at a major White House Conference on Philanthropy and the nonprofit, in turn, highlighted Timberland as a star corporate partner in community service. The company found itself sharing the spotlight of public acclaim with much bigger companies like IBM and Coca-Cola, a positioning that it would not have achieved without its cross-sector strategic alliance that had evolved from simple philanthropy to an integrative stage relationship.

Corporate involvement with nonprofits takes many forms beyond financial assistance. In the philanthropic and transactional stages a firm may facilitate employees' working as volunteers with nonprofits. One common volunteer modality for executives is service on nonprofits' boards of directors (Austin 1998). This personal governance role applies the managers' professional skills to the strengthening of the nonprofits. Such board service often enables the manager to interact closely with leaders from other sectors. The resultant personal relationships often become an intangible asset for the company that may be useful in dealing with other business issues that could require support from these other leaders. Companies often view their multiple forms of involvement with nonprofits as "banking social credits." That balance of good deeds and image of social responsibility may have to be drawn down if and when a company encounters either problems that expose it to criticism or the need arises for special approvals for some of its business activities. Cross-sector collaboration can be an effective vehicle for institutional marketing, and the stronger the alliance the more powerful the effect. Now let us turn to a more specific form of marketing strategy and collaboration.

CAUSE-RELATED MARKETING
AND TRANSACTIONAL COLLABORATIONS

Cause-related marketing (CRM) is a form of transactional stage collaboration that has grown rapidly in importance to businesses and nonprofits. In all instances the company is promotionally associated with the nonprofit partner's name and cause. In return, the nonprofit generally receives payments based on a percentage of consumer transactions during the campaign, or licensing fees from the use of the organization's logo, or simply publicity for the nonprofit's cause. CRM also encompasses event sponsorships.

CRM does contribute to the general image enhancement sought by institutional marketing, but falls into the second stage of cross-sector collaboration because it is a clearly delineated activity that involves an important two-way value exchange. Businesses use it as a marketing tool for brand and product differentiation. A Cone/Roper national survey revealed that 65% of consumers and 89% of teenagers would switch brands to a company associated with a good cause (Cone, Inc.

2000). For teens' purchasing decisions, a company's commitment to a good cause ranks second in importance after quality and before advertising, price, and celebrity endorsements. Females and Hispanics are particularly disposed to purchasing holiday gifts from companies supporting a cause (Cone, Inc. and Opinion Research 2000). Consumers in other countries are also influenced by cause association: half of the UK consumers in one survey reported that they switched brands, tried a new product, or increased purchases of a known product due to its link to a charity's cause (Farquason 2000). Even higher propensities for brand switching were reported in Italy, Australia, New Zealand, India, and Belgium (Business 1999). Over half of the 1,350 Mexican consumers in a 1999 survey indicated they would pay a 5-10% premium for products supporting a social cause (Promoting 2001).

There is considerable experiential evidence that specific promotional campaigns donating a share of the purchase price to a cause can generate significant sales increases. American Express pioneered this affinity marketing two decades ago by donating a percentage of each credit card purchase and a fixed amount for each new card application to the fund for restoration of the Statue of Liberty. The campaign prompted a 28% first-month increase in card usage, a 45% jump in applications, and generated overall $1.7 million for the restoration fund. Coca-Cola's promise in 1997 to donate 15 cents to Mothers Against Drunk Driving for every case of soft drink sold spurred a 490% increase in sales during the six-week promotion (Gray 1998). Some collaborations have business value because of the direct access to the nonprofit's client base. In another effort, Coca-Cola's $60-million, ten-year deal with Boys & Girls Club of America gave the company vending machine access to the over 2,000 clubs and three million youth members. CRM can differentiate advertising. The Norwich Union insurance company in Britain doubled consumer awareness of its advertising compared to competitors by promoting a nonprofit ambulance center's first aid courses. Twenty percent of the consumers indicated that they were more likely to consider Norwich as their insurer of choice.

In exchange for these benefits, companies have provided nonprofits over $1.5 billion in fees annually, a five-fold increase over the past decade (Gray 1998). Generally such payments came out of corporations' marketing budgets rather than their philanthropic giving budgets, which totaled $11 billion in 1999 (AAFRC 2000). Most recently, CRM has also entered the new Internet fundraising space of ePhilanthropy (Austin 2001). For example, in Click & Donate Internet sites corporations provide donations to particular causes and nonprofits when users click on the companys' logo. CRM has played an important role in expanding the total flow of funds from the corporate to the nonprofit sector. The collaboration value to the nonprofits, however, is more than fees. The publicity provides enormous name exposure, far beyond what the nonprofit could have ever afforded on its own. This builds the organization's brand recognition and image, which is critical to increasing memberships and donations.

More multifaceted CRM collaborations can create more value by using a company's core capabilities, as illustrated by Starbucks' alliance with the international development and relief agency CARE. To help celebrate CARE's 50th anniversary, Starbucks created in each of its outlets banners and displays describing CARE's mission and community development projects in several countries (from which Starbucks also sourced coffee). In addition, they sold canister sets of coffee from those countries, with proceeds going to CARE. This highly professional, massive consumer exposure was far more valuable to CARE than a simple check. The value emerged because the company was deploying its world class point-of-purchase skills and access to its massive client base. CARE could never have purchased that. It is also doubtful, however, that Starbucks would have made this effort had it not considered its relationship with CARE to be a strategic alliance of the stage II or III nature rather than simply a stage I philanthropic involvement.

One of the complications in executing the value exchange in these transactional relationships is determining their worth. The more narrowly prescribed and tightly tied the transaction, then the more feasible the setting of a "price." For example, a specific CRM campaign in which a certain percentage of sales or amount per transaction is destined to the nonprofit is directly tied to the revenue generated during a set period and can be compared to the cost-effectiveness of alternative promotional vehicles. However, it is often difficult a priori for the nonprofit or even the business to predict what the consumer response will be, so fixed absolute fees imply risks for both. The CRM market still does not have clear and easily verifiable pricing standards, and nonprofits particularly find it difficult to know what their brand is worth. And when the collaborations are multifaceted, which characterizes most Stage II and all Stage III partnerships, assessing value is even more complicated. But this also is true of many business-to-business strategic alliances, so it is a complication that comes with the collaboration territory. This places special importance on the capacity to understand your partner's needs and communicate clearly about how to meet them. Critical to making this process work effectively is the intangible asset of trust that is built up over time.

These CRM relationships are not without risks to the collaborators. One worry expressed by nonprofits is that their missions will be diverted or tainted (Andeasen 1996). The 150-year-old American Medical Association, suffering from a cash squeeze, entered into an agreement with Sunbeam Corporation for the use of the A.M.A.'s name and logo on its health-related products in return for royalties estimated at $1-million annually (Haddad 2001). This collaboration triggered intense criticism from some of its 290,000 medical doctor members, consumer advocates, and even *The New York Times* as compromising the integrity of the organization and being inconsistent with its mission. As a result, the A.M.A. pulled out of the contract but was forced to pay Sunbeam damage fees of $7.9 million plus another $2 million in legal fees and expenses (Associated Press 1998).

It is critical that the nonprofit and business both make sure that the arrangement will be acceptable to their key stakeholders. Sometimes the mutual mission fit will be clear. For example, Ralston Purina, one of the world's largest producers of pet food, joined with the American Humane Association, a national grouping of abandoned animal shelters, to sponsor a program to increase pet adoptions thereby reducing animal euthanasia. Both partners had a clear shared interest in keeping more animals alive. Other times one has to work to find the fit. Visa entered into a collaboration with Reading Is Fundamental that promotes literacy. This was not an obvious fit but a company survey of its cardholders revealed highest interest in literacy. Some nonprofits exclude a priori some types of corporations whose products are incompatible with the organization's mission, e.g., Jumpstart, a nonprofit working with at-risk preschoolers to develop their learning readiness, will not accept donations from alcohol or cigarette companies. In all cases, however, both nonprofits and businesses should engage in thorough due diligence to ensure that the stated values and actual practices of the potential partner are acceptable.

Care must also be taken that the nature of the relationship is clearly communicated in the promotions. The state attorneys general have been quite concerned about CRM campaigns misleading consumers into thinking that a nonprofit was endorsing a product. Smith-Kline Beecham, for example, agreed to alter its advertisements for its smoking cessation product to remove the possible interpretation that the American Cancer Society endorsed the product in exchange for a company donation to its research and education program (Abelson 1999).

Criticism and controversy still surround CRM collaborations, including understandable concerns about company logos and commercials cluttering and intruding on public places, such as sports arenas, parks, museums, and even public schools (Barber and Ostergard 2001). Twenty-one percent of the consumers in one survey doubt the charitable motives of corporations' CRM activities (Pringle 1999). However, the majority of the public seems to think otherwise. The 1999 Cone/Roper national survey revealed that 74% considered cause-related marketing to be acceptable and 61% even stated that it should be a standard business practice (Cone/Roper, op. cit.). The fundamental issue is not some form of altruistic purity such as philanthropic anonymity, but whether the social benefits generated exceed the costs. Nonetheless, research does suggest that consumers' attitudes toward a company and its CRM are more positive if the collaboration also encompasses additional forms of support and engagement (Drumwright 1996). In effect, the further a firm migrates along the Collaboration Continuum in terms of multifaceted transactional activities or even further into organizational integration, then the more effective the CRM component will likely be.

MARKET DEVELOPMENT
AND INTEGRATIVE COLLABORATIONS

Whereas institutional marketing deals with enhancing a company's general image and community relationships and CRM aims more specifically at sales boosts for current products, collaborations can also play a role in developing new markets. In these collaborations there is a close meshing of missions, combining of core competencies, and a long-term commitment. For example, Hewlett Packard provides funding and equipment to LINCOS, a Costa Rican nonprofit that created, in collaboration with MIT's Media Lab, mobile digital community centers. These are housed in recycled, 20-foot shipping containers that provide wireless Internet access to rural dwellers. HP sees these centers as fulfilling an unmet need in telecommunication infrastructure throughout the developing world. One HP manager stated, "Down the road the five-year vision is that it's a significant business in size" (Longstreth 2001).

Monsanto, a global producer of agricultural inputs, is using alliances with nonprofits to develop the market of small farmers in developing countries. The company sees this as an overlooked and potentially huge market segment. However, these farmers differ radically from the larger commercial scale farmers that represent the main markets for input companies. Consequently, Monsanto has entered into alliances with local nonprofit organizations whose missions are the betterment of the lives of these low-income farmers and their families. The nonprofits know the farmers' situations much better than Monsanto and have long-standing trust relationships with them. Accordingly, the company provides the agricultural inputs and funding to enable the nonprofits to introduce the new inputs to the farmers and to evaluate the results in terms of net benefits to the farmers. The alliances derive their value largely from the shared mission and the combination of the complementary core capabilities of each partner. The company is investing resources with the nonprofits to learn about and develop this underserved market.

Timberland and City Year collaborated to create new products. The first were called City Year Gear, consisting of t-shirts, backpacks, and other items carrying social cause messages. The products were sold through Timberland's retail outlets and carried information about the Timberland-City Year alliance. A later and more ambitious effort went to the heart of the company's product line: boots. The idea for producing a red boot, rather than the company's traditional yellow leather, came from the City Year youth and it was aimed at the youth market. Both partners were contributing to the concept and design of the products. Timberland was combining its core competency in boot production with City Year's direct knowledge of the urban youth market.

The nonprofit Local Initiatives Support Corporation (LISC) is an example of market development led by a nonprofit. LISC was originally funded by the Ford Foundation with the goal of stimulating inner-city community development. In this sphere there was market failure in the sense that the commercial marketplace was not meeting the social needs, particularly for low-income housing. LISC helped create a national network of local nonprofit community development corporations (CDCs) that would be low-income housing developers. LISC was also instrumental in getting federal legislation passed providing tax credits for developers of low-income housing. These tax credits were disbursed to the CDCs developing such housing projects. As untaxed nonprofits they could not use the tax credits directly, so LISC aggregated these rights to tax benefits and sold them to banks and corporations that used them to offset their taxes.

In effect, the nonprofit was playing the purely entrepreneurial role of creating a new financial market for Low Income Housing Tax Credits. Its relationships with the corporate buyers of the tax credits became multidimensional with many of the corporations also providing donations to LISC or the local CDCs and sometimes becoming board members of the nonprofits. In the early years, becoming involved with CDCs and their projects was perceived as highly risky. Consequently, LISC received a healthy fee for its financial intermediary services of marketing the tax credits. Over time, it became clear that the CDCs and their projects were not overly risky, particularly if one aggregated the projects. Accordingly, many commercial organizations were attracted into this new market space and began providing similar financial services, thereby causing the fee levels to drop, a clear sign of market development and maturity. In effect, the nonprofit corrected the market failure by reducing the real and perceived risks through developing innovative fiscal and financial mechanisms and demonstrating the viability of working with community-based nonprofits.

LISC also played a key role in stimulating inner-city commercial development through The Retail Initiative, in which it created a collaboration between capital providers (banks and insurance companies), supermarket chains, and local CDCs. LISC's market development role was first in perceiving the consumer need and then mobilizing the capital and technology (supermarket management). However, it also played an important role as a "guide" to help the supermarkets connect with the local community through alliances with CDCs and to navigate the political arena to obtain the necessary approvals for commercial development. Nonprofit organizations have characteristics and capacities that can be extremely valuable to the market development process in partnership with corporations.

INTERNAL ORGANIZATIONAL MARKETING AND INTEGRATIVE COLLABORATIONS

Institutional marketing, CRM, and market development are all oriented primarily toward external stakeholders, but cross-sector collaborations can also be focused on strengthening the company's internal organization.

Companies that support social causes and are meaningfully engaged with nonprofit organizations create a competitive advantage in recruiting employees. Salaries can be easily matched, but community engagements are more complex and difficult to duplicate, particularly if they are at the integration end of the Collaboration Continuum. Our company interviews indicate that a corporation's social sector activities are often reported as the tipping point in attracting and hiring new talent. These activities also help retain employees. One study revealed that

90% of employees of companies supporting causes "feel proud of their companies' values" compared to 56% in companies not supporting social causes; furthermore, 87% of the employees in the cause-supporting companies "feel a strong sense of loyalty" to their organization compared to 67% in the other companies (Cone, Inc. 1999).

Companies also recognize the value of getting their employees involved in volunteer work with nonprofits. A Conference Board survey of 454 companies revealed that 90% have formal employee volunteer programs (The Conference Board 1993). This is a form of job enrichment, and increasingly employees are given paid time off for such community service. Timberland allows its employees up to 40 hours annually. One senior executive of a financial services firm stated the rationale for promoting employee service: "It's important to keep the people within my ranks involved and happy in the community to avoid being attracted to move elsewhere. If they have ties with a charity, it's going to be a lot harder for them to uproot and move elsewhere."

In addition to increased satisfaction, motivation, and loyalty, volunteer service also has proven to be an effective vehicle for developing skills and attitudes that contribute positively to work performance. For example, Helene Curtis Inc. identifies opportunities for employees to practice 28 business skill areas through involvement with nonprofits. William Madar, former CEO of Nordson Corporation, stated that community service reinforces the company's culture: "The values that are key to making a responsive organization to customers, to suppliers, and to each other are the very same values of caring that lead to concern for our neighbors and participation in the community. Community involvement is part of the whole. It is integral to the success of the business."

Volunteer service with nonprofits is often an important vehicle for broadening the collaboration engagement beyond a philanthropic check-writing relationship. While my study of business-nonprofit alliances reveals that top-leadership commitment is essential to establishing a strong partnership, equally important to institutionalizing the collaboration is the widening and deepening of inter-organizational personal relationships. Volunteer involvement is a powerful way to make those connections. In the integrative stage personnel from each partnering organization will often be using their talents to provide assistance to the other. For example, Timberland's financial executives helped City Year strengthen its financial systems, and City Year's staff helped Timberland with diversity training.

Internal communications is a critical component in strengthening the relationship. It is important that top leadership of both the company and the nonprofit communicate to their employees the importance of the alliance to their organization. When this "blessing" is accompanied by strong delegation to the organization to make the partnership work, it has an empowering and energizing effect that unleashes impressive creativity in creating and capturing collaboration synergies. Internal marketing is as important as external. Starbucks accomplished this by incorporating into its orientation sessions for new hires a description of its alliance with CARE and why that was important to the company's values.

THE COLLABORATION IMPERATIVE

Cross-sector collaboration will become even more prevalent in this new century. The growing complexity of the socioeconomic problems facing societies transcends the capabilities of single organizations and separate sectors. The sectoral boundaries between business, civil society, and government are increasingly overlapping. Societal expectations of business to contribute to the resolution of social problems are rising. So too are donors' expectations of superior performance and accountability from nonprofit organizations.

In this growing realm of cross-sector collaboration, it is clear that marketing plays important and evolving roles. Institutional marketing has long been and will continue to be a motivating force behind traditional philanthropic stage collaborations. However, as companies have begun to think more strategically about philanthropy, they have shifted to more complex forms and stages of collaboration. The institutional marketing strategies have accordingly become more sophisticated and multifaceted. Cause-related marketing has been one of the fastest growing areas in marketing and this has opened up important new funds mobilization avenues for nonprofits. CRM is still maturing and both nonprofits and businesses will continue to discover opportunities for collaboration gains as well as mechanisms for managing the accompanying risks. Collaboration for the purpose of market development is one of the less developed areas and it holds high potential for mutual benefit. Cross-sector collaboration provides an important internal organizational marketing vehicle for enriching the institutional cultures and work environments with high payoffs in terms of recruiting, retention, and motivation.

In the arena of cross-sector collaboration, clearly the marketing function, discipline, and perspective have much to contribute. And much to learn. Hopefully, the analytical framework manifested through the Collaboration Continuum will provide a useful framework to explore further the strategic areas of institutional marketing, CRM, market development, and internal marketing as well as many other important avenues of study.

AUTHOR NOTE

James E. Austin is Snider Professor of Business Administration at the Harvard University Graduate School of Business Administration, where he has been a member of the faculty since 1972. He is chair of the Harvard Business School Initiative on Social Enterprise and teaches and researches social entrepreneurship, strategic management of nonprofits, and nonprofit board governance. Austin, whose work as a scholar and teacher has been acclaimed in such publications as the *Financial Times*, *The Wall Street Journal*, and *The New Yorker* magazine, is the author of fifteen books, dozens of articles, and a multitude of case studies. For the past three and a half decades, he has served as an advisor to businesses, nonprofit organizations, and governments throughout the world.

REFERENCES

AAFRC (2001), "Giving USA 2001," *AAFRC Trust for Philanthropy*, available online on July 3, 2001, at *http://www.aafrc.org/giving*

Abelson, R. (1999), "Marketing Tied to Charities Draws Scrutiny from States," *New York Times*, May 3, 1999, p. 1.

Andeasen, Alan R. (1996), "Profits for Nonprofits: Find a Corporate Partner," *Harvard Business Review*, November-December.

Associated Press (1998), "Broken Deal Costs A.M.A. $9.9 Million," *New York Times*, p. 12, col. 6, 8/3/98.

Austin, James E. (Fall 1998), "Business Leaders and Nonprofits," *Nonprofit Management & Leadership*, 9 (1).

Austin, James E. (Spring 1998), "The Invisible Side of Leadership," *Leader to Leader*.

Austin, James E. (2000a), *The Collaboration Challenge*. San Francisco: Jossey-Bass.

Austin, James E. (2000b), "Strategic Collaboration Between Nonprofits and Businesses," *Nonprofit and Voluntary Sector Quarterly*.

Austin, James E. (2001), "The E-Philanthropy Revolution Is Here To Stay," *The Chronicle of Philanthropy*," March 8, 2001.

Barber, Bejamin R. (2001), "No: Always an Angle." *Across the Board*, May-June, available online at *http://www.conference-board.org/atb/ATBmayjune2001.cfm*

Business for Social Responsibility (1999), "BSR Education Fund," in A.C. Nielsen, "Good As Gold–The Stillwater/AC Nielsen Report," available online on July 3, 2001, at *www.acnielsen.co.nz*

Cone, Inc. and Opinion Research Corporation International (2000), "2000 Cone Holiday Trend Tracker."

Cone/Roper, op. cit.

Cone, Inc. and Roper Starch Worldwide, Inc. (2000), "Survey Finds Teen Interest in Corporate Social Responsibility," *Philanthropy News Digest*, 6 (35), available online on July 3, 2001, at *http://fdncenter.org/pnd/20000822/003585.html*

Cone, Inc. and Roper Starch Worldwide, Inc. (1999), "1999 Cone/Roper Cause Related Trends Report: The Evolution of Cause Branding, Boston: Cone, Inc., 1999." *Philanthropy News Digest*, 5 (44), 24, available online on July 3, 2001, at *http://fdncenter.org/pnd/19991102/bookreview.html*

Drumwright, Minette, (1996) "Company Advertising with a Social Dimension: The Role of Noneconomic Criteria," *Journal of Marketing*, 60 (4) 71-87.

Farquason, Andy (2000), "Cause and Effect," *The Guardian*, November 11, 2000.

Gray, Susan and Holly Hall (1998), "Crashing In on Charity's Good Name," *The Chronicle of Philanthropy*, July 30, 1998.

Haddad, Kimberly A. and Ashish Nanda (2001), "The American Medical Association-Sunbeam Deal (A)-(D)." *Harvard Business School Case Study* (pp. 801-329).

Longstreth, Andrew (2001), "The Littlest Mobile Office," *Smartbusinessmag.com*, May 2001.

Ostergard, Paul (2001), "Yes: A Golden Age," *Across The Board*, June 2001.

Pringle, Hamish and Marjorie Thompson 1999), "Brand Spirit: How Cause Related Marketing Builds Brands," West Sussex, England: John Wiley & Sons Ltd.

Promoting Public Causes, Inc. (2001), "Mexico's Consumer Survey on Cause Related Marketing," available online July 2, 2001, at *http://www.publiccauses.com/resources/resource-mexico.htm*

The Conference Board (1993), "Corporate Voluntary Programs: Benefits to Business," Report Number 1029.

The Conference Board, (2001), "Should Corporations Be Praised for Their Philanthropic Efforts?" *Across the Board*, May-June, available online at *http://www.conference-board.org/atb/ATBmayjune2001.cfm*

Weiser, John and Simon Zadek (2000), "Conversations with Disbelievers: Persuading Companies to Address Social Challenges," New York: The Ford Foundation.

Theory of Alliances:
Partnership and Partner Characteristics

Easwar Iyer

SUMMARY. Alliances have been referred to by many other terms such as symbiotic marketing, horizontal integration, collaboration, or strategic partnerships. There is a lot of literature on alliances, although most of that has generally focused upon the nature of alliances, e.g., formality, symmetry, and number. Much less has been written about the characteristics of the alliance partners, e.g., strategic goals, administrative structures, range of activities, etc. There are also very few empirical studies in this area. Based on the limited empirical evidence that is available, the author will integrate *partnership* and *partner* characteristics to develop a comprehensive theory of alliances. Such an integration will considerably enhance development of alliance theory as well as help potential partners better understand themselves and their partnerships. *[Article copies available for a fee from The Haworth Document Delivery Service: 1-800-HAWORTH. E-mail address: <getinfo@haworthpressinc.com> Website: <http://www.HaworthPress.com> © 2003 by The Haworth Press, Inc. All rights reserved.]*

Easwar Iyer, PhD, is Associate Professor of Marketing, Isenberg School of Management, University of Massachusetts, Amherst, MA 01003. He is actively engaged in researching various topics that are within the intersection of business strategy, consumer pro-social behavior and environmentalism. Examples of such topics on which he has published include green advertising, environmental alliances, corporate environmentalism and consumer recycling behaviors.

[Haworth co-indexing entry note]: "Theory of Alliances: Partnership and Partner Characteristics." Iyer, Easwar. Co-published simultaneously in *Journal of Nonprofit & Public Sector Marketing* (Best Business Books, an imprint of The Haworth Press, Inc.) Vol. 11, No. 1, 2003, pp. 41-57; and: *Nonprofit and Business Sector Collaboration: Social Enterprises, Cause-Related Marketing, Sponsorships, and Other Corporate-Nonprofit Dealings* (ed: Walter W. Wymer, Jr. and Sridhar Samu) Best Business Books, an imprint of The Haworth Press, Inc., 2003, pp. 41-57. Single or multiple copies of this article are available for a fee from The Haworth Document Delivery Service [1-800-HAWORTH, 9:00 a.m. - 5:00 p.m. (EST). E-mail address: getinfo@ haworthpressinc.com].

KEYWORDS. Alliances, partner characteristrics, partnership characteristics, alliance theory

Alliances can be of various sorts and have been referred to by many
other terms. A number of high profile alliances between for-profit businesses (henceforth referred to merely as *businesses*) and nonprofit organizations (henceforth referred to merely as *nonprofits*) were reported in
the academic, business and popular press during this period. Witness,
for example, the many nonprofits promoting environmental awareness
through alliances with other like-minded nonprofits, government agencies or businesses instead of solely relying on confrontation. Some researchers have noted this change and called it the new willingness to
"work within the system" (Milne, Iyer, and Gooding-Williams 1996).
In the past a number of closely related concepts like symbiotic marketing (Varadarajan and Rajaratnam 1986) and co-marketing alliances
(Bucklin and Sengupta 1993) have been used to describe such relationships. In the extreme, almost every relationship can be conceptualized
to be an alliance of sorts, to the extent that there is a mutual dependence
and interaction. However, to be called an alliance, there has to be much
more than just mutual dependence or interaction. I will begin with a
brief discussion on what constitutes alliances. Two sections will follow
this; first, I will discuss partnership characteristics and second, I will
discuss partner characteristics. Finally I will conclude with summary
comments and some recommendations.

ALLIANCES

Alliance can be defined as the bond or connection between two or
more individuals or institutions. Commonly used synonyms include association, federation and union. Of course, the more fundamental and
key question pertains to the motives of individuals or institutions in
seeking out other individuals or institutions to form such associations,
federations or unions. In other words, why are alliances formed? I will
return to this question later and provide a more detailed theoretical analysis, but for the moment it will suffice to say that in a capitalist economic system promoting free and open markets, the primary motive to
form alliances is based on the expectation that the result of an alliance
will produce an outcome far greater than anything that each individual
could have produced independently. In other words, the synergistic in-

crease in effectiveness resulting from the alliance is the primary motive in its formation.

As stated earlier, almost any business relationship produces an outcome that neither individual entity could have achieved independently and in that extreme sense all business relations can be thought of as alliances. For example a movie theater cannot survive without viewers, and viewers cannot have the movie experience without theaters. This is not an alliance; it is more an issue of marketing-the theaters seek out its viewers and the viewers seek out theaters. However, suppose that the same movie theater decides to "work" with a local bookstore and promote the book on which the movie was based. This could be described as an alliance between the movie theater and the local bookstore. This example makes evident the differences and leads us to a more formal definition of an alliance.

Adapting from Anderson and Narus (1990), an alliance can be defined *as a working partnership in which there is mutual recognition and understanding that the success of each firm depends in part on the other firm/firms*. There are two variations in my adaptation of the original definition. First, Anderson and Narus (1990) restricted their attention to partnerships between businesses only and hence included the notion of satisfying customer needs in their expanded definition. I did not include that aspect in our definition of an alliance because our focus is beyond partnerships between just two businesses; I include partnerships between nonprofits and businesses, between two nonprofits, between businesses and governmental agencies (henceforth refereed to merely as *government* or *agency*), and between nonprofits and government (Iyer and Gooding-Williams 1999, Milne, Iyer and Gooding-Williams 1996). Thus, our definition and scope of alliances includes businesses, nonprofits and government. Second, Anderson and Narus (1990) seemed to implicitly (and maybe unintentionally) restrict their attention to only alliances between two firms. Although two-firm alliances are probably the most common, it is conceivable to have multi-firm alliances. Toward the end I will introduce a new theoretical basis that more readily recognizes this fact. In all other respects I fully concur with the central theme of the original definition according to which no matter who and how many the partners are, all partners in the alliance realize that their capabilities can be combined to mutual advantage and that the success of the alliance depends on every one of the partners. The pooled advantages can stem from each organization's strengths *compensating* for the other's weaknesses or from *amplifying* or *enhancing* their combined strengths. This is an important point that I will return to even as I continue with the presentation.

Why are alliances formed? As I stated earlier on, there is the expectation, grounded in some theoretical logic, that a partnership will somehow produce an outcome greater than the simple addition of the two parts; in other words, 2 + 2 > 4. Such an outcome would be possible if each partner had a particular resource or capability that was lacking in the other, and the alliance would not only overcome that deficiency but also endow the partnership with enhanced strength. This framework, generally referred to as "Resource Dependence Theory" (RDT) (Heide 1994), has been widely used in organizational analysis (Cyert and March 1963, Pfeffer and Salancik 1978) and has its roots in sociology (Emerson 1962) and social psychology (Thibaut and Kelley 1959). The basic premise in RDT is that both partners in the potential alliance lack key resources, which acts as a driver in their seeking out partnerships. Funds, market access, technology, power, influence and many other resources that are lacking may be sought out when forming an alliance. In this theory, there is the implicit assumption that organizations will seek to compensate for these deficiencies when seeking alliance partners. While that may be true sometimes, at other times, organizations may wish to amplify or enhance their strengths and capabilities instead of merely overcoming their deficiencies. This alternative theoretical rationale will be more fully developed later on.

In the 1970s and 1980s businesses tended to favor outright mergers as opposed to forming alliances. The classic example of this would be the merger between Ciba and Geigy (Aaker 1984), two Swiss companies that, after the merger, became a large multinational company. Ciba was renowned in the pharmaceutical sector whereas Geigy was well established in the agricultural chemicals sector. The merger, it is generally believed, was motivated by a desire to combine their unique market access and back it with a massive R&D effort (Varadarajan and Rajaratnam 1986). More recently the merger between AOL and Time Warner was motivated to leverage AOL's brand and digital infrastructure and Time Warner's entertainment, news, and cable operations (*Business Week* 2001). However, mergers are very different from alliances in that strong efforts are directed at replacing the distinct individual identity of each organization with that of a single combined organization. Whether the merged parties are successful in their efforts to forge a unique identity is an entirely different question outside the scope of this discussion.

Alliances, on the other hand, tend to protect the individual identities and cultures of the two partners largely, but not completely, intact. They also tend to be smaller and very targeted in their scope. Even though alliances became more commonplace in the 1980s and later on, they generally tended to be between businesses. Alliances that included nonprofits or government are of much more recent vintage. An early and good example of a business-nonprofit alliance formed in 1989 is the one involving Loblaws, the largest food retailer in Canada, and Pollution Probe, a nonprofit promoting environmental issues (Kohl 1990, Westley and Vredenburg 1991). Another preeminent example is the alliance between Environmental Defense Fund (EDF) and McDonald's (Prince and Denison 1992). In the summer of 1990, as the result of an alliance between EDF and McDonald's, the Solid Waste Task Force was created. This task force's primary objective was to prepare an action plan that would guide McDonald's in their effort to reduce the solid waste produced at their over 8,500 restaurants worldwide. Their final recommendations included 42 initiatives that when implemented were predicted to cut McDonald's solid waste by more than 80%.

So, how do alliances differ from mergers? In all the illustrative examples–mergers or alliances–the parties involved had a unique resource they brought to the union. In case of AOL-Time Warner merger, AOL had the digital infrastructure and Time Warner had the contents for consumer entertainment. In case of the Loblaw-Pollution Probe alliance, Loblaw's had the distribution capability and Pollution Probe had access to the testing technology and credibility. In that sense, resource dependence was the primary driver behind the mergers or alliances illustrated above. However, when it comes to a question of identity, mergers and alliances differ considerably. Notice that in both the examples of alliances all involved parties maintained their independent identities and came together with a fairly specific agenda, unlike in case of mergers, wherein a new identity was born out of the union.

In general, forming an alliance should start with the strategic vision and conscious decision by two parties to form an associative union, although sometimes alliances are formed for lesser reasons. There are two basic issues that need to be clearly understood when forming an alliance: the "*rules*" on which the union rests, i.e., what governs the proposed relationship, and the "*nature*" of the partner, i.e., what are the makeup of each individual organization. I will refer to them as *partnership characteristics* and *partner characteristics*; these will be the focus of the following discussion. After these two sections, I will offer some summary remarks and recommendations in conclusion. The proposed theory of alliances is represented in Figure 1, which also serves as a template for the ensuing presentation.

PARTNERSHIP CHARACTERISTICS

By partnership characteristics I mean the manner in which the alliance is structured and governed. In other words, what are the rules that govern this relationship? The notion of governance is implicit in the effort by any two parties to form an alliance; after all the parties have to agree upon the "ground rules" on which the relationship is to be organized, continued and possibly dissolved. Such an agreement considerably helps in regulating future exchanges and is referred to by Williamson and Ouchi (1981) as a "mode of organizing transactions." The notion of continuation and possible dissolution of the alliance is best captured in Palay (1984), who defines governance to be a "shorthand expression for the institutional framework in which contracts are initiated, negotiated, monitored, adapted and terminated." In other words, "governance is multidimen-

FIGURE 1

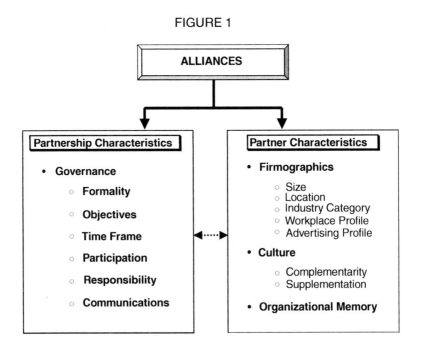

sional phenomenon" (Heide 1994) that includes various subordinate phenomena.

Governance

The concept of governance as discussed until now generally includes the more formal and often written part of an agreement. There are a host of unwritten and implicit "rules" that govern any alliance. Thus, the term *partnership characteristics* will include all *written and unwritten, formal and informal* agreements to be used in the governance of the alliance. Although there are a variety of sub-characteristics, the overarching theme is one of formality: how formal is the agreement? Obviously a formal written agreement represents one end of the continuum and an informal unwritten agreement represents the other end. Formality cannot be simply dichotomized, i.e., the agreement is *formal* or *informal*; there are various degrees of formality. Thus, even two formal written agreements can differ in terms of their language, length, specificity or scope. For instance Iyer and Milne (1994) found that environmental nonprofits had the longest written agreements governing their alliances with government (5.19 pages) as compared to shorter written agreements (1.28 pages) governing their alliances with other nonprofits. Using the number of pages as an indicator of the formality of an alliance agreement, one could conclude that nonprofit-government alliances are much more formal than nonprofit-nonprofit alliances. Whether there is a formal written agreement or just an informal unwritten one is just one aspect of partnership characteristics, which comprises of a number of other subordinate issues. Whereas there are many such subordinate issues, I will restrict my attention to the following five: *objective, time frame, participation, allocation of responsibility and communication systems*, and discuss each one in seriatim.

Objective. Objective refers to the desired outcome of the alliance. As stated earlier itself, alliances are formed primarily to achieve outcomes that may otherwise have not been possible. However, the objective of the alliance may be stated in very broad and general terms, e.g., to understand consumer recycling behaviors, or in very narrow and specific terms, e.g., to increase consumer recycling participation by 25% within 5 years. There is no particular reason to state the alliance's objectives broadly or narrowly. For instance, if the alliance wants to advance its knowledge of consumer recycling behaviors as opposed to actually influencing consumer recycling behaviors, then a broad statement of objective would be more appropriate. The specificity of the objective statement is also a function of how closely the partners agree upon their objectives. In general, the greater the agreement between the partners, the easier it would be to design a specific and narrow statement of objectives. On the other hand, if the partners disagreed in the stated objective, the likelihood of problems increases manifold. Sometimes the parties appear to be in agreement although their deeper motives may have been different. For instance, even though Pollution Probe and Loblaw's framed their alliance as an environmental initiative, their real motives were different (Stafford and Hartman 1996). Pollution Probe's motivation was financial and Loblaw's was to increase its market share. The apparent agreement was very fragile and the relationship between the two partners was fraught with problems until its eventual dissolution in 1991, just two years after the alliance was launched.

Time Frame. Time frame refers to the period for which the alliance will exist. Sometimes alliances are formed with a "sunset" clause that clearly fixes a date for dissolution of the partnership, whereas some other partnerships leave the duration open and vague. In other words, the time frame for an alliance can be very short, medium or long term. Generally short-term alliances also tend to be very specific in their objectives and long-term alliances tend to be less specific in their objectives. For instance the alliance between the Environmental Defense Fund and McDonald's (Stafford and Hartman 2000) was formed with a very specific and short-term objective of reducing the waste generated in the process of McDonald's conducting its business. Although there was no specific mention of a sunset clause, this alliance lasted a little under two years and was dissolved immediately after it made its recommendations. On the other hand, alliance between The Nature Conservancy and Georgia Pacific (Stafford and Hartman 2000) is not only long term but its objective is also broadly stated as protecting the ecosystem and enhancing biodiversity. This alliance was formed in 1994 and is still functional at the time of this research.

Participation. Participation includes trust, level and distance in the relationship between the two partners in the alliance. *Trust* is a function of the commitment expressed by one to another and the other's judgment of the likelihood of that commitment being upheld (Schurr and Ozanne 1985). There are two aspects included in this description. First, there is the expression of commitment, and second, there is the assessment of whether or not that commitment will be honored. Sometimes trust is like an "input" in that negotiations for forming alliances can begin based on some presumed level of trust, albeit at a low level. At other times, trust is like an "output" in that past alliance relationships help create and foster trust. The participation between members of the two alliance partners can be at various *levels* in their organizational hierarchy (Rajan and Rajaratnam 1986). Some alliance could be at the highest corporate levels and encompass many functions whereas other alliances could be at the functional level and be restricted to specific functional areas such as marketing or R&D. *Distance* refers to the gap in the relationship between the alliance partners; it can either be close and proximate or aloof and at an arms-length (Rajan and Rajaratnam 1986). The alliance between Greenpeace and Foron Household Appliances (Stafford and Hartman 2000, Hartman and Stafford 1997) is a premier example of one that was at the highest *corporate level* and *very close* in its relationship. On the other hand the alliance between Pollution Probe and Loblaw's (Westley and Vredenburg 1991), was at the *functional level* and at an *arms-length*. Very rarely can there be a relationship that is at an arms-length as well as close. One such rare example is the alliance between the American Oceans Campaign and various oil companies; even though this nonprofit works very closely with the oil companies in oil recycling programs, it remains one of the oil industry's harshest critics (Hartman and Stafford 1997).

Allocation of Responsibility. Responsibility refers to the allocation of tasks to the two partners involved in the alliance. Recall that the objectives can be broad and vague or narrow and specific. In either case, a successful alliance must clearly and explicitly define and circumscribe the tasks that are implied in the objectives. Moreover, there must be a matching of the task with each partner with their full understanding that they are accountable for those tasks. Nonetheless, this may be one of the weaker aspects in any partnership characteristic. Generally speaking, if the resource dependence pertains to a tangible component, e.g., payment of funds, access to R&D facilities, then the follow through becomes easier. However, if the resource dependence pertains to something intangible, e.g., opening markets, then the follow through and accountability may be harder. To a large extent, allocation of responsibility will be easier when objectives are clearly defined and both parties have open communications systems.

Communication Systems. Communication systems pertain to the formality, frequency, and level at which the information exchange occurs. Whereas more formal communications, e.g., written monographs and reports, are often desirable, sometimes the less formal communications, e.g., an e-mail or a telephone conversation, allow for easier and quicker flow of information. In general a combination of the two will likely be the best, and that brings me to frequency of communications. How fre-

quently must the alliance partners meet and exchange reports? There is
no magic number, but at least once a month or so will be needed for the
more formal exchanges. As for the informal exchanges, they must be allowed to occur at their natural frequency that either partner finds most
comfortable. If the informal exchanges occur at their natural and comfortable frequency, it may even be possible to reduce the frequency of
the more formal communications. The level at which the information
exchange occurs is very critical. There must be free and open access to
members from all levels to participate in the information exchange. Ad-
equate attention must also be paid to internal communications. Thus,
for instance, if the Director of R&D in one organization makes a particular commitment to his counterpart in the other organization, this must
be communicated quickly and completely to other members from both
organizations who may be part of the alliance team. Lacking such quick
and complete information may not only impede meaningful interaction
between other members but also may lead to bad blood.

PARTNER CHARACTERISTICS

By partner characteristics I mean to include all those factors that go to
describe the makeup of any organization. These include firmographics,
i.e., size, location, industry category, workforce profile, advertising profile, etc. (Hawkins, Best and Coney 2001, p. 678, Iyer and Gooding-Williams 1999), organizational culture (Detert, Schroeder and Mauriel 2000),
and organizational memory (Berthon, Pitt and Ewing 2001).

Firmographics

Firmographics includes all the attributes of an organization that are
used to describe it. *Size* is an important attribute of any organization.
Size can be conceptualized in terms of certain financial profiles, e.g.,
sales turnover, market capitalization, or in terms of its workforce, i.e.,
number of employees, although these two tend to be correlated. In other
words, firms with large sales also tend to have a large number of employees. In case of nonprofits, the concept of sales turnover does not apply; instead the organization's annual budget could serve as an indicator
of size (Iyer and Gooding-Williams 1999). Size is a continuous variable, although for this discussion I will be categorizing it into three:
large, medium, and small. Larger organizations will more often have a
greater range of skills represented in its workforce and thus will more

likely have specialists assigned to specific tasks. While this may be an advantage from a task knowledge and allocation perspective, it may pose problems in regards to communications. On the other hand, smaller organizations will have fewer employees; this may be a problem for allocating tasks but decisions may be more easily forthcoming.

Location refers to the geographic site of the organization. Location[1] can be conceptualized as an inter-national variable, i.e., country, global affiliations, or as an intra-national variable, i.e., state, region, etc. The differences between countries are well known in popular and academic communities. If the alliance partners come from different countries, time difference becomes one of the key issues, although such differences may manifest even within one country. *Industry category* refers to the type of business any organization is engaged in. This is an important variable because the type of industry it is operating in will influence much of the firm's perceptions. For instance, a chemical manufacturing company may categorize itself as operating in the "chemicals sector." If so, it may not want to seek alliances with any nonprofit it sees as threatening, e.g., Greenpeace, that often criticizes chemical companies for polluting the environment. However, if the same company were to categorize itself differently, say, as operating in the "energy sector," it may seek alliances not only with other energy producers, such as oil, coal, and natural gas producers, but also with nonprofits that try to promote "clean energy" and "energy conservation." In fact, such an alliance may considerably enhance the company's image resulting in forestalling regulations or in opening up newer markets.

Workforce profile refers to the number of employees and their skill levels (Iyer and Gooding-Williams 1999). It would be synonymous with size, if it only included the number of employees. However, workforce profile also includes the range of skills represented in a firm's employees. For instance, a traditional manufacturing firm may have to employ many craftspeople or those with moderate levels of education, whereas a high-tech firm may have to employ people with advanced degrees and high technical skills. This will play an important role in the formation and management of an alliance. When a business with few PR skills but significant managerial capability forms an alliance with a nonprofit with excellent PR skills but poor managerial capability, the resulting alliance can benefit by complementing the two partners' skills and capabilities. However, the presumed advantage of blending complementing skills is not universally true, and as an example, an engineering business may have a difficult time blending with a nonprofit that has no engineers in its payroll because of differing organizational cultures.

Advertising profile refers to the volume and types of advertising that a firm engages in. Whether an organization–business, nonprofit or government–engages in advertising or not and the amount and types of advertising serve as a critical indicator of the firm's style of operation (Iyer and Gooding-Williams 1999). In their study, Iyer and Gooding-Williams (1999) found that one type of nonprofit, best exemplified by The Nature Conservancy and Keep America Beautiful, advertised heavily and relied quite extensively on direct mail to deliver their message. On the other hand, another type of nonprofit, epitomized by the Upper Mississippi River Conservation Committee and The Rye Nature Center and Association, did not engage in any form of advertising at all. Businesses forming alliances with Old Solicitors may find it easy to advertise and promote their alliances, whereas businesses partnering with the Old Fashioned nonprofits may have a harder time because of the lack of emphasis on advertising. The volume and type of advertising also can vary from one firm to another. To some degree, volume of advertising is related to a firm's size, but various other factors such as the firm's perceptions of the effectiveness of advertising will determine the volume of advertising. Choice of media and frequency will also likely vary from firm to firm, with some choosing more traditional media, e.g., newspaper, radio, or television, and other choosing newer media, e.g., direct mail or the Internet.

Organizational Culture

Culture has been the focus of much work in anthropology and sociology for well over 100 years. However, its introduction and popular use in the business and management literature is of more recent vintage. The most widely used term is *organizational culture*, although more and more researchers use the term *corporate culture* as a synonym. Without getting into the debate, it is important to point out that many scholars view culture as something an organization *has*–implying that culture is a property of an organization and that the organization can have an existence independent of culture–whereas others view culture as something an organization *is*–implying that culture is intrinsic to the very existence of an organization (Meglino and Ravlin 1998, Smircich 1983). No matter which view one favors, clearly there has to be some compatibility between the cultures of the alliance partners, and often successful alliances are preceded by preliminary foundation work that aims to "understand" each other's cultures (Maron and vanBremenn 1999).

In the past decade or so researchers have speculated that the business performance–measured in terms of market share, profitability, size, and comparative growth rate–will be influenced by organizational culture (Deshpande, Farley and Webster 1993). In their exploratory research on Japanese firms, Deshpande, Farley and Webster (1993) proposed four categories of companies based primarily on their differences in organizational cultures: Clan, Adhocracy, Hierarchy, and Market. Organizations with a *clan* culture adopted organic processes and internal maintenance and tend to promote a sense of family by emphasizing loyalty, tradition and commitment. Organizations with an *adhocracy* culture adopted organic processes and external positioning and tend to emphasize creativity, innovativeness and risk taking. Those that adopted mechanistic processes and internal maintenance, and highlighted order, uniformity and rules were categorized as *hierarchy* cultures. Lastly, those adopting a *market* culture accepted mechanistic processes and external positioning by stressing superiority, competitiveness and goal achievement. Organizations with market cultures were associated with the best performance, followed by those adopting adhocracy and clan cultures, and organizations with hierarchy cultures were the worst performers.

Whereas these results are interesting from business strategy point of view, what does it mean for forming alliances? To derive any implications for forming alliances, I have to go back to the original rationale of alliance formation and introduce the concepts of *complementarity* and *supplementation*. Recall that as per the RDT, alliances are formed because partners in the prospective alliance lack one or more key resources, and they seek out alliance partners to remedy that lacuna. This view assumes that organizations are primarily driven by a desire to overcome their present weakness and that there would be significant advantages to pooling resources. Recall that at the beginning I had stated that the pooled advantages could stem from each organization's strengths *compensating* for the other's weaknesses or from *amplifying* or *enhancing* their combined strengths. In other words, two organizations could form an alliance that combines and amplifies their objectives. The common principle of "strength in numbers" best captures this perspective. Thus, rather than seeking an objective all by itself, an organization may benefit from partnering with other like-minded organizations, thus providing an amplification or enhancement. The fundamental question is: does the organization wish to *complement* or *supplement* the partnering organization? I will elaborate on these two principles here below.

Complementarity in an alliance refers to the idea that two partnering organizations having unique and non-overlapping capabilities wish to form an alliance that will overcome each other's limitations. This would be an effective guiding principle if overcoming the weaknesses was of primary concern and without complementing, the alliance would not be as successful. A case in point would be the alliance between Greenpeace and Foron Household Appliances (Stafford and Hartman 2000, Hartman and Stafford 1997). This alliance was formed with the objective of promoting HC-based refrigerator coolants, reported to be ozone-friendly, in lieu of HFCs and HCFCs that are more commonly used and believed to cause ozone depletion. Greenpeace had credibility and technology and Foron had manufacturing capability and underutilized capacity; the alliance was successful in marketing over 40 million household refrigerators in various parts of the world (Stafford and Hartman 2001). This alliance clearly exemplifies the RDT and underscores the value of one organization complementing the other.

Supplementation in an alliance refers to the idea that two partnering organizations having certain strengths that they wish to magnify form an alliance. The proposed logic for an alliance is not consistent with RDT; rather, it speaks to the value of Capability Enhancement. In other words, the two organizations seek an alliance so that their combined capability will be considerably greater that either one individually. An example cited in Iyer and Gooding-Williams (1999) is the Wildlife Center of Virginia that got together with other local nonprofits interested in parks and land conservation so that they could fulfill their mission much more effectively. Another example is the alliance between The Nature Conservancy, Ducks Unlimited, The California Waterfowl Association and the California Rice Industry Association (Stafford and Hartman 2000). In this case, they enhanced their combined visibility and credibility by supplementing each other and successfully persuaded the U. S. Bureau of Reclamation in allowing rice farmers to flood their fields as an alternative way of disposal of excess rice straw. These examples demonstrate the value of combining capabilities in order to magnify visibility or credibility.

Organizational Memory

All employees in any organization are transitory and move on to other working environments at one stage or another for one reason or another. Yet organizations tend to "remember" the policies and behaviors of the recently departed employee, and a new employee "introduces" policies and behaviors learned from the old organization to the new environment. In other words, even as the workforce changes, organizations seem to have a core set of values, beliefs, processes and schema that can be termed *organizational memory* (Berthon, Pitt and Ewing 2001). What role does organizational memory play in the formation of alliances? To a large extent the answer to this question depends on the larger organizational culture and organizational memory can either assist or inhibit alliance formation, depending on the situation and context. If there is the tendency to analyze past experiences as a learning vehicle, then it could assist alliance formation. If, however, there is a tendency to never look beyond past experiences, then it could inhibit alliance formation.

CONCLUSION

Alliance formation was the focal point of this article. After defining and reviewing past literature, I proposed two concepts, i.e., partnership characteristics and partner characteristics, as the primary conceptual basis to frame the presentation. Each of these concepts had many sub-concepts that I explored in detail. I will conclude by highlighting the salient issues discussed in this article.

- Alliance can be formed as a result of Resource Dependence or Capability Enhancement.
- Partnership Characteristics is the manner in which the alliance is structured and governed and must be discussed before forming an alliance.
- Partnership Characteristics includes Governance, Objective, Time Frame, Participation, Allocation of Responsibility and Communication Systems and is a vital part of any alliance.
- Partner Characteristics includes all those factors that go to describe the makeup of any organization.
- Partner Characteristics includes Firmographics, Organizational Culture and Organizational Memory.
- Partnership Characteristics and Partner Characteristics interact with each other and jointly influence the success of any alliance.

What should a firm look for when seeking alliance partners? First of all, the firm has to have a strategic vision and be convinced that it needs a partner to advance its objectives. Next, the firm must decide whether overcoming its deficiencies or enhancing its capabilities is critical to attain its objectives. If overcoming deficiencies is seen as critical, then it should seek partners with characteristics that will complement its own. For instance, a firm lacking presence in a region may be able to take advantage by partnering with another that has a significant presence in that region. If enhancing capabilities is seen as vital, then a firm must look for partners with characteristics to supplement its own. Three or four nonprofits that combine their resources so as to communicate more resoundingly with a government agency will best exemplify this point. No matter what the rationale, all aspects of the partnership will have to be carefully and clearly identified for the alliance to have any prospects of success.

NOTE

1. I have included location in firmographics even though some might suggest that it is correlated to "regional culture," because it is more of a descriptive variable.

REFERENCES

Aaker, David (1984), *Strategic Marketing Management*. New York: Wiley.

Anderson, James C. and James A. Narus (1990), "A Model of Distributor Firm and Manufacturer Firm Working Partnerships," *Journal of Marketing*, 54 (January), p. 42-57.

Berthon, Pierre, Leyland F. Pitt and Michael T. Ewing (2001), "Corollaries of the Collective: The Influence of Organizational Culture and Memory Development on Perceived Decision-Making Context," *Journal of the Academy of Marketing Science*, 29:2 (Spring), p. 135-150.

Bucklin, Louis P. and Sanjit Sengupta (1993), "Organizing Successful Co-Marketing Alliances," *Journal of Marketing*, 57 (April), p. 32-46.

Business Week (2001), May 14, Industrial/technology edition; p. EB28.

Cyert, Richard M. and James G. March (1963), *A Behavioral Theory of the Firm*. Englewood Cliffs, NJ: Prentice-Hall, Inc.

Deshpande, Rohit, John U. Farley and Frederick E. Webster, Jr. (1993), "Corporate Culture, Customer Orientation, and Innovativeness in Japanese Firms: A Quadrad Analysis," *Journal of Marketing*, 57:1 (January), p. 23-37.

Detert, James R., Roger G. Schroeder and John J. Mauriel, (2000), "A Framework For Linking Culture and Improvement Initiatives in Organizations," *Academy of Management Review*, 25:4 (October), p. 850

Emerson, Richard M. (1962), "Power-Dependence Relations," *American Sociological Review*, 27 (February), p. 31-41.

Hartman, Cathy L. and Edwin R. Stafford (1997), "Green Alliances: Building New Business with Environmental Groups," *Long Range Planning*, 30:2, p. 184-196.

Hawkins, Del I., Roger J. Best and Kenneth A. Coney (2001), *Consumer Behavior: Building Marketing Strategy*, New York: Irwin McGraw-Hill.

Heide, Jan (1994), "Interorganizational Governance in Marketing Channels," *Journal of Marketing*, 58 (January), p. 71-84.

Iyer, Easwar S. and Sara Gooding-Williams (1999), "How to Form Good Alliances," in *Green Marketing*, Martin Charter and Michael J. Polonsky, Eds. London UK: Greenleaf Publishers, p. 181-195.

_____ and George R. Milne (1994), "Environmental Organizations and their Co-Marketing Practices," Report produced for the members of the National Wildlife Federation.

Kohl, Helen (1990), Are They Nature's Choice?" *Financial Post Moneywise*, (April), p. 16-29.

Maron, Rebecca M. and Lee vanBremen (1999), "The Influence of Organizational Culture on Strategic Alliances," *Association Management*, (April), p. 86-92.

Meglino, B. M. & Ravlin, E. C. (1998), "Individual values in organizations: Concepts, controversies, and research," *Journal of Management*, 24, p. 351-389.

Milne, George R., Easwar S. Iyer and Sara Gooding-Williams (1996), "Environmental Organizational Alliance Relationships within and Across Nonprofit, Business and Government Sectors, *Journal of Public Policy and Marketing*, 15 (Fall), p. 203-215.

Palay, Thomas (1984), Comparative Institutional Economics: The Governance of Rail Freight Contracting," *Journal of Legal Studies*, 13 (June), p. 265-288.

Pfeffer, Jeffrey and Gerald. R. Salancik (1978), *The External Control of Organizations: A Resource Dependence Perspective*. New York: Harper & Row.

Prince, S. Jackie and Richard A. Denison (1992), "Launching a New Business Ethic: The Environment as a Standard," *Industrial Management*, 34:6 (Nov/Dec) 1992, p. 15-19.

Smircich, Linda (1983), "Concepts of culture and organizational analysis," *Administrative Science Quarterly*, 29, p. 339-358.

Stafford, Edwin R. and Cathy L. Hartman (2001), "Greenpeace's 'Greenfreeze' Campaign," in *Ahead of the Curve*, Ken Green, Peter Groenewegen, Peter S. Hofman, Amsterdam, Holland: Kluwer Academic Publishers, p. 107-131.

Stafford, Edwin R. and Cathy L. Hartman (2000), "Environmentalist-Business Collaborations: Social Responsibility, Green Alliances, and Beyond," in *Advertising Research: The Internet, Consumer Behavior and Strategy*, George Zinkhan, Ed., Chicago, IL: American Marketing Association.

_____ and (1996), "Green Alliances: Strategic Relations Between Businesses and Environmental Groups, *Business Horizons*, 39 (March-April), p. 50-59.

Thibaut, John W. and Harold H. Kelley (1959), *The Social Psychology of Groups*. New York: John Wiley & Sons, Inc.

Varadarajan, P. "Rajan" and Daniel Rajaratnam (1986), "Symbiotic Marketing Revisited," *Journal of Marketing*, 50 (January), p. 7-17.

Westley, Frances and Harrie Vredenburg (1991), "Strategic Bridging: The Collaboration Between Environmentalists and Business in the Marketing of Green Products," *Journal of Applied Behavioral Science*, 27 (March), p. 65-90.

Williamson, Oliver E. and William G. Ouchi (1981), The Markets and Hierarchies Program of Research: Origins, Implications, Prospects," in *Perspectives on Organization Design and Behavior*, A. H. Van de Ven and W. F. Joyce, Eds., New York: John Wiley & Sons, Inc., p. 347-370.

Dangerous Donations?
The Effects of Cause-Related Marketing
on Charity Attitude

Debra Z. Basil
Paul M. Herr

SUMMARY. How might cause-related marketing affect attitudes toward the charity involved? Could charity attitudes be harmed? These questions were addressed in a controlled laboratory study. Positive/negative fit between the organizations was manipulated, and company attitude was measured. The results suggest that charity attitude may be negatively impacted if consumers' attitudes toward the company are negative, or if the organizations have negative fit. Alternatively, CRM may improve charity attitude if company attitude is positive or the organizations share positive fit. The effect of fit is stronger than the effect of company attitude, so positive fit may compensate for pairing with a company toward which consumers' attitudes are negative. *[Article copies available for a fee from The Haworth Document Delivery Service: 1-800-HAWORTH. E-mail address: <getinfo@ haworthpressinc.com> Website: <http:// www.HaworthPress.com> © 2003 by The Haworth Press, Inc. All rights reserved.]*

Debra Z. Basil, PhD, is Assistant Professor of Marketing, University of Lethbridge.
Paul M. Herr, PhD, is Associate Professor of Marketing, University of Colorado, Leeds School of Business.

Address correspondence to: Debra Z. Basil, Faculty of Management, University of Lethbridge, 4401 University Drive, Lethbridge, Alberta, Canada, T1K 3M4 (E-mail address: debra.basil@uleth.ca).

[Haworth co-indexing entry note]: "Dangerous Donations? The Effects of Cause-Related Marketing on Charity Attitude." Basil, Debra Z., and Paul M. Herr. Co-published simultaneously in *Journal of Nonprofit & Public Sector Marketing* (Best Business Books, an imprint of The Haworth Press, Inc.) Vol. 11, No. 1, 2003, pp. 59-76; and: *Nonprofit and Business Sector Collaboration: Social Enterprises, Cause-Related Marketing, Sponsorships, and Other Corporate-Nonprofit Dealings* (ed: Walter W. Wymer, Jr. and Sridhar Samu) Best Business Books, an imprint of The Haworth Press, Inc., 2003, pp. 59-76. Single or multiple copies of this article are available for a fee from The Haworth Document Delivery Service [1-800-HAWORTH, 9:00 a.m. - 5:00 p.m. (EST). E-mail address: getinfo@haworthpressinc.com].

KEYWORDS. Cause-related marketing, charity attitude change, experiment, within-subjects ANOVA

INTRODUCTION

The financial survival of non-profit organizations depends upon the ability of these organizations to secure much needed funding from both the general public and corporate entities. The nature of corporate donations appears to be changing, and this could have a major impact on non-profit organizations. First, companies are under more pressure to give back to the communities in which they operate (Benezra, 1996). Second, companies are looking for greater corporate benefit for their philanthropic dollar (Dienhart, 1988). Taken together, these two trends suggest that companies will be seeking a means of making charitable donations that is highly visible to the general public. This may account for the increasing popularity of cause-related marketing (Cone/Roper 1999).

Cause-related marketing (CRM) occurs when a company and a charity or non-profit organization form an agreement such that a portion of the proceeds from the company's sales is donated to the charity (Varadarajan & Menon, 1988). In return the company gains the right to publicize their CRM efforts, which has been shown to improve consumer attitudes toward the company (Ross, Patterson, & Stutts, 1992). A recent survey of corporate members of the Promotional Marketing Association and leaders of major non-profit organizations indicated that over 85% of corporations and 65% of non-profit organizations had participated in some form of CRM (PMA/Gable Group, 2000). A similar survey, conducted by Roper Starch Worldwide for Cone Inc., found that 92% of businesses surveyed had participated in some form of CRM (Blum, 2000). Some examples of successful CRM campaigns include Avon's breast cancer awareness campaign that generated $22 million, American Express' efforts for hunger relief that generated $20 million, and Visa USA's children's literacy campaign that generated $1 million (Davidson, 1997). The Cone/Roper survey indicated that funding for CRM campaigns usually comes from the company's corporate-giving program or company-related foundation (Blum, 2000). This suggests that funds formerly donated to charities in other ways now come to charities through CRM partnerships. In order to continue to receive these corporate funds, then, charities may need to look toward CRM partnerships.

CRM offers charities an opportunity to gain both revenue and publicity. But at what cost? Could CRM have a negative impact on a charity? If, for example, Nike formed a CRM partnership with the Special Olympics, the Special Olympics could potentially gain a great deal of revenue and additional publicity for their cause. If associating with Nike negatively affects donors' attitudes toward the Special Olympics, however, the CRM partnership may be more of a liability than an asset. This research seeks to address whether CRM may change consumer attitudes toward the charity involved. If the CRM partnership itself harms individuals' attitudes toward the charity, the short-term financial gains of the CRM partnership may not be worth the potential loss of donor support. This research looks at the effect an individual's attitude toward the company in a CRM pairing can have on his or her attitude toward the charity. Additionally, the effect of fit between the company and charity is examined. Finally, the relative size of each of these effects is considered, to determine whether one can compensate for the other. A controlled laboratory experiment with student subjects is used to assess these issues, in an effort to demonstrate causality and control extraneous variables.

THEORETICAL DEVELOPMENT AND HYPOTHESES

As the incidence of CRM has increased, so has research relating to CRM. Varadarajan and Menon (1988) wrote the first major academic article relating to CRM, putting forth a number of managerial issues corporate leaders should consider when contemplating a CRM partnership. These include, for example, considering corporate objectives for the campaign such as increasing sales or offsetting negative publicity. Subsequent research has demonstrated that CRM can improve consumer attitudes toward the company's product or service (Berger, Cunningham, & Kozinets, 1996; Lafferty, 1997), and that CRM can increase consumer intention to buy the product (Coy, 1996). Perceptions of a company's motive for forming the CRM partnership can influence the effect the partnership has on consumer attitudes, with consumers responding negatively when they perceive corporate motives to be self-serving (Barone, Miyazaki, & Taylor, 2000). Additionally, personal support for the cause helps to improve consumer response to CRM partnerships (Sen & Bhattacharya, 2001). Even the nature of the product can influence consumers' CRM purchases, with consumers preferring CRM partnerships that are associated with hedonic rather than utilitarian products (Strahilevitz & Meyer, 1998). Research relating to the more general notion of corporate social responsibility also has been increasing (e.g., Brown & Dacin, 1997; Drumwright, 1996), suggesting a stronger focus on social responsibility issues within the field of marketing. These lines of research have provided valuable information regarding the effects of CRM on corporate performance, consumers' attitudes toward the company, and consumers' purchase intentions. Some research has also examined the effects of CRM on consumer attitudes toward the charity (e.g., Webb & Mohr, 1998), but this research is less plentiful. The present research seeks to contribute to this latter area by addressing the effects of CRM partnerships on consumers' charity attitudes.

Since CRM involves pairing a company and a charity, in considering how a CRM partnership might affect attitudes toward the charity, two important factors to consider are individuals' pre-existing attitudes toward the company, and individuals' attitudes toward pairing that specific company with the charity. First we will address the issue of attitude toward the company.

Previous CRM research has used a variety of theoretical frameworks in an effort to understand the consumer. Berger, Cunningham, and Kozinets contrasted the Elaboration Likelihood Model (Petty, Cacioppo & Schumann, 1983) with the Motivation, Opportunity, and Ability framework (MacInnis, Moorman, & Jaworski, 1991) in an effort to clarify how consumers cognitively process CRM advertisements. Strahilevitz and Myers (1998) used a complementarity framework examining multiple outcomes (Linville & Fischer, 1991) in order to understand how consumer responses to CRM campaigns differ for hedonic versus utilitarian products. Webb and Mohr (1998) developed their own typology of responses to CRM partnerships in order to gain richer insight into the CRM consumer. In each case, the selection of a theoretical framework was based upon the specific question at hand and the nature of the hypotheses being tested. In the present research an Associative Network frame was used, because this framework offers a clear indication of how concepts become linked with one another in an individual's mind. This issue is highly relevant to the question of organizational fit addressed in the present research.

The associative network view conceptualizes memory as a large, spider web-like structure. The general idea of associative networks can be traced back to British philosophers such as Locke and Hume (Gilbert, Fiske, & Lindzey, 1998). This concept was later adopted and extended within cognitive psychology (Collins & Quillian, 1969; Collin & Loftus, 1975; Anderson, 1983; and Fiske & Taylor, 1991). In an associative network individual nodes represent concepts, and these nodes are linked together (as though with the thread of a spider web). When an individual recalls a concept, that node is "activated" in memory. Related concepts that are linked to that node are also activated, with the level of activation decreasing for nodes that are farther removed from the activated node. This pattern of concept activation is known as spreading activation (e.g., Anderson, 1983).

New links can be formed when two previously unrelated concepts are experienced or thought of together (Gilbert, Fiske, & Lindzey, 1998). For example if the Special Olympics forms a CRM partnership with Nike, a link between these two organizations will be formed in individuals' associative networks. Once this link has been formed, when the Special Olympics node is activated in an individual's associative network, the Nike node will also be activated, albeit not as strongly. Concepts linked to Nike will also be activated, though again less strongly. If these concepts are negative (such as the use of sweat shops), then negative affect will be activated. This pattern of activation continues through all links, with the strength of activation declining the farther removed the concept is from the Special Olympics node within the individual's associative network. A concept directly linked to the Special Olympics (such as developmental disabilities) will be activated fairly strongly when the concept of the Special Olympics is activated, whereas a concept that is separated from the Special Olympics by several separate links (such as athletic wear) will only be weakly activated. If individuals hold negative attitudes toward Nike, then this negative affect becomes linked to the Special Olympics. Activation of the Special Olympics node in memory will cause activation of this negative affect. Thus if a charity pairs with a company toward which individuals hold negative attitudes, the individual's attitude toward the charity may become more negative.

On the surface it may appear odd to consider pairing with a company toward which individuals hold negative attitudes. It is quite possible, however, for a charity to partner with a company toward which its donors hold negative attitudes, perhaps even without the charity's management realizing this. It is important to recognize that attitudes can differ between groups of individuals. A company may be well liked by the general public, thus resulting in excellent product sales, making the company appear to be an appealing partner for CRM pairings. However, the charity's supporters may dislike the company, perhaps due to some negative behavior on the part of the company (e.g., involvement with "sweatshops" or poor environmental practices). Nike, for example, received a great deal of negative publicity for a time due to involvement with "sweatshops." After the furor died down, concern within the general public seemed to dissipate. Nike might be an acceptable CRM partner if concern within a charity's key donor groups also dissipated. However, concern such as this can dissipate differentially–one group may hold onto such concerns longer than other groups. If the charity's key donor groups still harbored negative affect toward Nike, then this partnership might be detrimental. It is proposed that such a situation could lead to short-term revenue increases for the charity, as the charity benefits from the CRM-linked product sales. However, pairing with a company that charity donors dislike might harm key donors' attitudes toward the charity, decreasing non-CRM related charity donations. It is important then, for the charity to consider both the general public's attitudes toward the company, in order to assess potential CRM product sales, and key donors' attitudes toward the company, in order to assess potential impact on non-CRM related donations.

Although charity managers would most likely prefer to partner with companies toward which attitudes are positive, willing partners may not always be available. It may be easier for charities to find willing partners among companies that face some form of negative consumer evaluation, since the company may use the CRM partnership to address such negative issues. For example, one of the groups Philip Morris has supported for years is Keep America Beautiful (http://www.philipmorrisusa.com). Keep America Beautiful seeks to reduce litter among other things. They are currently taking part in a joint effort to distribute ashtrays to public places, in an effort to reduce cigarette-butt litter. Keep America Beautiful supporters may hold negative attitudes toward Philip Morris, given the frequency with which cigarette butts are littered. Nonetheless they gain valuable financial support from Philip Morris. An associative network interpretation of this partnership suggests that this pairing may harm donors' attitudes toward Keep America Beautiful, because the organization has partnered with a company toward which donor attitudes may be negative (Philip Morris). This leads to the following hypothesis:

Hypothesis 1: Pre-existing company attitude will affect charity attitude such that a positive pre-existing company attitude will lead to positive change in charity attitude, whereas a negative pre-existing company attitude will lead to negative change in charity attitude.

The same reasoning can be used to understand individuals' responses to the actual partnership itself, regardless of pre-existing attitude toward the company. If a charity and a company become linked in an individual's associative network, both will be activated to some extent when the charity is activated in memory. Concepts that are linked to both the charity and the company should be more strongly activated than concepts that are only linked to one or the other (holding constant how far removed the concept is from the originally activated node). In a CRM partnership according to spreading activation theory whatever the two organizations have in common should be more strongly activated. If this concept is favorable, attitude toward the charity should become more favorable. If this concept is unfavorable, attitude toward the charity should become less favorable. For example, if Gerber baby food were to pair with the SIDS Foundation (Sudden Infant Death Syndrome), "babies" is the common node that should be activated. Most people have positive affect toward babies, so we would expect this partnership to result in more positive affect toward The SIDS Foundation. Conversely, if MADD were to pair with an alcohol company, "drunk driving" is the common node that would be activated in individuals' associative networks. The alcohol company could be seen as a facilitator for the practice of drunk driving, whereas MADD could be seen as a deterrent to the practice. Since drunk driving is a concept linked with negative affect, this partnership should result in negative attitude change toward MADD.

This conceptualization of examining the common element linking the company and charity is similar to the concept of fit in other literatures. Fit, and the similar concept of relatedness, was first conceptualized in the brand extension literature. Aaker and Keller (1990) defined "fit" in terms of three constructs: whether the extension and core brand were complements, whether they were substitutes, or whether knowledge gained from producing the core brand would be uniquely helpful in producing the extension. Good fit between a brand extension and the company's current brand offerings (Aaker & Keller, 1990) and similarity, typicality, or relatedness between the extension and the core brand (Boush & Loken, 1991; Broniarczyk & Alba, 1994; Dacin & Smith, 1994; and Herr, Farquhar, & Fazio, 1996) have been shown to foster more favorable consumer attitudes toward a brand extension.

The concept of fit was later applied to a co-branding situation. It was found that when two organizations' brands and products were viewed as fitting together, consumer attitudes toward the co-branding effort were more favorable (Simonin & Ruth, 1998). Conceptually extending

this, we would expect consumer attitudes to be more favorable to CRM partnerships that fit together as well.

Fit between two organizations in a co-branding situation can also be likened to fit between a celebrity and a product, in cases of celebrity product endorsements. According to the match-up hypothesis (Kamins, 1990), celebrity endorsements are more effective when the celebrity is seen to match with, or fit, the product. This is additional support for the importance of fit between two entities that join together. A conceptual extension of this again suggests the importance of fit between the organizations in a CRM partnership.

In the present research, organizations sharing a common concept carrying positive affect (such as Gerber and SIDS' shared concept of "babies") could be seen as "fitting" together in a positive way, or sharing positive fit. In contrast, organizations sharing a common element carrying negative affect (such as MADD and the alcohol company's shared concept of "drunk driving") could be seen as sharing negative fit. The present study, then, examines positive and negative fit between charities and companies. The concept of positive fit is similar to the concept of fit examined in previous research. However the concept of negative fit is quite different from the concept of no fit examined in previous research. No fit in other research has generally meant that no common concept existed. The concept of negative fit, on the other hand, suggests that the organizations share a common concept, but that concept has negative valence. Positive fit is expected to improve charity attitude, whereas negative fit is expected to harm charity attitude. This suggests the following hypothesis:

> Hypothesis 2: If the common element linking a company and charity generally carries positive affect (positive fit), the CRM partnership will have a more positive effect on charity attitude than if the common element linking the two generally carries negative affect (negative fit).

Both company attitude and positive/negative fit are proposed to influence change in charity attitude. If both were negative, we would expect a negative change in charity attitude. If both were positive, we would expect a positive change in charity attitude. What if one is negative and one is positive? The final issue this research examines is whether one of these factors can serve to overcome the negative effects of the other. Can positive fit compensate for pairing with a disliked company? Can pairing with a well-liked company compensate for negative fit? These questions have strong implications for charities. A charity might be willing to form a CRM partnership that would result in no appreciable change in charity attitude, because the CRM partnership would provide the charity with revenue. A charity most likely would not be willing to enter into a CRM partnership that would make charity attitude more negative, because this could have negative effects on charitable donations. This research seeks to determine whether company attitude can compensate for negative fit, and/or whether positive fit can compensate for negative company attitude. If so, charities would need only one of these attributes to be positive before considering a CRM partnership, thus opening more options in the selection of a CRM partner. This issue is put forth as a research question:

Research Question: Can positive company attitude compensate for the effect of negative fit on charity attitude change? Alternatively, can positive fit compensate for the effect of negative company attitude on charity attitude change?

METHOD

The research reported here was part of a larger study utilizing a controlled laboratory experiment. Sixty undergraduate business students at a major university in the Western United States participated in the study for extra course credit. The study was a 2 (fit) × 6 (CRM pairings) within-subjects design. Each subject completed paper and pencil questionnaires relating to 12 different CRM pairings, 8 of which were used in the present research. Four of those used in this research were pairings with positive fit, and 4 were pairings with negative fit. The pairings were randomly ordered. The actual pairings were fictitious, but the companies and charities used were real. The use of real company and charity names allowed for an examination of pre-existing attitudes, helping to improve external validity. The company and charity pairings used are shown in Table 1.

Subjects first indicated their attitudes toward a wide variety of for-profit and non-profit organizations, within which the target organizations were embedded. At this point subjects had not been exposed to any CRM information, so their attitude measures were not affected by information regarding the CRM partnerships. Subjects then read an explanation of cause-related marketing which included an example for

TABLE 1. Pairings Used in Study

Company	Positive Fit Charity	Positive Commonality	Negative Fit Charity	Negative Commonality
Nike	American Heart Association	Stronger hearts	Feed the Children	Disadvantaged children
Velveeta	Feed the Children	Food	American Heart Association	Heart disease
Smith and Wesson	National Rifle Association	Responsible gun use	Youth at Risk	Youth gun use
Nintendo	Youth at Risk	Youth activities	National Rifle Association	Youth gun use

clarity. Next subjects assessed the CRM partnerships. For each pairing subjects were instructed to imagine that the company and the charity had formed a CRM partnership. They then were asked to respond to scale-item questions regarding their reactions to the partnerships. Responses were measured on 11-point scales, ranging from −5 to +5.

Results

A 2 (fit) × 4 (CRM pairing) repeated-measures ANOVA was conducted to test Hypotheses 1 and 2 and the Research Question. Positive fit/negative fit and the non-theoretical pairing variable (which company was involved in the pairing) served as within-subject factors. Charity attitude change in each of the eight different scenarios served as the dependent variable. Pre-existing company attitude was a varying covariate.

Supporting Hypothesis 1, charity attitude improved significantly more when pre-existing company attitudes were positive, compared to negative pre-existing company attitudes ($t = 4.70$, $eta^2 = .28$, $p < .001$; see Figure 1). Supporting Hypothesis 2, the ANOVA showed that positive fit improved charity attitude ($F [1, 57] = 98.22$, $eta^2 = .63$, $p < .001$[1]). Subjects' attitudes toward the charity became significantly more positive when the organizations had positive fit than when they had negative fit (see Figure 2). Addressing the research question, the effect size for positive/negative fit was much larger than the effect size for company attitude ($eta^2 = .63$ versus $eta^2 = .28$ respectively), suggesting that the effect of fit is stronger than the effect of company attitude.

FIGURE 1. Company Attitude Main Effect

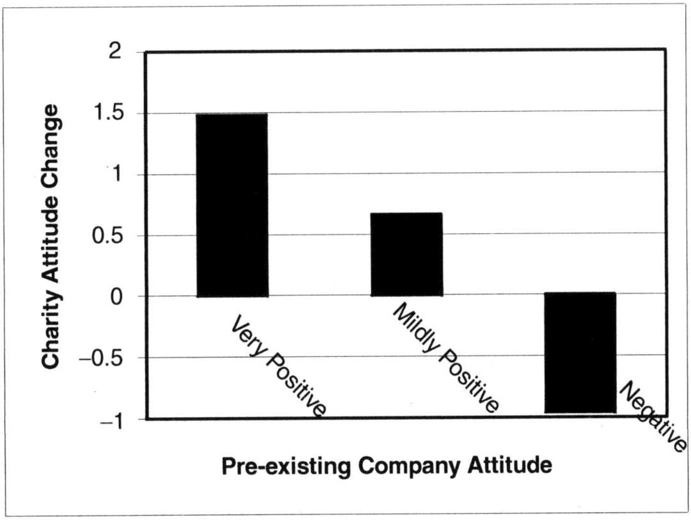

To further address the Research Question, the interaction between positive/negative fit and company attitude was assessed. ANOVA does not test covariate by factor interactions, therefore separate repeated-measures ANOVAs were necessary to perform this test. A separate 2 (fit) × 3 (company attitude) ANOVA was run for each company (Nike, Velveeta, Smith and Wesson, Nintendo), for a total of 4 ANOVAs. Fit served as a within-subject factor. Company attitude served as a between-subjects factor. Charity attitude change was the dependent variable used in each ANOVA. In each case company attitude was trichotomized, creating three separate attitude groups of approximately equal size. Group 1 represented subjects with a negative attitude toward the company (these subjects circled negative numbers on the company attitude response scale), group 2 represented subjects with a neutral or mildly positive attitude toward the company (these subjects circled 0, 1, 2, or 3 on the company attitude response scale), and group 3 represented subjects with a very positive attitude toward the company (these subjects circled 4 or 5 on the company attitude response scale). Trichotomizing company attitude allowed for this variable to serve as a between-subjects factor in the ANOVA, thus allowing for an assessment of the fit by company attitude interaction. The fit by company attitude interaction was insignificant in three of the four pairings (Nike: $F[2, 57] = 1.24$, $eta^2 = .05$, $p < .3$;

FIGURE 2. Fit Main Effect

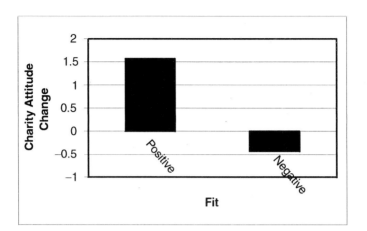

Velveeta: F[2, 57] = 1.19, eta^2 = .04, p < .3; Nintendo: F[2, 57] = 1.25, eta^2 = .04, p < .2; see Figure 3). Fit and company attitude significantly interacted in the Smith and Wesson pairings (F[2, 57] = 3.45, eta^2 = .11, p < .05; see Figure 4). An examination of the means for the Smith and Wesson ANOVA demonstrated that fit had a weaker impact when company attitudes were negative, compared to positive company attitudes. In the majority of cases, however (Nike, Velveeta, and Nintendo pairings), fit and company attitude did not interact, suggesting that a strong and consistent interaction between these two variables does not exist.

Discussion

Supporting Hypothesis 1, company attitude is an important determinant of the effect a CRM partnership will have on attitude toward the charity. A more positive company attitude leads to a significantly more positive charity attitude when the two partner for CRM. These results suggest that pairing with a popular company could lead to more positive charity attitudes. This approach could be especially useful for charities that are not well known. Pairing with a well-liked company could change neutral or non-existent attitudes to positive attitudes.

Conversely, the results suggest that pairing with a disliked company could harm charity attitude. Charity attitude became more negative when paired with a company toward which individuals held negative at-

FIGURE 3. Fit by Company Attitude Interaction for Nike, Velveeta, Nintendo

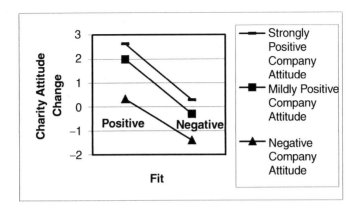

FIGURE 4. Fit × Company Attitude Interaction for Smith and Wesson

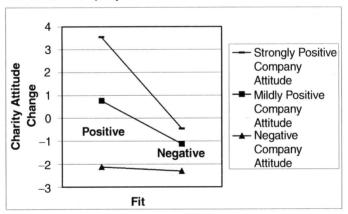

titudes. This finding is particularly important for non-profit managers. There are many companies that may enjoy positive consumer attitudes within the general population. As such pairing with these companies could prove profitable in the short-term for the charity. The popularity of the company would mean product sales, which would mean more money for the charity. If the charity's key donors held negative attitudes toward the company, however, the partnership could harm donors' attitudes toward the charity. This suggests the importance of assessing company attitudes for both the general product-purchasing public and for key donor groups when selecting a CRM partner, because pairing with a company donors dislike may in fact prove to be "dangerous" for the charity.

The results also supported Hypothesis 2. Fit is an important determinant of the effect a CRM partnership will have on charity attitude. When the organizations have positive fit, the partnership tends to lead to more positive attitudes toward the charity. When the organizations have negative fit, the effect of the CRM partnership on charity attitudes may be negative. This suggests that a charity should pair with positive fit companies. In other words the organizations should have some element in common, and attitude valence toward that element should be positive. Negative fit, much like negative company attitude, may prove to be "dangerous" for charities.

Assessment of the research question suggests that positive fit can compensate for negative pre-existing company attitude. Although generally pairing with a "negative" company leads to more negative attitudes toward the charity, the present results suggest that positive fit between the organizations may overcome this. Teaming with a company toward which key donors have negative attitudes may not always hurt the charity. Very little charity attitude change was evident in the Nike, Velveeta, and Nintendo conditions when the organizations had positive fit but pre-existing company attitude was negative. In such cases the charity could realize the financial benefits of the CRM without significantly harming (or helping) attitudes toward the charity. Charity attitudes did become more negative in the Smith and Wesson pairing when company attitudes were negative, even when the organizations had positive fit. This suggests that pairing with a company toward which donors have negative attitudes should be done cautiously, as it may have negative repercussions for the charity. Even in this case, however, the negative impact on charity attitude was much less in the positive fit condition than in the negative fit condition, suggesting that positive fit may help to overcome the negative impact of pairing with a disfavored company. This somewhat surprising result offers non-profit managers more latitude in selecting CRM partners. Companies seeking CRM partners might be interested in overcoming negative consumer attitudes due to some practice which has put the company in a negative light. The present results suggest that if the organizations have negative fit, such a partnership may harm charity attitude. If the organizations have positive fit, however, negative company attitude may be compensated for by positive fit, leaving charity attitudes unscathed by the CRM partnership.

CONCLUSION

Both organizational fit and pre-existing company attitudes are important determinants of how a CRM partnership can change individuals' attitudes toward a charity. Charity attitudes tend to become more positive when the organizations have positive fit. Charity attitudes also tend to become more positive when paired with a company that enjoys positive attitudes. Negative fit between the company and charity can harm attitudes toward the charity. Finally, negative pre-existing company attitudes can harm charity attitudes as well. The effect of fit is much stronger than the effect of company attitude, suggesting that a charity may be able to safely pair with an organization donors do not like, as long as the organizations have positive fit. In such cases the charity may be able to realize the financial benefits of the CRM partnership without harming donors' attitudes toward the charity. Overall, these findings suggest that a charity must choose wisely when selecting a CRM partner. Negative fit and/or negative company attitude may in fact make contributions from a CRM partnership "dangerous donations" for the charity, if the partnership harms charity attitude. Ideally the corporate CRM partner will have positive fit with the charity, and both general public and donor attitudes toward the company will be positive. If only one of these is possible, however, positive fit appears to be more important than positive company attitude.

LIMITATIONS

This research provides insight into the effect a CRM partnership can have on consumers' attitudes toward charitable organizations. It is important to note, however, that this research consisted of a laboratory experiment, and that the experimental subjects were university students. Although university students are consumers, they represent a fairly homogenous subset of the overall consumer base. Additionally, demographic variables related to charitable donations were not assessed in this research. Demographic variables have been shown to affect charitable giving in previous research. A replication of this study using a more representative subject pool and including demographic variables would be valuable future research.

FUTURE RESEARCH

This research suggests that positive fit has a positive effect on charity attitude, and negative fit has a negative effect on charity attitude. This naturally leads to a question of neutral fit. What effect would neutral fit have on charity attitude? For example, what if the Special Olympics formed a CRM partnership with Honda? If the organizations did not share positive *or* negative associations, would consumer attitudes be affected? Future research should assess the effects of neutral fit on charity attitude.

NOTE

1. A significance level of $p < .05$ was used for this research. All statistical tests with significance levels at or below .05 were accepted as supportive of the proposed hypotheses. This indicates 95% certainty that we are correct in rejecting the null hypothesis.

REFERENCES

Aaker, D. A., & Keller, K. L. (1990). Consumer evaluations of brand extensions. *Journal of Marketing*, *54*(January), 27-41.

Anderson, J. R. (1983). *The architecture of cognition.* Cambridge: Harvard University Press.

Barone, M. J., Miyazaki, A. D., & Taylor, K. A. (2000). The influence of cause-related marketing on consumer choice: Does one good turn deserve another? *Journal of the Academy of Marketing Science*, *28*(2), 248-262.

Benezra, K. (1996). Cause and effect marketing. *Brandweek*, *37*(17), 38-40.

Berger, I. E., Cunningham, M. P., Kozinets, R. V. (1996). The process of cause-related advertising: Cues, arguments, biases, or motivators? *Advances in Consumer Research*, *23*, 91.

Blum, E. M., & Loken, B. (2000), "9 of 10 Companies Have Charity Marketing Deals: Two new surveys reveal 9 of 10 companies have charity marketing deals," available online at *http://www.daytontech.com/Power2/DT_P2/news_Detail.asp?New_Id=9.*

Boush, D. M., & Loken, B. (1991). A process-tracing study of brand extension evaluation. *Journal of Marketing Research*, *28*(February), 16-28.

Broniarczyk, S. M., & Alba, J. W. (1994). The importance of the brand in brand extension. *Journal of Consumer Research*, *31*(May), 214-228.

Brown, T. J., & Dacin, P. A. (1997). The company and the product: Corporate associations and consumer product responses. *Journal of Marketing, 61*(January), 68-84.

Collins, A. M., & Quillian, M. R. (1969). Retrieval time from semantic memory. *Journal of Verbal Learning and Verbal Behavior, 8*, 240-247.

Collins, A. M., & Loftus, E. F. (1975). A spreading-activation theory of semantic processing. *Psychological Review, 82*(6), 407-428.

Cone/Roper. (1999). *Cause related trends report.* Boston: Cone Inc., New York: Roper Starch Worldwide Inc.

Coy, J. (1996). Redesigning corporate philanthropy. In L. Dennis (Ed.), *Practical Public Affairs in an Era of Change.* Maryland: University Press.

Dacin, P. A., & Smith, D. C. (1994). The effect of brand portfolio characteristics on consumer evaluations of brand extensions. *Journal of Marketing Research, 31*(May), 229-242.

Davidson, J. (1997). Cancer Sells. *Working Woman,* 36-39.

Dienhart, J. W. (1988). Charitable Investments: A Strategy for Improving the Business Environment. *Journal of Business Ethics, 7*(Jan/Feb), 63-72.

Drumwright, M. E. (1996). Company advertising with a social dimension: The role of noneconomic criteria. *Journal of Marketing, 60*(October), 71-87.

Fiske, S. T., & Taylor, S. E. (1991). *Social Cognition.* (2nd ed.). New York: McGraw-Hill.

Gilbert, D. T., Fiske, S. T., & Gardner, L. (1998). *The handbook of social psychology.* (4th ed.). (Vol. 1). Boston: McGraw-Hill.

Herr, P. M., Farquhar, P. H., & Fazio, R. H. (1996). Impact of dominance and relatedness on brand extensions. *Journal of Consumer Psychology, 5*(2), 135-159.

Kamins, M. A. (1990). An investigation into the match-up hypothesis in celebrity advertising: When beauty may be only skin deep. *Journal of Advertising, 19*(1), 4-13.

Lafferty, B. A. (1997). *Advance in Consumer Research.* Paper presented at the Association for Consumer Research, Tuscon.

Linville, P., & Fischer, G. (1991). Preferences for separating and combining events. *Journal of Personality and Social Psychology, 60*(January), 5-23.

MacInnis, D. J., Moorman, C., and Jaworski, B. J. (1991). "Enhancing and measuring consumers' motivation, opportunity, and ability to process brand information from ads: Conceptual Framework and Managerial Implications," *Journal of Marketing,* 55 (October), 32-53.

PMA/Gable Group, (2000). Survey of cause marketing. Summary viewed online at *http://www.pmalink.org/,* October 19, 2001.

Philip Morris U.S.A. (2001). http://www.philipmorrisusa.com/default.asp, *Philip Morris U.S.A. homepage,* viewed October 16, 2001.

Petty, R. E., Cacioppo, J. T., & Schumann, D. (1983). Central and peripheral routes to advertising effectiveness: The moderating role of involvement. *Journal of Consumer Research, 10*(September), 135-146.

Ross, J. K., Patterson, L. T., & Stutts, M. A. (1992). Consumer perceptions of organizations that use cause-related marketing. *Journal of the Academy of Marketing Science, 20*(1), 93-97.

Simonin, B. L., & Ruth, J. A. (1998). Is a company known by the company it keeps? *Journal of Marketing Research, 35*(February), 30-42.

Strahilevitz, M., & Meyers, J. (1998). Donations to charity as purchase incentives: How well they work may depend on what you are trying to sell. *Journal of Consumer Research, 24*(4).

Varadarajan, P. R., & Menon, A. (1988). Cause-related marketing: A co-alignment of marketing strategy and corporate philanthropy. *Journal of Marketing, July*(52), 58-74.

Webb, D. J., & Mohr, L. A. (1998). A typology of consumer responses to cause-related marketing: From skeptics to socially concerned. *Journal of Public Policy & Marketing, 17*(2), 226-238.

The Effects of Prior Impressions of a Firm's Ethics on the Success of a Cause-Related Marketing Campaign: Do the Good Look Better While the Bad Look Worse?

Michal Strahilevitz

SUMMARY. This research examines the effect of the initial perception of the ethical nature of a firm on the effects of that firm participating in a cause-related marketing campaign. In two studies, the effects of a cause-related marketing campaign are examined for companies perceived as ethical, unethical and ethically neutral. It is found that firms initially perceived as ethical are least likely to be seen as having ulterior motives for running a cause-related marketing campaign, whereas firms initially perceived as unethical are most likely to be suspected of having ulterior motives. However, it is also found that firms perceived as ethically neutral gained the most from a cause-related marketing campaign

Michal Strahilevitz, PhD, is Assistant Professor of Marketing, University of Arizona, Tucson, 320 McClelland Hall, Marketing Department, Eller School of Business, University of Arizona, Tucson AZ 85719.

The author would like to thank the editors of the *Journal of Nonprofit and Public Sector Marketing* for inviting her to submit a paper for this special volume. She would also like to thank Jamie Kern for his helpful comments on an earlier version of this paper.

[Haworth co-indexing entry note]: "The Effects of Prior Impressions of a Firm's Ethics on the Success of a Cause-Related Marketing Campaign: Do the Good Look Better While the Bad Look Worse?" Strahilevitz, Michal. Co-published simultaneously in *Journal of Nonprofit & Public Sector Marketing* (Best Business Books, an imprint of The Haworth Press, Inc.) Vol. 11, No. 1, 2003, pp. 77-92; and: *Nonprofit and Business Sector Collaboration: Social Enterprises, Cause-Related Marketing, Sponsorships, and Other Corporate-Nonprofit Dealings* (ed: Walter W. Wymer, Jr. and Sridhar Samu) Best Business Books, an imprint of The Haworth Press, Inc., 2003, pp. 77-92. Single or multiple copies of this article are available for a fee from The Haworth Document Delivery Service [1-800-HAWORTH, 9:00 a.m. - 5:00 p.m. (EST). E-mail address: getinfo@ haworthpressinc.com].

in terms of improvements to their image. Implications and directions for future research are discussed. *[Article copies available for a fee from The Haworth Document Delivery Service: 1-800-HAWORTH. E-mail address: <getinfo@haworthpressinc.com> Website: <http://www.HaworthPress.com> © 2003 by The Haworth Press, Inc. All rights reserved.]*

KEYWORDS. Cause-related marketing, corporate image, perceived ethics

I will never forget the horrible fire that occurred in the Berkeley hills when I was a doctoral student at U.C. Berkeley. Many of my friends lost their homes and all their belongings. Much of the Berkeley campus seemed to be in mourning. People were collecting clothes, blankets, money, and anything else that could help those that had suddenly become homeless overnight.

It was during the week right after the fire that I found myself passing a street musician on the way to a seminar. He played well and I was running early, so I decided to sit and listen for a while. At some point, I was no longer running early, so I reached into my purse to leave him some change before heading off to class. I was about to place two quarters in his guitar case when I noticed there was a sign in front of it that read, "half the money I collect today will be contributed to a fund to help victims of the fire." Somehow, the combination of good music and helping the homeless struck a chord in me. I put the two quarters back in my purse and dug into my wallet for a five dollar bill. I put that five dollar bill in his guitar case and hurried off to class.

It was only later that day when I had a chance to think about the potential marketing implications of what had happened. That sign had caused my tip to the musician to increase by 900%. Furthermore, by promising to give half his revenues to a good cause, the street musician had just increased his net (after donation) revenues from me from $.50 to $2.50. Obviously, I felt good about paying for the good music and making the donation to victims of the fire. My guess is that he also derived satisfaction from helping to raise money for a worthy cause. I later wondered if he had not ended up collecting more than twice as much money with that sign as he would have without such a sign. Could it be that his "charitable" efforts might also prove profitable for him? Unfortunately, I never got a chance to ask that street musician all the questions I had. However, I realized then and there that I had just come up with a set of research questions that were truly intriguing to me: Can donations to charity be used to increase profits? If so, under what conditions will this method be most effective?

Years have passed since that experience and I am pleased to report that many scholars, including myself, have since made important progress in addressing such questions with regards to cause-related marketing. However, there are still many intriguing factors left to be explored regarding the variables that should be considered in deciding if and how to use charity as a purchase incentive. In this paper, I will discuss some of the important findings that have been reported to date. More importantly, I will address a question that came up two years ago when I told this story to a colleague. The colleague had asked me if I had not trusted this musician, would I have been so generous with my tip to him? This question can also be translated to the world of cause-related marketing. Is the perceived ethics of a firm, prior to becoming involved in a cause-related marketing campaign, going to influence the effectiveness of that campaign? The main goal of this paper is to begin to address this question. Although the research presented here offers new insights into the role of a firm's perceived ethics prior to a campaign, it also leaves many interesting questions unanswered. This allows me to address my second goal, which is to suggest directions for future work and hopefully encourage more scholars to become involved in studying this fascinating area.

CAUSE-RELATED MARKETING

The tactic of companies linking the purchases of their products with donations to charity is often referred to as "cause-related marketing." Cause-related marketing has been described as a versatile marketing tool capable of accomplishing a wide range of marketing objectives (Varadajan and Menon 1988). Total spending on cause-related marketing in the United States alone exceeds $1 billion annually (Smith and Stodghill 1994, Tate 1995) and such efforts at linking sales to charitable donations continue to grow in popularity (Hanft 2001). The fact that each year thousands of marketers use charitable donations to promote their products demonstrates that many companies consider cause-related marketing to be a valuable marketing tool (Strahilevitz 1999).

Yet, the benefits of such campaigns are not always obvious, and they can vary depending the nature of the product or service being promoted (Strahilevitz and Myers 1998), the specific charity chosen (Lafferty

1996), the perceived quality of the product being promoted (Folkes and Kamins 1999), the size of the donation (Holmes and Kilbane 1993, Dahl and Lavack 1995, Strahilevitz 1999), the interaction between donation size and product type (Strahilevitz 1999) and the way that the cause-related marketing plan is communicated to the target market. In this paper I investigate another factor, which is whether the initial perception of a firm's ethics might also influence the effectiveness of a cause-related marketing campaign.

POSSIBLE EFFECTS
OF CAUSE-RELATED MARKETING CAMPAIGN

Some of the benefits to using charitable donations as purchase incentives include improving the image of and attitude towards the sponsoring firm (Ross, Patterson, and Stutts 1992, Brown and Dacin 1997, Berger, Cunningham and Kozinets 1996, Creyer and Ross 1996), differentiating a brand from its competitors (Murphy 1997, Brown and Dacin 1997, Berger, Cunningham and Kozinets 1996) and potentially increasing short term sales (Sen and Morwitz 1996, Murphy 1997, Strahilevitz and Myers 1998, Strahilevitz 1999). In addition to appealing to customers, cause-related campaigns can improve a company's image with other important constituencies such as employees and investors (Aldrich 2001). However, not all cause-related campaigns are equally effective in all these ways, and some cause-related marketing campaigns may be completely ineffective.

THE EFFECT OF THE NATURE OF THE PRODUCT

The nature of the product being promoted can influence how effective a cause-related marketing campaign might be (Strahilevitz and Myers 1998). More specifically, charity incentives have been found to be more effective in generating short terms sales with products perceived as pleasure-oriented and frivolous than with products perceived as goal-oriented and practical. The explanation given for this effect is based on a wide body of prior research which has shown that experiencing either pleasure (Isen, Shalker, Clark, and Karp 1978, Cunningham 1979) or guilt (Baummann, Cialdini and Kenrick 1981, Ghingold 1981) can significantly affect an individual's willingness to engage in charitable behavior. Since hedonic products tend to evoke more pleasure and guilt than utilitarian products, it follows that charity incentives should be most effective with pleasure-oriented products. This phenomenon is referred to as affect-based complementarity because the emotions generated by hedonic products appear to complement the feelings generated from contributing to charity (Strahilevitz and Myers 1998).

However, the tactic of linking donations to sales of hedonic products is not without its social critics. In a recent article on cause-related marketing in *Worth* (2001), writer Adam Hanft writes "Cause marketing is transforming the very nature of acquisition: It has become a mechanism to both indulge and do good, a new kind of heroic hedonism. Through this conflation of giving and getting, marketers have found a devise for sanctioning away any remaining guilt over the need to own stuff."

THE ROLE OF PRODUCT QUALITY

Product quality may also influence the effectiveness of a cause-related marketing campaign. Folkes and Kamins (1999) found that the effect of a firm engaging in pro-social behavior depends on the perceived quality of the products being promoted. In particular, the authors found that superior product attributes enhance attitudes towards ethically behaving firms more than toward unethically behaving firms. However, when product quality was seen as inferior, the firm's ethical behavior had less of an effect. In addition, Folkes and Kamins found that attitudes towards superior products varied depending on whether a firm was simply not involved in unethical behavior (e.g., not using child labor) or whether the firm was active in prosocial behavior (e.g., helping victims of child labor abuse).

THE PERCEIVED ETHICAL NATURE OF THE FIRM

Drumwright (1996) has pointed out that one factor that can influence the effectiveness of a given campaign is whether consumers perceive the cause-related marketing relationship to be beneficial or exploitative of the charity. In the current paper, I examine whether the effectiveness of a cause-related marketing campaign is affected by the initial perceived ethics of the company involved (i.e., is this perceived as a "ethical," "unethical," or "neutral" firm to begin with). The research investigates how the initial impression of a company influences whether a cause-related marketing campaign is viewed with admiration or suspicion, as well as how the initial impression affects the degree to which a firm's image will be improved by a cause-related marketing campaign.

Folkes and Kamins (1999) have made an interesting connection between how firms are judged as a function of their actions and how individuals are judged by their actions. Hamilton and Sherman (1996) suggest that organized groups, like individuals, are often perceived as having dispositional qualities or characteristics, and thus organizations, like people, are often perceived as being "good" or "bad." Several scholars have demonstrated the role of brand personalities and people's relationships with them in how companies are perceived by consumers (Aaker 1997, Fournier 1998, Muniz and O'Guinn 2001). All this suggests that prior research on how individuals are judged as a function of their ethical behavior is likely to be helpful in predicting how organizations will be judged as a function of their ethical behavior.

In judging individuals, research has shown that information about ethical and unethical actions have an asymmetrical influence on attitudes towards individuals, such that bad deeds detract from attitudes more than good deeds enhance them (Reeder & Brewer 1979, Skowronksi & Carlston 1987a). Skowronski and Carlston (1987b) point out that immoral acts are seen as stronger indicators of one's true nature than moral ones, because even immoral people will occasionally perform moral acts (e.g., the mafia hit man who is good to his children) or refrain from immoral acts (e.g., the thief who does not rob every house he enters).

One of the questions to be investigated in this research is whether the effect of a company participating in a cause-related marketing campaign (a good deed) will be evaluated differently as a function of the firm's perceived ethics before the campaign. More specifically, I examine whether the motives ascribed to having a cause-related marketing campaign are affected by the perceived ethics of the firm prior to the campaign. I also examine whether a company being perceived as ethical or unethical prior to a cause-related marketing campaign can affect how much that company's image will improve from participating in that campaign.

HYPOTHESES

Prior work suggesting individuals often judge organizations in the same way they judge people (Hamilton and Sherman 1996) is the foundation of the three hypotheses presented here. The first hypothesis is based on prior work documenting that unethical and ethical behavior have an asymmetrical influence on attitudes, such that unethical behavior has a stronger effect on how individuals are judged by others. This is attributed to the fact that negative information is weighted more heavily than positive information in judgments of individuals (Reeder and Brewer 1979, Skowronksi and Carlston 1987). In addition, in judging the ethics of individuals, we often look both at the actions they are currently taking and at actions they have previously taken. We tend to trust the motives of those that we consider "good" or "ethical." We also tend to suspect the motives of those that we consider "bad" or "unethical." This advances the following hypothesis:

(H1) The more ethical a firm is perceived to be initially, the more likely it is to be judged as having altruistic motives for getting involved in a cause-related marketing campaign. The less ethical a firm is perceived to be initially, the more likely it is to be judged as having ulterior motives for getting involved in a cause-related marketing campaign.

Yet perceptions of the motivation of a firm for getting involved in a cause-related marketing campaign may not be the only factor of concern to a firm. Disconfirmation theory (Oliver and Swan, 1989) predicts that expectations are set and form the reference point to which outcomes are compared to determine satisfaction or disatisfaction. If expectations are realized (e.g., a firm perceived as ethical helps a good cause) positive confirmation occurs. However, if expectations are exceeded (e.g., a firm perceived as neutral or unethical supports a good cause), positive disconfirmation occurs, leading to an even higher level of satisfaction. In addition, firms already perceived as highly ethical have less room for improvement in terms of their perceived ethics. Thus, a cause-related marketing campaign should have a stronger positive effect on the image of a firm with a neutral image or unethical image to begin with than on a firm that is already perceived as highly ethical. This advances the following hypothesis:

(H2) Firms that are initially perceived as highly ethical will benefit less in terms of improvements to their image as the result of a cause-related marketing campaign than will firms initially perceived as either neutral or unethical.

However, in comparing ethical firms to unethical firms, the fact that negative information is weighted more heavily than positive information (Reeder and Brewer 1979, Skowronksi and Carlston 1987a) works in the opposite direction of the fact that firms that are already perceived as ethical have less room for improvement and less of a chance to positively surprise consumers with their ethical behavior (Oliver and Swan 1989). Thus, it is unclear whether unethical or ethical firms will benefit more from a cause-related marketing campaign in terms of improvements to their image. However, firms perceived as ethically neutral have neither negative information that can be heavily weighted, nor do they have such a positive image that there is almost no room for improvement. Thus, it follows that firms perceived as neutral may benefit most from a cause-related marketing campaign in terms of improvements to their image. More formally:

(H3) Firms that are initially perceived as unethical will benefit less in terms of improvements to their image as the result of a cause-related marketing campaign than will firms initially perceived as neutral in terms of their ethics.

Combined, H2 and H3 suggest that neutral firms will improve their image most as the result of participating in a cause related marketing campaign. All three hypotheses were tested in two experiments.

STUDY 1

Method

Subjects were 76 undergraduate business students at a public university. Each subject was assigned to one of three conditions in a single-factor between-subject design. Depending on the condition to which they were assigned, subjects were given a description of one of three conditions of a shoe company that was depicted as either extremely ethical (employing the homeless mothers, encouraging volunteer work among employees, surpassing all environmental standards), ethically neutral (nothing ethical or unethical, meets basic environmental standards) or extremely unethical (uses child labor, underpays employees, fails to meet basic environmental standards). Regardless of the condition to which they were assigned, subjects were told that the company they had just read about had decided to run a cause-related marketing campaign contributing 5% of the profits from the sale of their shoes to charity. Within each condition, half the subjects were told the money would go to underprivileged kids and half were told that it would go to helping protect endangered wildlife. This was to make sure that the results obtained were not specific to the charity used.

Regardless of the condition to which they were assigned, subjects were asked to rate the motives of the company for participating in the campaign using a 5 point scale. The scale ranged from -2 (motivated only by ulterior motives), to 2 (motivated only by altruistic motives), with 0 indicating that the company was equally motivated by ulterior motives and altruistic motives. On the bottom of the scale it was explained that examples of ulterior motives would be a desire to increase sales or to improve the company's own image. It was also explained that examples of altruistic motives would be a genuine desire to contribute to the cause or to make the world a better place. Subjects were next given another scale and asked to rate how the cause-related campaign would affect their perceptions of the firm in terms of its ethics on a 5 point scale that ranged from -2 (the firm would seem much less ethical than before), to 2 (the firm would seem much more ethical than before).

Results

A one-way ANOVA was conducted to test for the significance of these differences at the aggregate level. The dependent variable was the rating on the altruism/self-interest scale. Because there was no effect for which of the two charities were used, the results are aggregated here for purposes of analysis. H1 had predicted that firms likely to be perceived as unethical to begin with would be more likely to be judged as having selfish motives for carrying out a cause-related marketing campaign. As predicted, the ethical firm was seen as the most altruistic in its motives, with an average rating of 0.56. The neutral firm was perceived as less altruistic with a mean rating of 0.04. Finally, the unethical firm was the only one judged as having the relatively selfish motives, with a mean of -0.65. The overall difference among the three conditions was significant ($F(2, 73) = 6.12, p < .005$). I also tested whether the differences were significant between the various pairs of conditions. In comparing the neutral firm to the ethical firm, the difference was in the predicted direction, but not significant ($F = 2.02, p < .20$). However, in comparing the neutral firm to the unethical firm, the difference was both in the predicted direction and significant ($F = 4.02, p < .05$). Finally, in comparing the ethical to the unethical firm, the difference was also significant ($F = 12.77, p <$

.001). These results strongly support the first hypothesis, which predicts that firms that are perceived as less ethical run a higher risk of having their cause-related marketing campaign ascribed to selfish motives.

The second and third hypotheses dealt with the relationship between the perceived ethical nature of a firm and the effect of a cause-related marketing campaign on improvements in the firm's image. Again, a one-way ANOVA was conducted to test for the significance of these differences at the aggregate level. For the ethical firm, the improvement was relatively small at 0.60. For the ethically neutral firm the improvement was relatively high at 1.28. Finally, for the unethical firm the improvement was somewhere in between at 0.88. The overall difference among the three conditions was significant ($F(2, 73) = 5.36, p < .01$). I also tested whether the differences were significant between the various pairs of conditions. As predicted by H2, comparing the neutral firm to the ethical firm, the neutral firm benefited more than the ethical one ($F = 9.55\ p < .005$). In comparing the neutral firm to the unethical firm, as predicted by H3, the unethical firm benefited significantly less than the neutral firm in terms of an improvement to its image ($F = 4.50, p < .05$). Interestingly, in comparing the ethical firm to the unethical firm, although the unethical firm appeared to benefit slightly more, the difference was not significant ($F = 1.66, p < .20$). These results support the second and third hypotheses and suggest that the firms that have no strong ethical identity (either positive or negative) may have the most to gain from participating in a cause-related marketing campaign.

STUDY 2

Method

Study 2 was identical to study 1 except that instead of using descriptions of companies as either ethical or unethical, well known companies were pretested to come up with those that were already perceived as either very ethical, very unethical, or ethically neutral. Thirty undergraduate students, who had not participated in study 1 and who would not be participating in study 2, were given a list of 12 well known companies, several of which seemed they would be likely to be perceived as either highly ethical or unethical, and asked to classify them as on a scale of -3 to 3, with 3 being highly ethical and -3 being highly unethical. In addition, one well-known product for each company was listed and pretest participants were asked to rate that product relative to its competition on a scale with −2 representing very low quality and 2 representing very high quality. The company that had the lowest score was chosen for the unethical company for study 2. This company was Phillip Morris, which had a mean score of −2.4. The ethical company chosen in the pretest was Ben and Jerry's, which had a mean ethics score of 2.2. The company chosen as neutral was Timex, which was classified as a 0 (neutral) by the majority of the subjects and had a mean rating of −.07. All three of the companies chosen for study 2 were also judged to have products perceived to be of high quality relative to their competition within their product category (all three firms scored above "1" on a 5 point scale where "−2" is very low quality and "2" is very high quality). Companies perceived to make high quality products (relative to their competition) were chosen to avoid creating a confound with the effect of product quality, which has been shown to affect how ethical and unethical behavior by companies are judged (see Folkes and Kamins 1999).

Subjects in study 2 were 97 undergraduates who had not participated in either the pretest or the first study. Similar to the first study, they were each assigned to one of three conditions. In the unethical condition, Phillip Morris was described as having a campaign linked to Marlboro cigarettes. In the ethical condition, Ben and Jerry's was described as having a campaign linked to the sale of their pint-sized ice cream. In the neutral condition, Timex was described as having a campaign linked to the sale of their sports watches.

For each condition, subjects were told that 5% of the profit from the products for the months of December and January would be donated to Big Brothers and Big Sisters of America. This charity was chosen because a prior pretest had found this to be a cause that almost all students considered worthy of support and that no students found offensive. The cause was also chosen because it was not particularly related to cigarettes, watches or ice cream.

Results

As in study 1, a one-way ANOVA was conducted to test for the significance of these differences at the aggregate level. The dependent variable was the rating on the same altruism/self-interest scale that had been used in the first study. The first hypothesis predicted that the more unethical a firm is judged to be, the more likely it will be perceived as having selfish motives for carrying out a cause-related marketing campaign. As predicted, the ethical firm (Ben and Jerry's) was seen as the most altruistic in its motives, with an average rating of 0.69. The neutral firm (Timex) was perceived as less altruistic with a mean rating of −0.06. Finally, the unethical firm (Phillip Morris) was judged as having the most selfish motives with a mean of −1.06. The overall difference among the three conditions was significant ($F(2, 94) = 18.03, p < .001$).

It was also relevant to test whether the differences were significant between the various pairs of conditions. In comparing the neutral firm to the ethical firm, the difference was in the predicted direction and significant ($F = 5.46\ p < .05$). Similarly, in comparing the neutral firm to the unethical firm, the difference was also significant and in the direction predicted ($F = 5.69, p < .05$). Finally, as the first hypothesis would predict, the difference between the ethical and unethical firm was both significant and in the predicted direction ($F = 42.94, p < .001$). As in study 1, study 2 confirmed that companies perceived as unethical to begin with run a higher risk of having their cause-related marketing campaign ascribed to selfish motives.

As in the first study, to test the second hypothesis, a one-way ANOVA was conducted to examine how a cause-related campaign would affect improvements (or lack thereof) to a company's image as the result of a cause-related marketing campaign. For the unethical firm, the improvement was 0.813. For the ethically neutral firm the improvement in image was greater at 1.15. Finally, for the ethical firm the improvement was 0.75. Although, as predicted, the firm perceived as ethically neutral gained the most in terms of improvements to its image, the overall difference among the three conditions was not significant ($F(2, 94) = 2.01, p < .15$). It was also important to test whether the differences were significant between the various pairs of conditions. In comparing the ethical firm to the neutral firm, the difference was also only marginally significant, although in the predicted direction ($F = 3.73, p < .06$), thus supporting H2. In comparing the neutral firm to the unethical firm, the difference was marginally significant in the direction predicted ($F = 3.01, p < .10$), thus supporting H3. In comparing the ethical and unethical firms, the difference was not significant ($F = 0.07, p < .80$). As in study 1, the firm that appeared to benefit the most from the campaign was the one that had been judged ethically neutral to begin with.

Discussion

This research shed new light on factors that might affect the results of a cause-related marketing campaign. The findings reported here suggest that firms should first try to sense how they are perceived in terms of ethics by their target market. They should then ask if their goal is to be perceived as altruistic and caring or simply to improve their current image. One of the more interesting findings here was that firms perceived as ethical are least likely to be seen as having selfish motives for running a cause-related marketing campaign. Yet, in terms of improving their image, ethical firms and unethical firms gained significantly less than neutral firms from participating in a cause-related marketing campaign. This suggests that companies that have a strong image as either ethical or unethical may have less to gain from being involved in cause-related marketing campaigns than companies that are not perceived as particularly ethical or unethical.

Limitations and Future Research

While the work presented here addresses important questions regarding the role of perceptions of a firm's ethics prior to a cause-related marketing campaign on the possible effects of such a campaign, it was not without its limitations. First of all, only student subjects were used and it is possible that different results might be obtained using a non-student sample. Furthermore, no measures were taken to rule out alternative explanations for the results observed. In addition, in the case of support for H2, measures of improvements in a company's image as the result of a cause-related marketing campaign did not involve pre-campaign and post-campaign measures. Thus, it is not clear if the reason that neutral firms benefited most is that they started at a lower point than firms perceived as highly ethical to begin with, or that perhaps some other phenomenon was driving the effect observed. Fortunately, all of these limitations provide opportunities for future research addressing these weaknesses.

In addition, many important questions remain unanswered. For example, both non-profit and for-profit organizations need to be concerned with the effect that a cause-related marketing campaign will have on their image. It would be interesting to see how the perceived ethics of the marketer might affect consumers' judgments of the non-profit organizations that choose to team up with them. It might also be interesting to see if there might be an interaction between the perceived ethics of a firm and the type of charity they choose to support in their cause-related marketing campaign. For example, if a firm that makes cigarettes were to consider linking sales of their products to donations to the American Lung Association, they would likely be judged more harshly than if they supported a cause unrelated to any negative side effects associated with their product. On the other hand, a company that sells books might gain the most from supporting a cause that is related to the positive effects of their product, such as a literacy fund or an organization that provides free books to underprivileged children. Other factors such as the perceived quality of the products being marketed (see Folkes and Kamins 1999), the size of the donation (see Holmes and Kilbane 1993, Dahl and Lavack 1995, Strahilevitz 1999), and the hedonic nature of the products being marketed (see Strahilevitz and Myers 1998) could also interact with the perceived ethics of the firm that existed prior to a cause-related marketing campaign.

It is also worth noting that the initial image that a firm has is probably not the only factor that will affect how the motives of a cause-related marketing campaign are judged. Other influencing factors could be the size of the donation or whether the relationship between a given charity and marketer are long lasting or simply short term. There is great variation in both the size of donation made (ranging from 100% of profits to less than 0.01% of profits) and the duration of commitment made in such campaigns. For example, companies such as Patagonia, the Body Shop and Ben and Jerry's consistently give a significant portion of their income to several charities. Such companies are likely to be judged quite differently from those that contribute only incremental amounts or get involved with cause-related marketing only during certain promotional periods. Barone, Miyazaki and Taylor (2000) suggest that perceived commitment to a cause might also be affected by whether the company's employees are encouraged to get involved by programs such as paid release time for volunteering or donation drives within the company. Further research as to how these factors might interact with a firm's initial image could be of great interest to marketers.

It would also be valuable to take a closer look at the mediating factors that might have affected the results presented in this paper. To illustrate, in future research, one could ask subjects to give explanations as to why they judged companies as they did. These explanations could be analyzed to gain a deeper understanding of the phenomenon I have observed here. Finally, this paper focused on how consumers' perceptions are affected by a cause-related campaign. Yet it has been noted that employees and investors might also prefer to be associated with a firm that they consider ethical and/or that contributes to society by supporting good causes. Future research could examine how cause-related marketing campaigns affect the morale of employees and perhaps even shareholders.

REFERENCES

Aaker, Jennifer L. (1997), "Dimensions of Brand Personality," *Journal of Marketing Research*, 34 (3), 347.

Aldrich, Nelson W., Jr (2001), "The New Power Giving: Corporate Donations Are on the Rise as Charitable Aspirations Among the New Money Crowd," *Worth*, (December/January), 104.

Barone, Michael J., Anthony D. Miyazaki and Kimberly A. Taylor (2000), "The Influence of Cause-Related Marketing on Consumer Choice: Does One Good Turn Deserve Another?" *Journal of the Academy of Marketing Science*, 28 (2), 248-262.

Baumann, D.J., R.B. Cialdini and D.T. Kenrick (1981), "Altruism as Hedonism: Helping and Self-gratification as Equivalent Responses," *Journal of Personality and Social Psychology*, 40 (June), 1039-1046.

Berger, Ida E., Peggy H. Cunningham and Robert V. Kozinets (1996), "The Processing of Cause-related Marketing Claims: Cues, Biases or Motivators?" *1996 AMA Summer Educators Conference: Enhancing Knowledge Development in Marketing*, 7, Cornelia Dröge and Roger Calantone, eds. Chicago; American Marketing Association, 71-72.

Brown, Thomas J. and Peter A. Dacin (1997), "The Company and the Product: Corporate Associations and Consumer Product Responses," *Journal of Marketing*, 61 (January), 68-84.

Creyer, Elizabeth H. and William T. Ross, Jr (1996), "The Impact of Corporate Behavior on Perceived Product Value," *Marketing Letters*, 7 (2), 173-185.

Cunningham, M.R. (1979), "Weather, Mood, and Helping Behavior: Quasi-experiments with the Sunshine Samaritan," *Journal of Personality and Social Psychology*, 37, 1947-1958.

Dahl, Darren W. and Anne M. Lavack (1995), "Cause-Related Marketing: Impact of Size of Cause-Related Promotion on Consumer Perceptions and Participation," *1995 AMA Winter Educators Conference: Marketing Theory and Applications*, 6, David W. Stewart and Naufel J. Vilcassim, eds. Chicago: American Marketing Association, 476-481.

Drumwright, Minette E. (1996), "Company Advertising with a Social Dimension: The Role of Noneconomic Criteria," *Journal of Marketing*, 60 (October), 71-87.

Folkes, Valerie S. and Michael A. Kamins (1999), "Effects of Information About Firms' Ethical and Unethical Actions on Consumers' Attitudes," *Journal of Consumer Psychology*, (March), 243-259.

Fournier, Susan (1998), "Consumers and Their Brands: Developing Relationship Theory in Consumer Research," *Journal of Consumer Research*, 24 (4), 343-373.

Ghingold, Morry (1981), "Guilt Arousing Communications: An Unexplored Variable," K. Monroe (Ed.), *Advances in Consumer Research*, 8, 442-448.

Hamilton, D.L. and S.J. Sherman (1996), "Perceiving Persons and Groups," *Psychological Review*, 103, 336-355.

Hanft, Adam (2001), "And Profits to Boot: Cause Marketing Has Mushroomed Into One of the Most Visible Forms of Corporate Philanthropy, Involving Every Major Corporation. That is a Problem," *Worth*, (December/January), 112-113.

Holmes, John H. and Christopher J. Kilbane (1993), "Selected Effects of Price and Charitable Donations," *Journal of Nonprofit & Public Sector Marketing*, 1 (4), 67-83.

Isen, A.M., T.E. Shalker, M. Clark and L. Karp (1978), "Affect, Accessibility of Material in Memory and Behavior: A Cognitive Loop?" *Journal of Personality and Social Psychology*, 36, 1-12.

Lafferty, Barbara A. (1996), "Cause-Related Marketing: Does Cause Make a Difference in Consumers' Attitudes and Purchase Intentions Toward the Product?" working paper, Department of Marketing, Florida State University.

Muniz, Albert M., Jr. and Thomas C. O'Guinn (2001), "Brand Community," *Journal of Consumer Research*, 27 (4), 412-432.

Murphy, I. P. (1997), "Pillsbury Proves Charity, Marketing Begins at Home," *Marketing News*, (February 17), 16.

Oliver, Richard L. and John E. Swan (1989), "Equity and Disconfirmation Perceptions as Influences on Merchant and Product Satisfaction," *Journal of Consumer Research*, 16 (December), 372-383.

Reeder, G. and M. Brewer (1979), "A Schematic Model of Dispositional Attribution in Interpersonal Perception," *Psychological Review*, 86, 61-79.

Ross, John K. III, Larry T. Patterson, and Mary Ann Stutts (1992), "Consumer Perceptions of Organizations that use Cause-Related Marketing," *Journal of the Academy of Marketing Science*, 20 (1), 93-97.

Sen, Sankar and Vicki G. Morwitz (1996), "Consumer Reactions to a Provider's Position on Social Issues: The Effect of Varying Frames of Reference," *Journal of Consumer Psychology*, 5 (1), 27-48.

Skowronski, J.J. and D.E. Carlston (1987a), "Social Judgment and Social Memory: The Role of Cue Diagnosticity in Negativity, and Extremity Biases in Impression Formation: A Review of Explanations," *Psychological Bulletin*, 105, 131-142.

Skowronski, J.J. and D.E. Carlston (1987b), "Social Judgment and Social Memory: The Role of Cue Diagnosticity in Negativity, Positivity and Extremity Biases," *Journal of Personality and Social Psychology*, 52, 689-699.

Smith, Geoffrey and Ron Stodghill II (1994), "Are Good Causes Good Marketing?" *BusinessWeek*, (March 21), 64-66.

Strahilevitz, Michal (1999), "The Effects of Product Type and Donation Magnitude on Willingness to Pay More for a Charity-Linked Brand," *Journal of Consumer Psychology*, (March), 215-241.

Strahilevitz, Michal and John G. Myers (1998), "Donations to Charity as Purchase Incentives: How Well They Work May Depend on What You Are Trying to Sell," *Journal of Consumer Research*, 24 (4), 434-446.

Tate, Nancy T. (1995), "And Now a Word From Our Sponsor," *American Demographics*, (June), 46.

Varadarajan, P. Rajan and Anil Menon (1988), "Cause-Related Marketing: A Coalignment of Marketing Strategy and Corporate Philanthropy," *Journal of Marketing*, 52 (July), 58-74.

Effect of Cause-Related Marketing on Attitudes and Purchase Intentions: The Moderating Role of Cause Involvement and Donation Size

Mahmood M. Hajjat

SUMMARY. The purpose of the present research was to examine the role of involvement and donation in moderating the effect of cause related marketing (CRM) and ordinary marketing (OM) on consumer attitudes and purchase intentions. It is proposed that the level of involvement (i.e., high or low involvement) may make either veridical information (i.e., high involvement) or peripheral cues (i.e., low involvement) in the message more salient, and hence, more relevant and more important in the formation of attitudes and purchase intentions. Therefore, the level of donation size (i.e., high or low level) may be perceived either as an important element in the message (i.e., high involvement) or as a peripheral cue (i.e., low involvement). It is hypothesized that in conditions where there is a *match* between levels of involvement and donation (i.e., high-high or low-low), CRM would be superior to OM in creating favorable attitudes and purchase intentions whereas in conditions where there is a *mismatch* between (i.e., high-low and low-high), OM would be superior to CRM. To test these hypotheses, half of the subjects were shown

Mahmood M. Hajjat, PhD, teaches Marketing and Consumer Behavior at Sultan Qaboos University, Al Khod, P.O. Box 20, Muscat, Oman 123 (E-mail: temara@squ.edu.om).

[Haworth co-indexing entry note]: "Effect of Cause-Related Marketing on Attitudes and Purchase Intentions: The Moderating Role of Cause Involvement and Donation Size." Hajjat, Mahmood M. Co-published simultaneously in *Journal of Nonprofit & Public Sector Marketing* (Best Business Books, an imprint of The Haworth Press, Inc.) Vol. 11, No. 1, 2003, pp. 93-109; and: *Nonprofit and Business Sector Collaboration: Social Enterprises, Cause-Related Marketing, Sponsorships, and Other Corporate-Nonprofit Dealings* (ed: Walter W. Wymer, Jr. and Sridhar Samu) Best Business Books, an imprint of The Haworth Press, Inc., 2003, pp. 93-109. Single or multiple copies of this article are available for a fee from The Haworth Document Delivery Service [1-800-HAWORTH, 9:00 a.m. - 5:00 p.m. (EST). E-mail address: getinfo@haworthpressinc.com].

93

painful images (i.e., high cause involvement) and the other half were shown pleasant images concerning the cause (i.e., low cause involvement). In one half of the ads, 5% of sales were claimed to be donated (i.e., high donation) and 0.1% in the other (i.e., low donation). In one half of the ads, a fictitious nonprofit organization (NPO) was affiliated with the experimental brand and claimed to work on the sponsored cause (i.e., CRM) and in the other half there was no mention of a specific cause (i.e., OM). Results from several ANOVA analyses supported the hypotheses and all hypotheses were accepted. *[Article copies available for a fee from The Haworth Document Delivery Service: 1-800-HAWORTH. E-mail address: <getinfo@haworthpressinc.com> Website: <http://www.HaworthPress.com> © 2003 by The Haworth Press, Inc. All rights reserved.]*

KEYWORDS. Cause related marketing, donation level, marketing strategy, attitudes, issue/cause involvement, purchase intentions

INTRODUCTION

Cause-related marketing (CRM) involves the integration of marketing activities of a for-profit firm with fund raising requirements of a not-for-profit organization (NPO). In its basic form, CRM campaigns try to persuade consumers to buy a certain product by promising to donate something in return to a specific cause. Research indicates that CRM is a good way to raise funds for social causes, can enhance the firm's image, create favorable attitudes toward its products, increase sales and profits, and provide additional support for the NPO.

As it becomes more difficult for companies to obtain and maintain competitive advantage, substantive and strategic cause related marketing (CRM) programs would become an extremely valuable marketing strategy that offer a point of differentiation (Murphy 1997; Tate 1995). As a strategy designed to promote the achievement of corporate objectives (e.g., sales volume), CRM has become corporate America's lexicon for working in financial concert with a charity and experienced phenomenal growth recently with total spending exceeding $1 billion annually in the U.S. alone (Smith and Stodghill 1994; Tate 1995).

Marketing programs with social dimensions are becoming mainstream as managers respond to higher consumer expectations of corporate social responsibility. According to Stewart-Allen (1998), CRM became the latest buzzword for U.K. marketing at the close of the last century. It was reported in a series of studies, Business in the Community (BITC), that 83% of consumers believed that CRM yields positive image of the product and the producer and 86% said that when price and quality are equal they would be more likely to buy a brand if it was associated with a cause (BITC 1996a, 1996b, 1997). In another study, 64% of respondents reported that they would be prepared to pay a little more for a CRM-supported product (Gray 1997).

Presumably, CRM should be more effective than ordinary marketing in terms of creating positive brand attitudes and purchase intentions. The success of CRM reflects, at least in part, consumer favorable responses to a company's support of a cause. It is suggested, therefore, that consumers' perceptions of social responsibility can influence their beliefs and attitudes of the product and the producer (Brown and Dacin 1997, Gray 1997). However, given the complexity and uncertainty of CRM campaigns, research that provides insights into whether and when CRM enhances brand attitudes and purchase intention is needed. Toward this end, the present research investigates whether the level of cause involvement and the Level of charity donation moderate the effect of CRM on consumers' attitudes and purchase intentions.

LITERATURE REVIEW

In its simplest form, CRM is the affiliation of company's identity to nonprofit organizations, good causes, and important social issues through corporate marketing and fund raising programs. In their seminal article on CRM, Varadarajan and Menon (1988) provide a comprehensive analysis of CRM and define it as "the process of formulating and implementing marketing activities that are characterized by an offer from the firm to contribute a specified amount to a designated cause when consumers engage in revenue-providing exchanges that satisfy organizational and individual objectives." Some advocates believe that CRM "may be the most creative and cost effective product strategy to evolve in years and one that directly addresses the issue of financial returns" (Smith and Alcorn 1991).

In spite of the prevalence and acceptance of CRM by both practitioners and consumers (Barnes and Fitzgerald 1992; Ross, Paterson, and Stutts 1992), research has only recently begun to investigate consumers' responses to, and understanding of CRM campaigns (Drumwright 1996; Webb and Mohr 1998). In a number of studies, it was found that most consumers view CRM favorably and a majority of them had favorable attitudes and purchase intentions (Carringer 1994; Kroll 1996; Murphy 1997; Ross, Patterson, and Stutts 1992; Ross, Stutts, and Patterson 1991; Smith and Alcorn 1991). However, Varadarajan and Menon (1988) caution that firms may incur "negative publicity and charges of exploitation of causes." Indeed, CRM has been shown to foster negative perceptions about a firm's motivation for engaging in cause-related activities and still other findings indicate that CRM has little impact on decision making ("It Pays To Behave" 1995; Smith and Stodghill 1994). In one study, Webb and Mohr (1998) reported that consumers believed that firms engage in CRM for egoistic reasons whereas NPOs participate for altruistic motives. Consequently, firms running CRM are more of a subject to negative consumer affective and behavioral responses than NPOs (Dahl and Lavack 1995; Ellen, Mohr, and Webb 1997).

A factor that could explain prior opposing results is issue involvement (i.e., cause involvement). Past research in CRM reported some evidence that consumers prefer local causes (i.e., involving causes) to national ones and disaster relief or curing diseases to other causes (Ellen, Mohr, and Webb 1996; Ross, Stutts, and Patterson 1991; Smith and Alcorn 1991). CRM was also shown to be more effective with luxury products (i.e., involving products) than practical ones (Strahilevitz and Myers 1995) and with large donations than small ones (Dahl and Lavack 1995). More recently, Lafferty (1996) found that consumers' responses were more positive when the cause was more important to them. She has also reported that control advertisements (i.e., with no cause mentioned in the ad) resulted in more positive attitudes and purchase intentions than a CRM advertisement supporting an unimportant cause.

Generally, involvement is viewed as personal relevance (Zaichkowsky 1985) or the degree of consumer engagement in different aspects of the consumption episode and is considered to have a primary influence on consumer responses (Chaiken 1980; Jain and Srinivasen 1990; Laaksonen 1994). Three main facets of the construct are evident in literature: product, response, and subject or issue involvement (Petty and Cacioppo 1979). Whilst all three perspectives are important, only issue involvement is taken in the present treatise to provide a framework for understanding consumer responses to CRM.

The focus of the present research is on the role of cause (i.e., issue) involvement in mediating the effect of CRM. High issue involvement occurs when an issue has personal relevance (Zaichkowsky 1985), or intrinsic importance (Sherif and Hoveland 1961), when people expect the issue to have significant consequences to their lives (Aspler and Sears 1968), or when concerns about immediate situational rewards are dwarfed by outcomes connected with the topic itself (Cialdini et al. 1976).

The extant literature on issue involvement proposes that highly involved individuals look for more information, use more criteria, consider fewer alternatives, and elaborate more on relevant information (Beatty and Smith 1987; Chaiken 1980; Petty and Cacioppo 1981). It is also suggested that they carefully scrutinize message elements and use their knowledge of the merits of the issue in making judgments of the validity of an advocacy (Petty, Cacioppo, and Schumann 1983). Depending on the level of involvement, Petty and Cacioppo (1983) propose two routes to persuasion and attitude formation, a central and a peripheral route. One or the other will work best depending on the elaboration likelihood of the message. When the individual is highly involved with the communication situation, message elaborations are more likely to occur. Therefore, informative advertising is likely to be more effective under high rather than low involvement since people are motivated to consider the true merits of the message (Petty, Cacioppo, and Schumann 1983). In the case of CRM, highly involved individuals with the cause will integrate the cause-related elements in the message with information recalled from memory in order to form a unitary opinion about the sponsoring product. One of the important informational elements is the size of contribution donated to the cause (the terms high and low donation will be used for consistency). Highly involved individuals in a cause want and expect high donations to be contributed to their cause by the sponsoring product. The attitudes and purchase intentions of highly involved consumers whose expectations were met (i.e., high donation level) in a CRM condition, therefore, should be higher than the attitudes and purchase intentions of those individuals whose expectations were not met in an OM condition (i.e., high donation to society but not to their cause). If the donation level is low, consumers in a CRM condition will be frustrated and their frustration will be reflected negatively on their attitudes and purchase intentions because they believe that the advertising firm is using the cause for egoistic rather than altruistic motives. Conversely, consumers in an OM condition who have no prior expectations of any contribution to charity will think that it is good from the advertising organization to donate a portion of its revenues, though small, to society. Consequently, consumers' attitudes and purchase intentions in an OM condition should be higher than the attitudes and purchase intentions of those in a CRM condition.

However, cause involvement is not always high for all individuals. Because people are often preoccupied with different aspects of their lives, low cause involvement may prevail. It is therefore important to examine the effect of CRM under low involvement conditions. The persuasion literature offers insights on this issue (Chaiken 1980; Petty and Cacioppo 1983). It is suggested that people are unlikely to scrutinize message elements diligently and combine all related thoughts into an overall attitude. Instead, peripheral cues rather than veridical information in the message will be used in the persuasion and attitude formation process. The size of the contribution will be used again but as a peripheral cue. Individuals watching a CRM advertisement but have little or may be no emotional or motivational association to the particular cause in the advertisement do not accept that a high portion of the price they pay be given away. They think that the firm is trying to take credit for doing something (i.e., helping society) on the expense of consumers. Instead, they think that they deserve this money in the form of price reduction or rebate. Individuals exposed to an OM advertisement, however, will perceive the large donation favorably. The reason is that each individual will think that several social causes will be served by giving large amounts of money back to the society. Therefore, the attitudes and purchase intentions of those individuals in an OM condition will be higher than their counterparts' in the CRM condition. Alternatively, people in a CRM condition see that giving away a small fraction of the price they pay to a social cause fulfills their philanthropic and altruistic feelings toward their society whereas individuals in an OM condition think that paying a little amount of money to society is a cheap price for increasing sales. Therefore, the attitudes and purchase intention of individuals in a CRM condition will be higher than their counterparts' in the OM condition. The preceding predictions are consistent with previous findings (Dahl and Lavack 1995; Ellen, Mohr, and Webb 1996; Ross, Stutts, and Patterson 1991; Smith and Alcorn 1991). In line with this argument, the following hypotheses will be tested:

H1: Under conditions of high cause involvement and high donation, CRM produces higher attitudes and purchase intentions than ordinary marketing.

H2: Under conditions of high cause involvement and low donation, CRM produces lower attitudes and purchase intentions than ordinary marketing.

H3: Under conditions of low cause involvement and high donation, CRM produces lower attitudes and purchase intentions than ordinary marketing.

H4: Under conditions of low cause involvement and low donation, CRM produces higher attitudes and purchase intentions than ordinary marketing.

METHODOLOGY

Subjects and Design: A total of 240 undergraduate students from a major university in the Middle East, where the researcher used to teach, participated in the present experiment. Thirty students were randomly assigned to each of the 2 (high versus low cause involvement) × 2 (cause versus ordinary marketing) × 2 (high versus low donation) experimental cells.

Stimulus Material: Two PowerPoint presentations and a booklet were prepared for this study. For one half of the subjects (i.e., high cause involvement), the PowerPoint presentation contained *painful* images of Palestinian children, women, and men under siege being shot, tortured, or terrified by occupation soldiers, their crops and trees being burned by settlers, and their houses being flattened by army bulldozers. For the second half of the subjects (i.e., low cause involvement), the PowerPoint presentation contained *pleasant* images of holy sites, tourist attractions, and crafts from Palestine.

The booklet contained magazine ads for real products (i.e., Gillette Mark III razors, Aquafresh toothpaste, Atta Ali ice cream, and Tiger candy bars). Different ads contained different information about the advertised products and pictures of the products in relevant and pleasant images. Imbedded in the booklet was the critical ad, ad number 3, for a fictitious fruit drink named FreshTop. For one half of the subjects (i.e., CRM), the ad was sponsored by a fictitious charity organization called Isra'a Org. that claimed to operate in Palestine helping distressed families. In one half of these ads (i.e., high donation), the ad claimed that 5% of all FreshTop's sales will go to Palestinian families through the sponsoring charity organization whereas in the other half of these ads (i.e., low donation) it was mentioned that only 0.1% of FreshTop's sales will be contributed to this cause. For the second half of the subjects (i.e., ordinary marketing), the ad for this product was not different from ads of other products except that it was claimed that part of the product sales would be given back to society (no mention of any specific cause). In one half of these ads (i.e., high donation), the ad claimed that 5% of all FreshTop's sales will be given to society whereas in the other half of these ads (i.e., low donation) it was mentioned that only 0.1% of FreshTop's sales will be given to society. Finally, the booklet contained several questions that assessed students' reactions to the ads and advertised products and several others about themselves. In all phases of the study, the mother language of the participants was used in order to enhance learning and comprehension.

Procedure: Students were approached in their respective classrooms and told that their task was to evaluate some print ads for class discussion. Participants in the same classroom were assigned to the same level of issue involvement and in different rooms to different levels. Students were told that they had to wait for a few minutes until ad booklets would be brought in and, in the meantime, the experimenter would like to show them some images from Palestine. Those in the high cause involvement condition watched the painful whereas those in the low cause involvement watched the pleasant images from Palestine. Additional verbal comments were also given by the experimenter during the PowerPoint presentations in order to create the desired levels of involvement. In the high cause involvement condition, the experimenter elaborated on the hardships and difficulties Palestinian families experience after a family member is killed, jailed, or permanently disabled, their house is demolished, or their crops are destroyed and how much and how urgent these families need assistance. In the low cause involvement condition, the experimenter said few words of enchantment about the beautiful elements in each scene. At the end of the power point presentation, the booklets were distributed to subjects. Ad viewing was timed to 3 minutes per ad and subjects were told when to go from one ad to another. At the end of ad viewing, subjects were asked to list all the thoughts that they had experienced during viewing the PowerPoint presentations and the ads, to answer few questions about the critical brand and some other questions about another brand, and to answer few questions about themselves. When subjects finished, they were briefed, thanked for their participation, and warned not to talk about the experiment.

Experimental Manipulations: (1) Involvement. Subjects in the high cause involvement condition viewed painful images of Palestinians being shot, tortured, or humiliated at the hands of occupation soldiers whereas those in the low cause involvement were shown pleasant images of holy sites, tourist attractions, and crafts from Palestine. Additionally, the experimenter in the high cause involvement condition elaborated on the cruelty of life Palestinian families live under occupation and how much assistance is urgently needed to provide to those families. In the low cause involvement condition, the experimenter said a few nice words about the beauty of each scene and how much the scene was enchanting. (2) Type of marketing. Subjects in the CRM condition were told that the contribution of the fruit drink would go to a specific cause, and that is to help distressed Palestinian families under occupation. Subjects in the ordinary marketing condition were told that the contribution of the advertised brand would be given back to society but with no mention of any specific cause or charity. (3) Donation level. Subjects in the high donation condition were told that the advertised brand would contribute a total of 5% whereas those in the low donation condition were told that the donation was 0.1%.

Measured Variables: (1) Involvement. Subjects were asked to list all the thoughts that they had while viewing the power point presentations and the product ads. The purpose of this task was to assess the cause-involvement manipulations. It was expected that the more (less) subjects feel involved with the cause, the more (less) thoughts that they would list about the cause and about FreshTop fruit drink and the less (more) about the pleasant images and about other products advertised. (2) Type of marketing. Subjects were asked on two 7-point scales how specific (general) the cause mentioned in the ad they believed was with 1 indicating that the cause was not very specific (general) and 7 indicating that the cause was very specific (general). (3) Donation level. In order to assess the level-of-donation manipulations, subjects were asked to indicate on two 7-point scales how high (low) they believed the level of the donation was with 1 indicating that the level was not very high (low) and 7 indicating that the level was very high (low). A third question asked subjects to write the exact percentage of FreshTop's sales to be donated. (4) Attitude toward the ad. Subjects indicated their overall evaluations of FreshTop ad on a six item semantic differential scale anchored at −3 and +3 (bad-good, boring-interesting, unpleasant-pleasant, depressing-comforting, surprising-expected, and sad-joyous). (5) Attitude toward the brand. Subjects indicated their attitudes toward FreshTop fruit drink on a seven-item Likert scale anchored at 1 and 7 (FreshTop is: refreshing, thirst quenching, filling, good value for the money, party pride, tasty, the drink for me). (6) Purchase intention. To assess purchase intentions, subjects were asked to indicate on a 7-point scale how likely they would purchase FreshTop the next time they needed a fruit drink. Finally, subjects responded to several questions about themselves concerning age, gender, family income, and several other questions about their perception of their adherence to religious teachings.

RESULTS

Manipulation Checks: (1) Involvement. The written responses on the thoughts that subjects recalled and listed about both painful and pleasant, types of images of Palestinians, and about the advertised products were used to assess the effectiveness of the involvement manipulations. Participants in the high involvement condition recalled more thoughts about the Palestinian painful images (M = 5.3) than participants in the low involvement condition (M = 1.27, F1, 238 = 37.85, p = 0.001) and recalled more thoughts about FreshTop (M = 3.7) than their counterparts in the low involvement condition (M = 1.84, F1, 238 = 18.73, p = 0.001). Conversely, participants in the low involvement condition recalled more thoughts about the Palestinian pleasant images (M = 3.8) than participants in the high involvement condition (M = 0.34, F1, 238 = 43.6, p = 0.0001) and recalled more thoughts about other products (M = 3.1) than their counterparts in the high involvement condition (M = 0.54, F1, 238 = 31.64, p = 0.001). (2) Type of marketing. Responses to two 7-point scales about subjects' beliefs about the specificity (generality) of the cause were used to assess whether the marketing type manipulation was effective. Participants in the CRM condition believed that the cause was very specific (M = 6.03), more than those in the ordinary marketing condition (M = 3.07, F1, 238 = 18.27, p = 0.01). Alternatively, subjects in the ordinary marketing condition thought that the cause mentioned in the ad was very general (M = 5.78), more than their counterparts in the CRM condition (M = 1.42, F1, 238 = 23.17, p = 0.001). (3) Donation level. Responses to two 7-point questions asking subjects how high (low) they believed the donation level was were used to assess the donation level manipulations. Subjects who learned that the donation was 5% thought that it was very high (M = 5.7), more than those who learned that the donation was only 0.1% (M = 1.7, F1, 238 = 47.32, p = 0.0001). Alternatively, Subjects who learned that the donation was 0.1% thought that it was very low (M = 4.5), more than those who learned that the donation was 5% (M = 1.3, F1, 238 = 45.87, p = 0.0001). When asked about the level of the promised donation, 83% of subjects recalled the exact level of the donation.

Attitudes and Purchase Intentions: Subjects responses to the attitude toward the ad, attitude toward the brand, and purchase intentions were analyzed in several 2 (high versus low involvement) $\times$ 2 (cause versus ordinary marketing) $\times$ 2 (high versus low donation) ANOVAs.

ANOVA performed on subjects' attitudes toward the brand revealed a two-way interaction of type of marketing by donation level as it is illustrated in Figure 1 for high involvement condition ($F1$, $236 = 41.56$, $p = 0.001$) and Figure 2 for low involvement condition ($F1$, $236 = 39.63$, $p = 0.001$). Similar interactions were found on the attitude toward the ad (high involvement condition: $F1$, $236 = 25.31$, $p = 0.001$; low involvement condition: $F1$, $236 = 19.85$, $p = 0.001$) and purchase intention measures (high involvement condition: $F1$, $236 = 17.53$, $p = 0.001$; low involvement condition: $F1$, $236 = 21.59$, $p = 0.001$).

Results of the ANOVA analyses were consistent with H1 and H2, which predicted that CRM would produce higher attitudes and purchase intentions than OM under conditions of high involvement when the donation level was high, but lower attitudes when the donation level was low. Specifically, when the donation level was high, cause related marketing produced under conditions of high involvement higher attitudes toward the ad ($M = 2.3$ versus 0.5, $F1$, $236 = 14.45$, $p = 0.001$), attitudes toward the brand ($M = 5.1$ versus 2.3, $F1$, $236 = 17.52$, $p = 0.001$), and purchase intentions ($M = 4.9$ versus 1.7, $F1$, $236 = 23.68$, $p = 0.001$), than ordinary marketing (see Figure 1). When the level of the donation was low, cause related marketing produced under conditions of high involvement lower attitudes toward the ad ($M = 0.7$ versus 2.5, $F1$, $236 = 21.15$, $p = 0.001$), attitudes toward the brand ($M = 3.1$ versus 5.3, $F1$, $236 = 27.12$, $p = 0.001$), and purchase intentions ($M = 1.9$ versus 4.7, $F1$, $236 = 31.38$, $p = 0.001$), than ordinary marketing (see Figure 1).

H3 and H4 predicted that CRM would produce lower attitudes and purchase intentions under conditions of low involvement when the donation level was high, but higher attitudes when the donation level was low. Indeed, when the donation level was low, CRM produced under conditions of low involvement higher attitudes toward the ad ($M = 2.9$ versus 1.7, $F1$, $236 = 23.38$, $p = 0.001$), attitudes toward the brand ($M = 5.9$ versus 2.3, $F1$, $236 = 31.38$, $p = 0.001$), and purchase intentions ($M = 4.8$ versus 1.3, $F1$, $236 = 17.65$, $p = 0.001$), than ordinary marketing (see Figure 2). When the donation level was high, cause related marketing produced under conditions of low involvement lower attitudes toward the ad ($M = 1.1$ versus 2.8, $F1$, $236 = 241.32$, $p = 0.001$),

FIGURE 1. Plot of the interaction effect of type of marketing by donation level on attitudes toward the brand under high involvement condition.

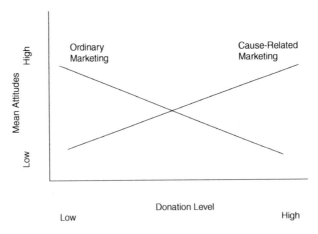

attitudes toward the brand (M = 1.6 versus 4.8, F1, 236 = 29.49, p = 0.001), and purchase intentions (M = 2.4 versus 4.6, F1, 236 = 34.26, p = 0.001) than regular marketing (see Figure 2). These findings lend support to all hypotheses H1 through H4.

DISCUSSION AND CONCLUSIONS

The present research was conducted in the Middle East where, to the knowledge of the researcher, CRM has not been known. Participants, however, were business undergraduate students who were familiar with most business concepts. Keeping this caveat in mind, the present research indicated that students understand and may even support CRM. The present research has demonstrated that CRM has a differential effect on consumers' responses depending on the level of cause involvement and the level of donation contributed to the cause. When the level of cause involvement was high, CRM had more effect on consumers' responses than ordinary marketing when the donation level was high; the opposite was true when the level of donation was low. Alternatively, when the level of cause involvement was low, CRM had more effect on consumers' responses than ordinary marketing when the donation level was low; the opposite was true when the donation level was high.

FIGURE 2. Plot of the interaction effect of type of marketing by donation level on attitudes toward the brand under low involvement condition.

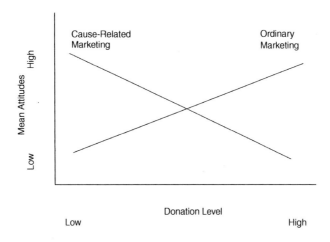

The findings of the present research are consistent with and build on those of past research and provide insight into several issues. First, they provide a means of reconciling opposing CRM effects found in some of the previously mentioned research. Second, the findings provide a theoretical framework for anticipating the conditions under which either CRM or ordinary marketing would be more effective in generating favorable responses toward the advertised product. Finally, the findings are consistent with current theory about the moderating role of involvement on behavioral responses to marketing stimuli (Baker and Lutz 2000; Broderick and Mueller 1999; Greenwald and Leavitt 1984; Petty, Cacioppo, and Schumann 1983). When cause involvement was high, students elaborated on the issue and the route to persuasion was through substantial processing of information. This is evident in the average number of thoughts generated by subjects about the cause (M = 5.3 in high involvement versus M = 1.27 in low involvement, F1, 238 = 37.85, p = 0.001) and about the advertised product (M = 3.7 in high involvement versus M = 1.84 in low involvement, F1, 238 = 18.73, p = 0.001). However, when the donation level was high, students assigned more positive weight to CRM than to ordinary marketing; and the opposite was true when the donation level was low. Alternatively, when cause involvement was low, participants did not give much thought to the message elements but instead used peripheral cues in arriving at their opinions. The level of the donation was the most important cue used by subjects. Approximately 83% of participants (n = 199) recalled the exact level of the promised donation. However, when the donation level was low, students assigned more positive weight to CRM than to ordinary marketing; and the opposite was true when the donation level was high.

It is possible that other extraneous factors may have contributed to the observed moderating effect of involvement. This possibility was investigated in a number of additional analyses. First, a 2 (involvement) × 2 (type of marketing) × 2 (gender) ANOVA for subjects exposed to the high donation condition indicated that the only two-way significant interaction was type of marketing × involvement (F 1, 112 = 15.36, p = 0.001). A similar ANOVA for subjects participating in the low donation condition produced similar results (F1, 112 = 13.74, p = 0.001). Second, a 2 (involvement) × 2 (type of marketing) × 4 (family income) for subjects in the high donation condition indicated that the only significant interaction was type of marketing × involvement (F1, 104 = 11.37, p = 0.01). Another ANOVA for subjects in the low donation condition produced comparable results (F1, 104 = 17.35, p = 0.01). Finally, a 2 (involvement) × 2 (type of marketing) × 4 (adherence to religion) for subjects in the large donation condition revealed that the only significant interaction was type of marketing × involvement (F1, 104 = 5.73, p = 0.02). ANOVA for subjects in the small donation condition produced similar results (F1, 104 = 7.48, p = 0.01).

The present research has also important implications for business marketers. Nevertheless, marketers should exercise extreme care when trying to incorporate experimental research into business strategies. The findings indicate that there are cause-adopting consumers who behaviorally respond favorably to CRM. Marketers, therefore, might be advised to employ CRM to appeal to those consumers if they intend to contribute substantially to their cause and to use ordinary marketing if otherwise. Marketers might also be advised to clearly communicate to consumers the actual amount being promised to the cause and may even the terms and results of the donation be communicated as the CRM campaign progresses. This practice may enhance consumers' trust in the company and in its products and communicate the impression that the company does not engage in CRM for exploitative purposes but rather to exercise a social responsibility. However, marketers should keep in mind that involvement with the cause was more of a factor in creating positive attitudes toward the brand than involvement with the product. From a practical standpoint, CRM can be used effectively whether the product is highly involving or not.

AUTHOR NOTE

Dr. Hajjat earned his PhD from the Ohio State University. He has taught in several other countries including the United States and Jordan. He has published several research papers in the areas of consumer attitude and behavior, structural equation modeling, marketing strategy, total quality management in a variety of international refeered outlets and has presented a number of papers in reputed professional conferences such as ACR and SMA.

REFERENCES

Aspler, R. and D. Sears (1968), "Warning, Personal Involvement, and Attitude Change," *Journal of Personality and Social Psychology*, 9 (June), pp. 162-66.

Barnes, N. and D. Fitzgerald (1992), "Strategic Marketing for Charitable Organizations," *Health Marketing Quarterly*, 9(3/4), pp. 103-114.

Beatty, S. and S. Smith (1987), "External Search Effort: An Investigation Across Several Product Categories," *Journal of Consumer Research*, 14, pp. 83-95.

Business In The Community (1996a, June), "Cause Related Marketing Research–The Winning Game," London: Research International (UK).

Business In The Community (1996b, November), "Cause Related Marketing Research–The Winning Game," London: BRMB Omnibus Survey.

Business In The Community (1997, November), "Cause-Related Marketing: The Game Plan," London: Research International (UK).

Brown, T. and P. Dacin (1997), "The Company and The Product: Corporate Associations and Consumer Product Responses," *Journal of Marketing*, 61 (January), pp. 68-84.

Carringer, P. (1994), "Not Just a Worthy Cause: Cause Related Marketing Delivers the Goods and the Good," *American Advertising*, 10 (Spring), pp. 16-19.

Chaiken, S. (1980), "Heuristic Versus Symantic Information Processing and the Use of Source Versus Message Cues in Persuasion," *Journal of Personality and Social Psychology*, 39 (November), pp. 752-56.

Cialdini, R., A. Levy, P. Herman, L. Kozlowski, and R. Petty (1976), "Elastic Shifts of Opinion: Determinants of Direction and Durability," *Journal of Personality and Social Psychology*, 34, pp. 663-72.

Dahl, D. and A. Lavack (1995), "Cause-Related Marketing: Impact of Size of Corporate Donation and Size of Cause-Related Promotion on Consumer Perceptions and Participation," in *Proceedings of the American Marketing Association Winter Educators' Conference*, vol. 6, D. Stewart and N. Vilcassim, eds, Chicago: AMA.

Drumwright, M. (1996), "Company Advertising with a Social Dimension: The Role of Noneconomic Criteria," *Journal of Marketing*, 60 (October), pp. 71-87.

Ellen, P., L. Mohr, and D. Webb (1996), "Consumer Reactions to Corporate Social Responsibility: Do Attributions Make a Difference?" working paper, Department of Marketing, Georgia State University.

Ellen, P., L. Mohr, and D. Webb (1997), "Can Retailers Benefit From Cause Marketing? Consumer Responses to Different Promotional Offers," working paper, Department of Marketing, Georgia State University.

Gray, R. (1997), "Cause for Thought," *Marketing*, (January) 2, pp. 20-23.

"It Pays To Behave" (1995), *Advertising Age*, (October), 23, p. 3.

Jain, K. and N. Srinivasen (1990), "An Empirical Assessment of Multiple Operationalizations of Involvement," in *Advances in Consumer Research*, 17, M. Goldberg, G. Gorn, and R. Pollay, eds., Provo UT: Association for Consumer Research, pp. 594-602.

Kroll, C. (1996), "Consumers Note Marketers' Good Causes: Roper," *Advertising Age*, (November) 11, p. 51.

Laaksonen, P. (1994), "Consumer Involvement: Concepts and Research," Routledge.

Lafferty, B. (1996), "Cause-Related Marketing: Does the Cause Make a Difference in Consumers' Attitudes and Purchase Intentions Toward the Product?" working paper, Department of Marketing, Florida State University.

Murphy, I. (1997), "Pillsbury Proves Charity, Marketing Begins at Home," *Marketing News*, (February) 17, p. 16.

Petty, R. and J. Cacioppo (1979), "Issue Involvement Can Increase or Decrease Persuasion by Enhancing Message Relevant Cognitive Responses," *Journal of Personality and Social Psychology*, 37 (October), pp. 1915-26.

Petty, R. and J. Cacioppo (1981), "Attitudes and Persuasion: Classic and Contemporary Approaches," Dubuque, IA: WM, C. Brown Co.

Petty, R. and J. Cacioppo (1983), "Central and Peripheral Routes to Persuasion: Application to Advertising," in *Advertising and Consumer Psychology*, L. Percy and A. Woodside, eds. Lexington, MA: Lexington Books, pp. 3-23.

Petty, Cacioppo, and Schumann (1983), "Central and Peripheral Routes to Advertising Effectiveness: The Moderating Role of Involvement," *Journal of Consumer Research*, 10 (September), pp. 135-46.

Ross, J., L. Paterson, and M. Stutts (1992), "Consumer Perceptions of Organizations that Use Cause-Related Marketing," *Journal of the Academy of Marketing Science*, 20 (1), pp. 93-97.

Ross, J., M. Stutts, and L. Patterson (1991), "Tactical Considerations for the Effective Use of Cause-Related Marketing," *Journal of Applied Business Research*, 7 (Spring), pp. 58-65.

Sherif, M. and C. Hoveland (1961), "Social Judgment," New Haven: Yale University Press.

Smith, S. and D. Alcorn (1991), "Cause Marketing: A New Direction in the Marketing of Corporate Social Responsibility," *Journal of Consumer Marketing*, 8 (3), pp. 19-35.

Smith, G. and R. Stodghill (1994), "Are Good Causes Good Marketing?" *Business Week*, (March 21), pp. 64-66.

Stewart-Allen, A. (1998), "Europe Ready for Cause-Related Campaigns," *Marketing News*, 32(4), p. 1.

Strahilevitz, M. and J. Myers (1995), "Donations to Charity as Purchase Incentives: How Well They Work May Depend on What You Are Trying to Sell," *Journal of Consumer Research*, 24 (4), pp. 434-46.

Tate, N. (1995), "And Now a Word From Our Sponsor," *American Demographics*, (June), p. 46.

Varadarajan, P. and A. Menon (1988), "Cause-Related Marketing: A Coalignment of Marketing Strategy and Corporate Philanthropy," *Journal of Marketing*, 52 (July), pp. 58-74.

Webb, D. and L. Mohr (1998), "A Typology of Consumer Responses to Cause-Related Marketing: From Skeptics to Socially Concerned," *Journal of Public Policy and Marketing*," vol. 17, no. 2, pp. 226-38.

Zaichkowsky, J. (1985), "Measuring the Involvement Construct," *Journal of Consumer Research*, 12 (December), pp. 341-350.

A Study on the Effect
of Cause-Related Marketing
on the Attitude Towards the Brand:
The Case of *Pepsi* in Spain

Iñaki García
Juan J. Gibaja
Alazne Mujika

SUMMARY. CRM is an effective tool for differentiating brands and for obtaining emotional positioning among consumers. However, an utilitarian use of this tool might be counteractive. This research aims to better understand the effect of CRM on attitude towards the brand. For this purpose, *Pepsi*'s CRM campaigns in Spain have been analyzed. Results show that, unexpectedly, CRM campaigns might lead to adverse effects as a result of the mercantilist abuse of the concept of solidarity. *[Article copies available for a fee from The Haworth Document Delivery Service: 1-800-HAWORTH. E-mail address: <getinfo@haworthpressinc.com> Website:*

Iñaki García is Associate Professor of Marketing, ESTE School of Management, University of Deusto, Paseo de Mundaiz 50, 20012 San Sebastián, Spain (E-mail: igarri@deusto.es).

Juan J. Gibaja is Assistant Professor of Marketing, ESTE School of Management, University of Deusto, Paseo de Mundaiz 50, 20012 San Sebastián, Spain (E-mail: jgibaja@deusto.es).

Alazne Mujika is Assistant Professor of Marketing, Faculty of Humanities, University of Deusto, Paseo de Mundaiz 50, 20012 San Sebastián, Spain (E-mail: almugica@deusto.es).

[Haworth co-indexing entry note]: "A Study on the Effect of Cause-Related Marketing on the Attitude Towards the Brand: The Case of *Pepsi* in Spain." García, Iñaki, Juan J. Gibaja, and Alazne Muijika. Co-published simultaneously in *Journal of Nonprofit & Public Sector Marketing* (Best Business Books, an imprint of The Haworth Press, Inc.) Vol. 11, No. 1, 2003, pp. 111-135; and: *Nonprofit and Business Sector Collaboration: Social Enterprises, Cause-Related Marketing, Sponsorships, and Other Corporate-Nonprofit Dealings* (ed: Walter W. Wymer, Jr. and Sridhar Samu) Best Business Books, an imprint of The Haworth Press, Inc., 2003, pp. 111-135. Single or multiple copies of this article are available for a fee from The Haworth Document Delivery Service [1-800-HAWORTH, 9:00 a.m. - 5:00 p.m. (EST). E-mail address: getinfo@haworthpressinc.com].

111

KEYWORDS. Cause-related marketing, attitude towards the brand,
consumer skepticism, Spain, *Pepsi*

CAUSE RELATED MARKETING

In a seminal piece, Varadarajan and Menon (1988:60) define CRM
as "the process of formulating and implementing marketing activities
that are characterized by an offer from the firm to contribute a specified amount to a designated cause when consumers engage in revenue-providing exchanges that satisfy organizational and individual
objectives."

Several European and American authors (Varadarajan and Menon
1988; Smith and Alcorn 1991; Andreasen 1996; Guardia 1998; Adkins 1999;
Fundación Empresa y Sociedad 1999; Meyer 1999; Pringle and Thompson
1999; Welsh 1999; Recio and Ortiz 2000; Fundación Empresa y Sociedad
2001) point out that CRM can be an effective tool for differentiating brands
and for obtaining emotional positioning among consumers. Its application would be of benefit to the interests of the firm as far as its market
position, social reputation and brand image are concerned. The positive outcome experienced by corporations in this area has led to a continuous growth in CRM activities (Brown and Dacin 1997). File and
Prince (1998:1537) conclude that CRM "has become an established
part of the marketing mix in privately held companies, confirming the
adoption of this marketing innovation in a new segment of business."
Smith (1994) states that corporate-NPO alliances, including CRM, are
becoming the fastest growing form of marketing today. According to
these authors, it seems as though causes, NPOs, corporations and society have benefited from corporate involvement with social issues.

In spite of its popularity, several authors (Varadarajan and Menon 1988;
Andreasen 1996) warn that corporations involved in CRM activities might
incur criticism and charges of potential abuse and exploitation of both
causes and NPOs. Due to these reasons Webb and Mohr (1998) found that
around half of the sample analyzed in their study expressed negative attitudes of skepticism or cynicism towards the firms that participate in CRM
campaigns. Polonsky and Wood (2001) also advice that using CRM programs to merge social objectives with commercial objectives might lead to

unexpected results. What they call "overcommercialization" of CRM may, in fact, harm those who should benefit from this new tool designed to support social causes.

In Spain, some current trends of CRM have also been criticized (García 2000a, 2000b; Ballesteros 2001) because it could be seen as a cynical use of solidarity with commercial aims. According to this argument, many of the Spanish firms that get involved in this kind of campaigns would do so, above all, in the hope that the image of the NPO with which they are associated will help to define, improve or repair their own image. To these authors the concept of solidarity might be spoiled as a result of its utilitarian abuse. Thus, CRM might become just another tool to improve brand image instead of making people aware of social injustices. In this light, CRM would not educate but would merely encourage consumption.

From the company's point of view, CRM is certainly an instrument that can offer favorable commercial results in the short term. However, it may also seriously harm its image if the firm's commitment to a cause is, in the long term, directly and exclusively linked to the firm's product consumption. It may be for this reason that in Spain, an increasing tendency to detach CRM from strictly promotion-orientated actions is currently being observed.

CAUSE-RELATED MARKETING IN SPAIN

Spanish consumers' purchase decisions are increasingly based on ethical and moral considerations. Tangible features of the product are no longer the sole purchase criteria. Spanish citizens show increasing sensibility towards social issues. According to a research carried out by Fundación Empresa y Sociedad[1] (1997), 63% of Spanish consumers admitted this support to non-profit organizations for the last year. Fernández et al. (1999) also found that nearly 61% of those surveyed worked in aid of a solidarity cause. Therefore, one can argue that there is a positive attitude among Spaniards to help those in need. These studies also confirm that the Spanish youth show more solidarity than other age groups, and more than they used to some years ago. Another report from Fundación Empresa y Sociedad (2001) evinces the results for Spain of international studies *"The Millenium Pool on Corporate Social Responsibility"* and *"European Survey of Consumers' Attitude Towards Corporate Social Responsibility."* This report also reveals that consumers in general, and Spaniards in particular, have a good mind to reward those socially concerned companies. So, while the social responsibility of a company is a "very important" factor for 25% of Europeans when purchasing a product, in Spain the rate grows to 47%, rising to 89% if we take into account those who regard it as "important", in contrast to the European average of 70%. Otherwise stated: consumers (especially youngsters) begin to wonder: Is the firm whose products I buy a "good citizen"? Spanish consumers are punishing "bad citizens" and rewarding the "good" ones.

Spanish consumers ask the firms to involve to a greater extent into social responsibility. It is for this reason that CRM has been undergoing a spectacular boom in the last few years. Proof of this is the fact that Fundación Empresa y Sociedad has declared the promotion of CRM campaign quality management to be a priority activity area. In this sense, it has recently created the "Solidarity Action" emblem, the first quality certificate for CRM programs in Spain (Fundación Empresa y Sociedad 1999).

The willingness of Spanish citizens to participate in CRM programs, especially those based on solidarity-orientated affairs, is very high. According to Fundación Empresa y Sociedad (1997) nine out of ten Spanish consumers are willing to pay more for products involved in a CRM campaign. They are also willing to switch brands when they are informed about the implication of a firm in a CRM campaign. However, even though Spanish consumers show excellent attitudes towards products associated with solidarity, they express a lack of confidence in the fund-gathering system used in CRM programs and in the final destination of funds. This implies an urgent need for the improvement of CRM program communication strategy in Spain (Fundación Empresa y Sociedad 1999).

Nevertheless, the recent and rapid acceptance of CRM by society and companies in Spain has not been sufficiently reflected in academic research. In Spanish marketing literature there are hardly any specific studies assessing the success of any particular CRM campaign. Barone, Miyazaki and Taylor (2000:249) also point out that "research is needed that provides insight into whether and when corporate sponsorship of social causes enhances brand choice." Therefore, the aim of this research is to shed light on the potential effects of CRM campaigns on brand image. For this purpose, *Pepsi's* CRM campaigns have been analyzed. The most relevant features of these campaigns are shown on the following pages.

THE PEPSI *CRM CAMPAIGNS IN SPAIN*

In 1997, *PepsiCo*-Spain obtained profits of approximately 3.6 million euros, while just one year before it had lost almost 43.3 millions (Salas 1998). The company thus emerged from a deep crisis which had started in the early nineties and which had seriously harmed the market share of its most emblematic brand–*Pepsi*–to the benefit of its eternal rival *Coca-Cola* (see Table 1).

1998 was the year in which the good prospects for *PepsiCo* consolidated in Spain, with approximate profits of 12.6 million euros. The importance of this new prospect comes across clearly in the words of Yiannis Petrides, Chairman of the company in Europe and key man behind this change, when he stated that "after the United States, Spain is the country with the highest volume of business for the company. It is therefore one of the strategic markets for continued growth of a profitable kind" (Gómez 2000).

During its Spanish crisis, *Pepsi* had discovered that its drastic reduction in price with regard to *Coca-Cola* had only contrived to harm its quality image. According to the marketing director of *Pepsi* in Spain, after carrying out many market research studies, the company had discovered that the differences in the market share with regard to *Coca-Cola* could not be put down to taste, price or distribution network, but to something much more complex: brand image (Cabrero 2000).

Being aware of this factor, in the last few years the company has started an ambitious brand image construction strategy for *Pepsi* in Spain. Using the implicit message that "we are the alternative to *Coca-Cola*", *Pepsi* wants to promote consumption among young Spaniards,

TABLE 1. The Cola Refreshments Market in Spain

Year	Sales in millions of litters		Market share in volume (%)		
	Coca-Cola	*Pepsi*	*Coca-Cola*	*Pepsi*	Others
1995	1,248.2	253.3	76.4	15.5	8.1
1996	1,270.0	232.0	77.1	14.1	8.8
1997	1,415.0	227.0	79.2	12.7	8.1
1998	1,520.0	247.0	80.3	13.1	6.6
1999	1,649.2	262.7	82.2	13.1	4.7
2000	1,780.0	280.0	81.5	12.8	5.7

Alimarket (2001, 2000, 1999a, 1999b, 1998a, 1998b, 1996)

introducing itself as a modern, non-conformist, provocative, rebel brand, which shares their concerns and values. As the president of *PepsiCo* for Europe states, "we shall maintain our policy of connecting with the younger generations by means of attractive advertising and promotion actions in environments this group feels most identified with: football, music and NPO cooperation" (Gómez 2000). These three basic pillars would be the cornerstones of the image of *Pepsi* in Spain in the new era. The first two were not new for the company, but the third was tried out at a public level for the first time. The challenge was a risky business, although as the marketing director of *Pepsi* in Spain put it, "associating ourselves with solidarity makes sense for *PepsiCo*, because it fits in with our corporate culture and with the concerns of our consumers" (Cabrero 2000).

Thus, in December 1998, *PepsiCo* Spain signed a three-year general cooperation agreement with *Médicos sin Fronteras*[2] (MSF) Spain, a NPO that is well-known to and valued by *Pepsi*'s target public in Spain: young people between the ages of 12 and 24. In general terms, *PepsiCo* committed itself to the following points in the agreement:

- Giving support to and publicizing the work of MSF in heightening Spanish public opinion awareness.
- Helping MSF to attract new members.
- Providing economic funds for MSF's activities.

In the internal context, *PepsiCo* communicated the signature and aims of the agreement by means of a personal letter to all its employees. The company also took on the commitment to carry out specific informative action through its fortnightly bulletin *"Pepsi en Acción"* to make the activities of MSF known among its staff and thus attract potential members. *PepsiCo* also agreed to make a yearly donation to MSF equivalent to the membership fees of all the company's employees. A clause was also signed by virtue of which the company stated its opposition to different aspects of social injustices; namely, the use of child labor anywhere in the world; the exploitation, of any kind, in the engagement of workers; the harm of the environment, and the support of any form of totalitarian regimes (Médicos sin Fronteras 1999).

In the external context, apart from minor actions such as sending MSF Christmas cards to all *PepsiCo* suppliers and distributors, the company guaranteed the presence of MSF publicity and informative materials in establishments where *Pepsi* was on sale. They would also

organize activities, on a regular basis, aimed at encouraging brand consumers to contribute funds to MSF.

As regards this last point, apart from strengthening the consumer's
affective bond with the campaign, and considering that it was the first
time that *Pepsi* was launching out on an action of this type in Spain, the
firm also strove to find a more rational bond. This was obtained by
means of solidarity-orientated promotions. They provided a convenient
and elective mechanism for the consumer such as indicating, for example, that the campaign would donate 1% of *Pepsi*'s net sales in Spain to
MSF for a period of one month (Cabrero 2000). These promotional activities were widely publicized on television and at sale outlets over the
Christmas 1998 and 1999 periods. Thus, linking solidarity commitment
with the sale and consumption of *Pepsi* was, without doubt, the most
visible element of the CRM program for *Pepsi*'s target public.

A slogan used in the promotion campaigns, "Rebeldes con causa, 1%
¡YA!"[3] caused ill feeling among some Spanish NPOs. In this context,
critics pointed out that "it is reasonable to suppose that a group such as
the 0.7% Platform [4],–which has been struggling for years to ensure that
0.7% of the GNP goes to poorer countries–should feel a certain degree
of indignation at seeing that one of the large multinational companies
has taken over one of its war cries and one of its basic postulates. It is
not so much a question of the intellectual ownership of the slogan, but
rather that on saying 1% RIGHT NOW!, in red capital letters and with a
strongly imperative emphasis, it seems as if the company wants to insist
that they are asking for more than NPOs are, and that, in accordance
with the image of its target public, one must be a rebel with a cause and
ask for the impossible. Behind this message, there does not appear to be
a serious approach or a study stating why what is sought is in fact 0.7%
and not any other figure" (Ballesteros 2001:39).

The persisting presence of these promotional campaigns on the Spanish mass media, and the real risk involved in the Spanish public opinion
interpreting them as a cynical use of solidarity, may explain the fact
that, in late 2000, *PepsiCo* and MSF suddenly broke-off their cooperation agreement in Spain.[5]

PepsiCo immediately established a new cooperation agreement in
Spain with another NPO: *Save the Children*. The aim of the new agreement, in the words of the company, is "to give massive support to children and young people who lack shelter throughout the world over the
course of the year 2001." With this aim, *PepsiCo* designed a website
(www.daunpaso.com)[6] which was widely publicized on television at

Christmas 2000. According to the company, it was "the tool which will permit you to actively participate in *Pepsi*'s new solidarity stage."

The activity that *Save the Children* carries out in favor of children and young people in conflict areas around the world is explained on this website. The visitor is invited to go through its pages to discover the so-called "month's project" and to participate by means of a "solidarity click," in exchange for which *Pepsi* commits itself to make a donation-unspecified-to this NPO's projects. This campaign is currently under way in Spain.

RESEARCH HYPOTHESES

The goal of this experiment is to find out if Spanish young people's attitude towards *Pepsi* varies after discovering the contents of the CRM campaigns carried out by this brand in Spain.

Spanish research on consumers' attitude towards CRM (Fundación Empresa y Sociedad 1997, 1999, 2001) shows a wide acceptance of this activity by Spanish society. In a previous study, Mujika, García and Gibaja (2000) found that every group into which the global sample was divided (in terms of gender, consumption of the brand, and collaboration with a NPO) improved their attitude towards the brand after being acquainted with the contents of the CRM campaigns that the brand had performed. Fernández et al. (1999) also found favorable consumer attitudes towards CRM.

Bearing this in mind, the following research hypothesis about change in attitude towards the brand is suggested:

H1: Young people will improve their attitude towards *Pepsi* after knowing the contents of the CRM campaigns developed by the brand. This will also be true for every group defined in terms of gender, consumption of the brand, and collaboration with a NPO.[7]

Additionally, previous research on consumers' attitudes towards the firm, its products, and the NPO involved suggests that women, consumers of the brand and cooperators with an NPO have, respectively, a more favorable attitude than men (Ross, Stutts and Patterson 1990-1991; Ross, Patterson and Stutts 1992; Berger, Cunningham and Kozinets 1996), non-consumers of the brand (Sagarzazu and Gurrutxaga 2001) and non-cooperators with an NPO (Sagarzazu and Gurrutxaga 2001).

This led us to the following set of hypotheses about the strength of change in the attitude:

H2a: After being acquainted with the contents of the CRM campaigns, young women will improve their attitude towards *Pepsi* in a stronger way than young men will.

H2b: After being acquainted with the contents of the CRM campaigns, young people who cooperate with a NPO will improve their attitude towards *Pepsi* in a more noticeable way than young people who do not cooperate with a NPO.

H2c: After being acquainted with the contents of the CRM campaigns, young *Pepsi* consumers will improve their attitude towards *Pepsi* in a stronger way than young non-consumers will.

EXPERIMENT DESIGN

In order to test the research hypotheses, an instrument was developed to measure attitude towards the brand in the form of a self-administered questionnaire. Initially it was made up of a scale of 44 5-point semantic differentials. Approximately 75% of them were selected by a group of university marketing teachers after the translation and adaptation to the Spanish cultural context of items from two widely used scales based on the work of Osgood, Succi and Tannenbaun (1976). They were also thoroughly checked against marketing literature on attitude towards the brand measurement (Bruner and Hensel 1996, 1992; Bearden, Netemeyer and Mobley 1993). The remaining 25% were specifically developed for this experiment after their prior testing in a previous study of a similar nature (Mujika, García and Gibaja 2000).

In late March 2001, the scale was administered to students in the first years of the Humanities-Communication, Humanities-Business and Business Management degree courses at the University of Deusto in San Sebastián. This group of students was selected because they had no previous acquaintance with CRM, and, furthermore, they matched the target segment selected by *Pepsi* for their campaign in Spain.

Three days later, the two CRM campaigns carried out by *Pepsi* in cooperation with MSF and *Save the Children* in Spain were presented to these students. The presentation lasted about 20 minutes and special care was taken to transmit exclusively information and images that the target public had received from *Pepsi* during these campaigns. From the first campaign, therefore, the two television commercials made by

Pepsi at Christmas 1998 and 1999 were shown. In these advertisements, the fact that 1% of net sale was to be donated by the brand in Spain to MSF was made known. Several examples of the informative and advertising materials exhibited by *Pepsi* at the sales outlets were also shown. As regards the second campaign, the television commercial shown by *Pepsi* at Christmas 2000, explaining their new cooperation plan with *Save the Children* was also presented. A visit was also conducted to the website which explains the campaign and how to cooperate by means of the "solidarity click" in the so-called "month's project."

Six days later these students were again administered the same scale in order to detect the existence of any change in their attitude towards *Pepsi*. All in all, 104 pairs of valid observations were identified (see Table 2). The requirements that students are to meet in order to be regarded as a valid case are the following:

- To complete the questionnaire at both stages of the research.
- To attend the presentation of CRM campaigns performed by *Pepsi*.
- Not to have previous knowledge of CRM campaigns carried out by *Pepsi*.[8]

DATA ANALYSIS

Scale Reliability and Dimensionality Assessment

In order to evaluate the reliability and dimensionality of the scale, both analysis of internal consistency and principal component analysis were performed.

TABLE 2. Sample (n = 104) Analyzed in the Experiment

		N	Percentage
	Male	25	24.0
Sex	Female	75	72.1
	Missing	4	3.9
	Yes	13	12.5
Cooperates with a NPO	No	86	82.7
	Missing	5	4.8
	Yes	44	42.3
Pepsi consumer	No	60	57.7
	Missing	0	0.0

A final scale was attained after an iterative purification process of the preliminary measuring tool. This final version consisted of 22 5-point semantic differentials, which fulfilled the following conditions in both stages of the experiment (see Tables 3 and 4):

- They reach their maximum factor loading, in absolute value, on the first factor resulting from the principal components analysis.
- The factor loading on this first factor is greater, in absolute value, than .60.
- The deletion of the semantic differential does not imply an increase of the scale's internal consistency index.

The results of Table 4 show the unidimensional nature in the attitude towards the brand. According to Nunnally (1987), to affirm that unidimensionality exists in a construct two conditions are necessary. On the one hand, the first resulting factor in the principal component analysis must account for a substantially greater portion of the variance than the second one. On the other hand, the third factor must not entail much less variance than the second.

Furthermore, the high values of internal consistency reached by the scale, high above the limits normally accepted in studies of an exploratory nature, enables us to confirm that the constructed scale is a reliable tool to measure the attitude towards the brand.

Attitude Towards **Pepsi** *Before Becoming Acquainted with CRM Campaigns*

As a prior step, the attitude of individuals towards the brand before the presentation of the stimulus was analyzed. With this aim in mind, we proceeded to recode the scores given to the 22 semantic differentials into integer values between −2 (assigned to the least favorable extreme) and +2 (assigned to the most favorable extreme). This recoding process was consistent with the existence of semantic differentials whose right extreme indicated a favorable attitude towards the brand (e.g., "Bad-Good") and others whose right extreme denoted an unfavorable attitude (e.g., "Attractive-Unattractive"). After this process, a negative score given in a yet recoded semantic differential indicates a negative attitude as far as this differential is concerned, regardless of how it was originally formulated.

TABLE 3. Results of the Purification Process for Items in the Final Scale

Item	Before acquaintance with CRM campaigns		After acquaintance with CRM campaigns	
	Factor loading on the 1st factor	α if item deleted	Factor loading on the 1st factor	α if item deleted
Would not consume - Would consume	.782	.9523	.814	.9632
Unfavorable - Favorable	.730	.9531	.817	.9631
Worthless - Valuable	.643	.9542	.749	.9640
Annoying - Pleasing	.753	.9530	.696	.9645
Unappetizing - Appetizing	.787	.9523	.744	.9640
Disapprove - Approve	.773	.9526	.726	.9642
Attractive - Unattractive	-.661	.9540	-.717	.9642
Bad - Good	.763	.9526	.852	.9626
Unenjoyable - Enjoyable	.775	.9526	.782	.9637
Useless - Worthwhile	.796	.9524	.820	.9632
Inferior - Superior	.622	.9544	.602	.9653
Would support - Would not support	-.618	.9545	-.812	.9632
Disagreeable - Agreeable	.737	.9532	.820	.9632
Would recommend - Would not recommend	-.704	.9533	-.810	.9631
High quality - Poor quality	-.601	.9547	-.749	.9639
Dislike - Like	.731	.9533	.834	.9629
Would buy - Would not buy	-.727	.9532	-.754	.9641
Gentle - Harsh	-.719	.9535	-.702	.9644
Unsatisfactory - Satisfactory	.811	.9518	.843	.9627
Interesting - Boring	-.669	.9539	-.709	.9645
Does not match my image - Matches my image	.635	.9543	.609	.9652
Undesirable - Desirable	.835	.9519	.867	.9627

TABLE 4. Scale Reliability and Dimensionality Overall Results

	Before acquaintance with CRM campaigns	After Acquaintance with chairman campaigns
Cronbach's Alpha	.9553	.9653
Percentage of the variance put down to the first factor	52.498	59.026
Percentage of the variance put down to the second factor	6.816	6.193
Percentage of the variance put down to the third factor	4.658	4.124

Lastly, adding up the recoded scores given for the 22 items of the scale drew up an overall index for the attitude towards the brand. This overall index ranges from −44 to +44.

Let:

- X_{ij} be the recoded score given by the ith individual in the jth semantic differential before the CRM campaigns were known.
- S, the overall sample.
- M, the set of young men in the sample.
- F, the set of young women in the sample.
- V, the set of young cooperators with a NPO in the sample.
- NV, the set of those young people who do not cooperate with any NPO in the sample.
- C, the set of *Pepsi* young consumers in the sample.
- NC, the set of those young people who do not consume *Pepsi* in the sample.
- n_K, the number of cases in set K ∈ {S, M, F, V, NV, C, NC}.

Table 5 presents, in columns 2 to 8 respectively, the average value of every item in the scale for the whole sample, men, women, people who cooperate with an NPO, people who do not cooperate with an NPO, consumers of the brand, and not-consumers of the brand before being acquainted with the contents of the campaign. More precisely:

$$\frac{1}{n_k}\sum_{i\in k} X_{ij} \quad \begin{array}{l} j = 1 \ldots 22 \\ K \in \{S, M, F, V, NV, C, NC\} \end{array}$$

Furthermore, the last row in Table 5 presents the average value of the global scale for the groups previously defined, before being acquainted with the contents of the campaign. More precisely:

$$\frac{1}{n_k}\sum_{i\in K}\sum_{j=1}^{22} X_{ij} \quad K \in \{S, M, F, V, NV, C, NC\}$$

From Table 5 it can be inferred that before knowing *Pepsi* CRM campaigns in Spain:

- The overall sample shows a moderately negative attitude towards *Pepsi* (−1.77 in a range from −44 to +44).
- Both men and women express a moderate negative attitude towards *Pepsi*. However, the attitude of men (−3.29) is less favor-

able than that of women (−1.70), although the difference is not statistically significant.

- Both those who cooperate with a NPO and those who do not have a negative attitude towards *Pepsi*. However, the attitude is more favorable among those who do not cooperate with any NPO (−1.73) than among those who do (−5.62), although the difference is not statistically significant.

- *Pepsi* consumers are the only group that values the brand in a slightly positive way (+7.20). They contrast with non-consumers, who make up the group that gives the brand the worst evaluation (−8.19). The difference between the two groups is also statistically significant.

Attitude Towards Pepsi After Becoming Acquainted with Its CRM Campaigns

In this second stage, the semantic differentials were again recoded in the same way as in the first one. Considering the sample sets previously defined (S, M, F, V, NV, C, NC), let Y_{ij} be the recoded score given by the i-th individual in the j-th semantic differential after knowing the CRM campaigns.

Table 6 presents, in columns 2 to 8 respectively, the average value of every item in the scale for the whole sample, men, women, people who cooperate with a NPO, people who do not cooperate with a NPO, consumers of the brand and not-consumers of the brand after being acquainted with the contents of the campaign. More precisely:

$$\frac{1}{n_K}\sum_{i\in K} Y_{ij} \quad \begin{array}{l} j = 1 \ldots \ldots 22 \\ K \in \{S, M, F, V, NV, C, NC\} \end{array}$$

Furthermore, the last row in Table 6 presents the average value of the global scale for the groups previously defined, after being acquainted with the contents of the campaign. More precisely:

$$\frac{1}{n_K}\sum_{i\in K}\sum_{j=1}^{22} Y_{ij} \quad K \in \{S, M, F, V, NV, C, NC\}$$

The results of the analysis can be observed in Table 6.

From the analysis of Table 6 it can be inferred that all the groups into which the sample has been divided have once again a negative attitude

TABLE 5. Attitude Towards *Pepsi* Before Becoming Acquainted with CRM Campaigns

Item (1)	Full Sample (2)	Sex		Cooperates with NPO		*Pepsi* consumer		
		Male (3)	Female (4)	Yes (5)	No (6)	Yes (7)	No (8)	
Would not consume - Would consume	.05	−.12	.09	−.38	.07	.63	−.37	*
Unfavorable - Favorable	−.03	−.29	.03	−.31	−.05	.38	−.33	*
Worthless - Valuable	−.20	−.16	−.25	−.53	−.20	.05	−.38	*
Annoying - Pleasing	.28	.12	.31	.15	.26	.64	.02	*
Unappetizing - Appetizing	−.32	−.24	−.43	−.92	−.311	.47	−.88	*
Disapprove - Approve	.25	.20	.24	.15	.24	.63	−.03	*
Attractive - Unattractive†	−.01	−.24	.05	.23	−.03	.26	−.18	*
Bad - Good	−.17	−.16	−.23	−.31	−.21	.35	−.55	*
Unenjoyable - Enjoyable	.26	.12	.28	.15	.24	.77	−.12	*
Useless - Worthwhile	−.02	−.08	−.01	−.15	−.02	.42	−.35	*
Inferior - Superior	−.31	−.56	−.23	−.54	−.30	−.14	−.42	
Would support - Would not support†	−.08	−.20	−.04	−.15	−.07	.14	−.23	
Disagreeable - Agreeable	.17	.00	.20	.08	.16	.56	−.12	*
Would recommend - Would not recommend	−.07	−.16	−.05	−.23	−.08	.21	−.27	*
High quality - Poor quality†	.08	.20	.01	.08	.06	.28	−.07	
Dislike - Like	−.47	−.20	−.61	−.77	−.45	.35	−1.08	*
Would buy - Would not buy†	−.18	−.36	−.19	−.76	−.14	.51	−.70	*
Gentle - Harsh†	−.05	.04	−.09	−.31	−.04	.29	−.28	*
Unsatisfactory - Satisfactory	−.38	−.40	−.41	−.69	−.36	.40	−.92	*
Interesting - Boring†	−.02	.16	−.09	−.08	−.03	.33	−.25	*
Does not match my image - Matches my image	−.13	−.12	−.16	−.31	−.12	.09	−.30	*
Undesirable - Desirable	−.05	−.28	.00	.00	−.09	.42	−.40	*
SCALE	−1.77	−3.29	−1.70	−5.62	−1.73	7.20	−8.19	*

(†) Reversed in the recoding process.
(*) Significant difference (p < .05)

towards *Pepsi*. This finding is counterintuitive. Likewise, the most critical positions correspond once again to non-consumers of the brand (−10.96) and to those who cooperate with a NPO (−10.00), whereas the most favorable attitudes continue to correspond to brand consumers (+6.52).

TABLE 6. Attitude Towards *Pepsi* After Becoming Acquainted with CRM Campaigns

Item (1)	Full Sample (2)	Sex		Cooperates with NPO		*Pepsi* consumer		
		Male (3)	Female (4)	Yes (5)	No (6)	Yes (7)	No (8)	
Would not consume - Would consume	−.35	−.48	−.33	−.77	−.34	.35	−.87	*
Unfavorable - Favorable	−.24	−.44	−.17	−.46	−.22	.21	−.58	*
Worthless - Valuable	−.25	−.36	−.23	−.46	−.24	.07	−.49	*
Annoying - Pleasing	.06	.00	.05	.00	.05	.37	−.17	*
Unappetizing - Appetizing	−.43	−.36	−.51	−1.00	−.40	.23	−.92	*
Disapprove - Approve	−.03	−.36	.05	−.69	.06	.42	−.37	*
Attractive - Unattractive	−.02	.08	−.08	−.31	−.01	.47	−.36	*
Bad - Good	−.27	−.42	−.26	−.46	−.26	.24	−.64	*
Unenjoyable - Enjoyable	.12	.12	.11	.15	.08	.51	−.17	*
Useless - Worthwhile	−.17	−.42	−.13	−.46	−.15	.21	−.46	*
Inferior - Superior	−.49	−.48	−.51	−.85	−.45	−.33	−.60	
Would support - Would not support	.03	.12	−.03	−.46	.06	.44	−.27	*
Disagreeable - Agreeable	.04	−.04	.03	−.08	.01	.49	−.29	*
Would recommend - Would not recommend	−.20	−.24	−.23	−.31	−.23	.26	−.53	*
High quality - Poor quality	−.11	.04	−.18	−.38	−.12	.19	−.32	*
Dislike - Like	−.48	−.24	−.63	−.92	−.47	.37	−1.10	*
Would buy - Would not buy	−.32	−.60	−.28	−.69	−.30	.40	−.83	*
Gentle - Harsh	.05	.13	.01	−.08	.05	.42	−.22	*
Unsatisfactory - Satisfactory	−.43	−.48	−.47	−.69	−.41	.21	−.90	*
Interesting - Boring[†]	.12	.20	.08	.00	.12	.44	−.12	*
Does not match my image - Matches my image	−.13	−.32	−.08	−.46	−.09	.12	−.32	*
Undesirable - Desirable	−.17	−.36	−.15	−.62	−.15	.28	−.50	*
SCALE	−3.35	−4.96	−3.46	−10.00	−2.96	+6.52	−10.96	*

(†) Reversed in the recoding process.
(*) Significant difference ($p < .05$)

Change in the Attitude Towards Pepsi

A set of T-tests for correlated samples was performed in order to contrast hypothesis H1. Thus, taking Tables 5 and 6 as a basis, let us define a new variable in the following way:

$$D_{ij} = Y_{ij} - X_{ij}$$

This new variable represents the improvement (if the value is positive) or worsening (if negative) in the attitude towards *Pepsi* after becoming acquainted with the CRM campaigns.

Thus, Table 7 presents in columns 2 to 8 respectively, the average change in the attitude towards *Pepsi* of every item in the scale for the whole sample, men, women, people who cooperate with an NPO, people who do not cooperate with an NPO, consumers of the brand and not-consumers of the brand after being acquainted with the contents of the campaign. More precisely:

$$\frac{1}{n_K} \sum_{i \in K} D_{ij} \quad \begin{matrix} j = 1 \dots 22 \\ K \in \{S, M, F, V, NV, C, NC\} \end{matrix}$$

Furthermore, the last row in Table 7 presents the average change of the global scale for the groups previously defined, after being acquainted with the contents of the campaign. More precisely:

$$\frac{1}{n_K} \sum_{i \in K} \sum_{j=1}^{22} D_{ij} \quad K \in \{S, M, F, V, NV, C, NC\}$$

Analysis of Table 7 reveals that the overall sample undergoes a moderate-though statistically significant-worsening as regards its attitude towards *Pepsi*. The evaluation given is reduced by 2.38 points. Women significantly worsen their attitude towards the brand (−2.54), whereas in men this change is not statistically significant (−1.77).

Those who do not cooperate with any NPO also show a significant worsening in their attitude towards *Pepsi* (−1.96). Although those who cooperate with a NPO are the group that most clearly shows a negative shift towards the brand (−4.38), they do not do so in a statistically significant way. This phenomenon can be explained by the smaller size of this group.

Non-consumers of *Pepsi* also worsen their attitude towards the brand to a significant degree after knowing the CRM campaigns (−2.96). Although brand consumers also worsen their attitude, they do not do so in a significant way (−1.54).

Thus, hypothesis H1 must be rejected.

TABLE 7. Change in Attitude Towards *Pepsi* Because of the CRM Campaigns

Item (1)	Full Sample (2)	Sex		Cooperates with NPO		Pepsi consumer	
		Male (3)	Female (4)	Yes (5)	No (6)	Yes (7)	No (8)
Would not consume - Would consume	−.41*	−.36	−.43*	−.38	−.41*	−.28	−.50*
Unfavorable - Favorable	−.22*	−.21	−.20*	−.15	−.19*	−.19	−.25
Worthless - Valuable	−.04	−.20	.04	.08	−.02	.02	−.08
Annoying - Pleasing	−.23*	−.12	−.25*	−.15	−.22*	−.29*	−.18
Unappetizing - Appetizing	−.12	−.12	−.08	−.08	−.08	−.23	−.03
Disapprove - Approve	−.29*	−.56*	−.21	−.85	−.19	−.21	−.36*
Attractive - Unattractive	−.01	.33	−.13	−.54*	.02	.21	−.17
Bad - Good	−.09	−.21	−.03	−.15	−.04	−.10	−.08
Unenjoyable - Enjoyable	−.14	.00	−.17*	.00	−.16*	−.26*	−.05
Useless - Worthwhile	−.16*	−.33	−.12	−.31	−.13	−.21	−.10
Inferior - Superior	−.18*	.08	−.28*	−.31	−.15	−.19	−.18
Would support - Would not support	.11	.32	.01	−.31	.12	.30*	−.03
Disagreeable - Agreeable	−.15	−.04	−.19*	−.15	−.16	−.07	−.19
Would recommend - Would not recommend	−.13	−.08	−.17	−.07	−.15	.05	−.27*
High quality - Poor quality	−.18*	−.16	−.20	−.46	−.17	−.09	−.25
Dislike - Like	−.01	−.04	−.01	−.15	−.01	.02	−.02
Would buy - Would not buy	−.13	−.24	−.09	.08	−.16	−.12	−.13
Gentle - Harsh	.10	.08	.11	.23	.08	.12	.07
Unsatisfactory - Satisfactory	−.06	−.08	−.05	.00	−.05	−.19	.02
Interesting - Boring	+.13	.04	.17	.08	.15	.12	.13
Does not match my image - Matches my image	.00	−.20	.08	−.15	.02	.02	−.02
Undesirable - Desirable	−.13	−.08	−.15	−.62	−.06	−.14	−.10
SCALE	−2.38*	−1.77	−2.54*	−4.38	−1.96*	−1.54	−2.96*

(†) Reversed in the recoding process.
(*) Significantly different from 0 ($p < .05$)
Shaded cells indicate significantly different means

Strength of Change in the Attitude Towards the Brand

In order to test hypotheses H2a, H2b and H2c, a set of T-tests for independent samples was performed, based upon the "change" variables previously defined. Results of comparing mean values of D_{ij} between the appropriate groups (F and M, V and NV, C and NC) are also shown on Table 7 where shaded cells indicate statistically significant differences between mean values.

Results show that, against what was stated in hypothesis H2a, women's attitude towards *Pepsi* take a more significant turn for the worse than men's. However the difference is not statistically significant.

As regards hypothesis H2b, consumers who cooperate with a NPO worsen their attitude towards the brand in a stronger way than those who do not cooperate with a NPO. Again, the difference is not statistically significant.

Conversely, *Pepsi* consumers worsen their attitude in a less noticeable way than non-consumers of the brand. This finding aligns with what was stated in hypothesis H2c. However, the difference between these two groups is not statistically significant.

Therefore, hypotheses H2a to H2c must be rejected.

DISCUSSION

The exploratory research shows that the attitude towards *Pepsi* worsens after being acquainted with the contents of the CRM campaigns. One can thus wonder why this attitude takes a turn for the worse after the campaign, even though Spanish consumers, and particularly the youngsters, show a strong concern towards social issues.

There certainly exists evidence to argue that certain CRM campaigns may lead to adverse effects. According to Fundación Empresa y Sociedad (1997), even though around 50% of those surveyed agree with companies policies to support social causes, this fact does not affect their opinion about the brand. Eroski (1997), a Spanish cooperative of consumers, has also pointed out that some consumers distrust this initiative. In a seminal research in Spain, Eroski also shows that almost half of those surveyed think that the main reason for companies to support social causes is obtaining profit and improving brand image. Smith and Stodghill (1994) and Webb and Mohr (1998) determine that CRM programs can create a negative attitude within consumers, as they may distrust the reasons that made companies undertake this kind of program. Barone, Miyazaki and Taylor (2000:249) point out that "although skepticism towards CRM appears to be declining, consumers remain critical of these efforts, often questioning whether a company's support of a social cause is designed to benefit the cause or the company." This problem can worsen if there is not a clear correspondence between what the company manufactures or markets and the cause that is sponsored.

This finding, which at first might appear surprising, may have an explanation. During the presentation of the stimulus, respondents were informed about the persisting presence in the Spanish mass media of these *Pepsi* promotion campaigns, centered especially at the Christmas period.[9] This might have been interpreted by those surveyed as a cynical and mercantilist use of the concept of solidarity, and as a form of instrumentalization of those NPOs involved in the campaigns.

The fact that a leading multinational company such as *PepsiCo* should have, at some stage, used and even tried to improve on slogans associated with the Spanish NPO environment (remember the controversial "Rebeldes con causa. 1% "YA!"") may also have been punished by respondents. In this study it is thus to be observed that those who cooperate with NPOs are especially critical in their attitude towards *Pepsi* after knowing the contents of the campaigns.

Another factor to be taken into account when explaining these very critical attitudes is the lack of informative transparency shown by *Pepsi* so as to explain the quantity and destination of the funds obtained in their CRM campaigns. Young people, who have been overwhelmed by the commercials of *Pepsi* campaigns, do not actually know how much money has been raised by them, nor which specific aid projects this money has been allocated to (although this latter aspect seems to have been partially mitigated in the campaign carried out with *Save the Children*).

It is nonetheless true that *Pepsi's* social action in Spain goes well beyond what the company has conveyed to the public opinion in this kind of promotional campaign. Thus, for example, Spanish public opinion does not know that if an employee of PepsiCo donates to a NPO, then the firm donates the same amount. Nor is it aware of the fact that, if the employee works as a volunteer for that NPO, the company will donate double the amount given by the employee. Even in the CRM campaigns analyzed in this paper there have been actions that are unknown to the public (for example, the yearly donation made to MSF, equivalent to the membership fees of all *PepsiCo's* employees in Spain).

To sum up, the fact that *PepsiCo* should have mainly used promotional Christmas television commercials to convey its CRM campaigns to its target (thus making too much of a direct, and maybe even blatant association between its commitment to solidarity and the sale and consumption of *Pepsi*), may well have been nothing short of a blunder. Maybe respondents have understood these campaigns to be more cause-exploitative than cause-beneficial.

In this light, firms implementing these programs ought to consider the convenience of devising parallel communication campaigns so as to provide stakeholders with accurate and thorough information of objectives, procedure, results and thus avoid suspicion, and consequently a negative effect upon the brand. As García (2000a) points out, in order to achieve the success and reliability of CRM initiatives, companies must offer consumers clear spaces for participation so they can consider themselves as active elements in the social action they are indirectly supporting. If the customer's awareness of his/her participation is not accurate, nor is he/she fully aware of the values shared with both the NPO and the company, he/she could gradually dissociate from this support to the cause and underestimate his/her own effort. It would be advisable, therefore, to provide customers with means for participation other than monetary. It would also be convenient to make the most of the contact with consumers by informing them, involving them and making them aware of the cause and the reasons for supporting it.

CONCLUSIONS

CRM is a tool which more and more firms in Spain are using with the idea of improving their market share, their social reputation or their brand image.

In Spanish marketing literature there are practically no studies on the effectiveness of this kind of campaign. Therefore, this exploratory research was drawn up to determine if youngsters' attitude towards *Pepsi* varies after becoming acquainted with the CRM campaigns. Results unexpectedly show that awareness of the campaigns has a negative effect on the attitude towards *Pepsi*.

Maybe young people have evaluated these CRM campaigns depending on the perceived motivation underlying *Pepsi*'s efforts to support causes. Inappropriate reasons, such as an excessively utilitarian concept of CRM or overcommercialization of solidarity linked to the consumption of *Pepsi*, might have led to this worsening in the brand image.

LIMITATIONS AND DIRECTIONS FOR FUTURE RESEARCH

The exploratory nature of this research implies a series of limitations and opportunities for future research.

Future research on the effects of CRM on attitude towards a brand should adopt an experimental approach rather than the quasi-experimental approach followed in this research (see, for example, Barone, Miyazaki and Taylor 2000).

The sample is not a probabilistic one but a convenience one. Further research should take this limitation into account and, in addition, guarantee more representation for some groups (e.g., those who cooperate with an NPO).

This paper should be considered a case study of *Pepsi* and the CRM campaigns performed by the brand. Thus, results, findings and conclusions must not be generalized to other brands or consumers.

Finally, a more qualitative approach might add to this paper. These qualitative techniques might help to shed light on the effects of CRM on attitude towards the brand (e.g., a focus group might provide additional insight to gain a qualitative understanding of the underlying reasons and motivations of respondents).

NOTES

1. This institution was created in 1995 to encourage social action among Spanish firms.

2. Doctors Without Borders.

3. *"Rebels with a cause, 1% RIGHT NOW!"*

4. The so-called 0.7 question is a very extended grievance within the nonprofit organizations in Spain. It demands that the Public Administration sets aside 0.7% of its overall budget to support development-related projects in Third-World countries.

5. There is no official notice either from MSF-Spain or from *PepsiCo* explaining the reasons for this breaking. Yet, there might be evidence that the initiative comes from MSF. In the first place, the collaboration between *Pepsi* and MSF had already provoked some reluctance among a section of MSF's members–they had even written letters to MSF magazine in which they showed their concern about this issue. The opinion that the campaign did certainly involve a mercantilist use of solidarity was quite widespread among Spanish NPOs, even more after MSF was awarded with the Nobel Prize. In a review about CRM in Spain, García (2000a) regards the *PepsiCo*-MSF campaign as one of the most controversial ones in the country.

In the second place, it sounds certainly striking the fact that in the 2000 MSF Yearbook, *PepsiCo* is not listed under the acknowledgements to companies committed to the cause during that year. MSF seems to have learnt the lesson: after their joint venture with *Pepsi* they said, "[we] prioritize global involvement and long term commitments when devising collaboration with other firms. We avoid collaborations based on actions of solidarity-oriented promotions, in which MSF becomes a commercial seal supporting the consumption of a specific product. Those practices run the risk of promoting solidarity through consumption, not through real commitment" (Médicos sin Fronteras 2001a:21).

6. "Da un paso" may be translated as "Take a step."
7. Cooperation was assessed by the following questions: "Do you financially support any NPO?" and "Do you dedicate part of your spare time to help any NPO's activities?" If any of the answers was affirmative, respondent was considered a cooperator.
8. By means of a filter question those students who had previous knowledge about any of the campaigns presented in the experiment were excluded from the analysis.
9. In fact, all the TV advertisements shown in the CRM campaigns were centered only around Christmas period. They presented the decision to donate 1% of the brand net sales to the supported causes only during the Christmas period.

REFERENCES

Adkins, Sue (1999), *Cause Related Marketing. Who Cares Wins*, Oxford, United Kingdom: Butterworth-Heinemann.

Alimarket (2001), "Refrescos: aliarse para crecer," *Alimarket*, 140 (May), 217-230.

_____ (2000), "Refrescos: a la cola del líder," *Alimarket*, 129 (May), 221-236.

_____ (1999a), "El 'nuevo' Pepsico en España," *Alimarket*, 121 (September), 47.

_____ (1999b), "Refrescos: Coca-Cola revoluciona el sector," *Alimarket*, 118 (May), 131-146.

_____ (1998a), "Refrescos: a más venta, menos cuota," *Alimarket*, 107 (May), 147-158.

_____ (1998b), "Refrescos: Coca-Cola más líder en un mercado creciente," *Alimarket*, 103 (January), 38-39.

_____ (1996), "Refrescos: entre lo viejo y lo nuevo," *Alimarket*, 85 (May), 107-116.

Andreasen, Alan R. (1996), "Profits for Nonprofits: Find a Corporate Partner," *Harvard Business Review*, 74 (6), 47-50, 55-59.

Ballesteros, Carlos (2001), *Marketing con causa, marketing sin efecto. El marketing con causa y la educación para el desarrollo*, Madrid, Spain: Universidad Pontificia Comillas.

Barone, Michael J., Anthony D. Miyazaki, and Kimberly A. Taylor (2000), "The Influence of Cause-Related Marketing on Consumer Choice: Does One Good Turn Deserve Another?," *Journal of the Academy of Marketing Science*, 28 (2), 248-262.

Bearden, William O., Richard G. Netemeyer, and Mary F. Mobley (1993), *Handbook of Marketing Scales: Multi-item Measures for Marketing and Consumer Behavior Research*, Newbury Park, CA: Sage Publications.

Berger, Ida E., Peggy H. Cunningham, and Robert V. Kozinets (1996), "The Processing of Cause-Related Marketing Claims: Cues Biases, or Motivators" in *1996 AMA Summer Educators Conference: Enhancing Knowledge Development in Marketing*, Vol. 7, Cornelia Dröge and Roger Calantone, eds. Chicago, IL: American Marketing Association, 71-72.

Brown, Tom J. and Peter A. Dacin (1997), "The Company and the Product: Corporate Associations and Consumer Product Responses," *Journal of Marketing*, 61 (January), 68-84.

Bruner, Gordon C. and Paul J. Hensel (1996, 1992), *Marketing Scales Handbook. A Compilation of Multi-Item Measures*, Chicago, IL: American Marketing Association.

Cabrero, Elena (2000), "Pepsi y el Marketing Social," in *7" Aula de Marketing*, Conference given on November 23, San Sebastián, Spain: University of Deusto.

Eroski (1997), "Empresas: Deben comprometerse con las causas sociales," *Consumer*, 5 (November), 4-7.

Fernández Lucía, Irene Hernáez, Cristina Marco, Esperanza Montero and Gabriela Seco (1999), "Marketing con Causa: Solidaridad y Rentabilidad Económicas Unidas," *Universidad del País Vasco*, Bilbao, Spain, www.oc.lm.ehu.es/cupv/univ99/comunicaciones/bilbao10.html.

File, Karen M. and Russ A. Prince (1998), "Cause Related Marketing and Corporate Philanthropy in the Privately Held Enterprise," *Journal of Business Ethics*, 17 (14), 1529-1539.

Fundación Empresa y Sociedad (2001), *La empresa que viene. Responsabilidad y acción social en la empresa del futuro*, Madrid, Spain: Fundación Empresa y Sociedad.

_____ (1999), *Marketing con Causa. Cómo añadir valor a las marcas vinculándolas a proyectos sociales*, Madrid, Spain: Fundación Empresa y Sociedad.

_____ (1997), *La Estrategia Social de la Empresa. Un enfoque de valor*, Madrid, Spain: Fundación Empresa y Sociedad.

García, Bernardo (2000a), "El Valor de Compartir beneficios a través del Marketing Social Corporativo," *Boletín de Estudios Económicos*, 171 (December), 495-523.

_____ (2000b), "El Valor de Compartir Beneficios: las ONGD y el Marketing con Causa. Retos y Oportunidades," *Cuadernos Deusto de Derechos Humanos*, 7, 1-84.

Gómez, Mercedes (2000), "Entrevista al presidente para Europa de Pepsico," *El Mundo. Suplemento Nueva Economía*, 37, www.elmundo.es, June 11, 2000.

Guardia, Ramón (1998), *El beneficio de compartir valores. Marketing social corporativo, una nueva estrategia para diferenciar las marcas*, Bilbao, Spain: Ediciones Deusto.

Médicos sin Fronteras (2001a), "La empresa y Médicos Sin Fronteras: el fin no justifica los medios," *Médicos sin Fronteras*, 42 (May), 21.

_____ (2001b), "La empresa y Médicos Sin Fronteras," *Médicos sin Fronteras*, 43 (July), 43.

_____ (1999), "El convenio de colaboración con Pepsi," *Médicos sin Fronteras*, 32 (February), 17.

Meyer, Harvey (1999), "When the cause is just," *Journal of Business Strategy*, 20 (6), 27-31.

Mujika Alazne, Iñaki García and Juan J. Gibaja (2000), "Marketing con Causa e imagen de marca: el caso de los cigarrillos Fortuna y la campaña For 0'7," in *III Forum Internacional sobre las Ciencias, las Técnicas y el Arte aplicadas al Marketing. Ponencias académicas*, E. Ortega, L. González and E. Pérez eds., Madrid, Spain: Universidad Complutense de Madrid, 207-216.

Nunnally, Jum C. (1987), *Teoría Psicométrica*, México D.F., Mexico: Trillas.

Osgood, Charles E., George J. Succi and Percy H. Tannenbaum (1976), *La medida del significado*, Madrid, Spain: Gredos.

Polonsky, Michael J. and Greg Wood (2001), "Can the overcommercialization of cause-related marketing harm society?" *Journal of Macromarketing*, 21 (1), 8-22.

Pringle, Hamish and Marjorie Thompson (1999), *Brand Spirit: How Cause Related Marketing Builds Brands*, Chichester, United Kingdom: John Wiley & Sons.

Recio, Manuel and Ángel Ortiz (2000), "Marketing con Causa," *Harvard-Deusto Marketing y Ventas*; 36 (Jan/Feb), 26-33.

Ross, John K., Larry Patterson, and Mary Ann Stutts (1992), "Consumer Perceptions of Organizations that Use Cause-Related Marketing," *Journal of the Academy of Marketing Science*, 20 (1), 93-97.

_____, Mary Ann Stutts, and Larry Patterson (1990-1991), "Tactical Considerations for the Effective Use of Cause-Related Marketing," *Journal of Applied Business Research*, 7 (2), 58-65.

Sagarzazu, Izaskun and Aitor Gurrutxaga (2001), *Juventud y Marketing Social Corporativo. El caso de la alianza de MSC entre PepsiCo y Médicos Sin Fronteras*, Working paper, San Sebastián, Spain: University of Deusto.

Salas, Carlos (1998), "Malas noticias para nuestros enemigos: ganamos dinero," *El Mundo*, www.elmundo.es, June 10, 1998.

Smith, Craig (1994), "The New Corporate Philantropy," *Harvard Business Review*, 72 (3), 105-116.

Smith, Geoffrey and Ron Stodghill III (1994), "Are Good Causes Good Marketing?" *Business Week*, March 21, 64-66.

Smith, Scott M. and David S. Alcorn (1991), "Cause Related Marketing: A New Direction in the Marketing of Corporate Responsibility," *Journal of Consumer Marketing*, 8 (3), 19-35.

Varadarajan, P. Rajan and Anil Menon (1988), "Cause-Related Marketing: A Coalignment of Marketing Strategy and Corporate Philantropy," *Journal of Marketing*; 52 (3), 58-74.

Webb, Deborah J. and Lois A. Mohr (1998), "A Typology of Consumer Responses to Cause-Related Marketing: From Skeptics to Socially Concerned," *Journal of Public Policy & Marketing*; 17 (2), 226-238.

Welsh, Jerry C. (1999), "Good Cause, Good Business," *Harvard Business Review*, 77 (5), 21, 24.

www.csreurope.org

www.daunpaso.com

Cause-Related Marketing:
Keys to Successful Relationships
with Corporate Sponsors
and Their Customers

Linda I. Nowak
T. K. Clarke

SUMMARY. An increasingly popular method for nonprofits to raise awareness, educate the public, and receive financial support from corporations is through cause-related marketing. The distinctive feature of cause-related marketing is the corporate sponsor's contribution to a designated cause being tied to customers' participating in revenue-producing transactions with the sponsor. The sponsor benefits from favorable publicity and increased sales. This article discusses factors contributing to the potential success of a cause-related marketing campaign: the sponsor's product quality, fair pricing, and customer traits; the nonprofit's and the sponsor's reputation, shared values, good communication, and commitment; a well-planned and executed campaign, and specific terms that protect both party's assets and clearly outline each party's responsibilities. *[Article copies available for a fee from The Haworth Document Delivery Service: 1-800-HAWORTH. E-mail address: <getinfo@haworthpressinc.com>*

Linda I. Nowak, PhD, is Associate Professor of Marketing, and T. K. Clarke, PhD, is Professor of Marketing, both at the School of Business and Economics, Sonoma State University, 1801 East Cotati Avenue, Rohnert Park, CA 94928.

[Haworth co-indexing entry note]: "Cause-Related Marketing: Keys to Successful Relationships with Corporate Sponsors and Their Customers." Nowak, Linda I., and T. K. Clarke. Co-published simultaneously in *Journal of Nonprofit & Public Sector Marketing* (Best Business Books, an imprint of The Haworth Press, Inc.) Vol. 11, No. 1, 2003, pp. 137-149; and: *Nonprofit and Business Sector Collaboration: Social Enterprises, Cause-Related Marketing, Sponsorships, and Other Corporate-Nonprofit Dealings* (ed: Walter W. Wymer, Jr. and Sridhar Samu) Best Business Books, an imprint of The Haworth Press, Inc., 2003, pp. 137-149. Single or multiple copies of this article are available for a fee from The Haworth Document Delivery Service [1-800-HAWORTH, 9:00 a.m. - 5:00 p.m. (EST). E-mail address: getinfo@haworthpressinc.com].

137

KEYWORDS. Cause-related marketing, nonprofits, corporate sponsors, strategic alliances, relationship management

An increasingly popular method of image building for businesses is cause-related marketing. The distinctive feature of cause-related marketing is the firm's contribution to a designated cause being tied to customers' participating in revenue-producing transactions with the firm. Formally, cause-related marketing has been defined as "the process of formulating and implementing marketing activities that are characterized by an offer from the firm to contribute a specified amount to a designated cause when customers engage in revenue-providing exchanges that satisfy organizational and individual objectives" (Varadarajan and Menon 1988, p. 58). The firm benefits from favorable publicity and increased sales. Non-profits benefit by raising awareness, educating the public, and receiving financial support for their cause.

A nonprofit may engage in cause-related marketing activity for either strategic or tactical reasons. An example of a tactical activity would be a nonprofit connecting with a company for a limited time and fairly narrow purpose, such as a holiday charity program. A strategic approach would view a cause-related campaign as more long-term in nature. An example would be a long-term and consistent campaign focused at image-building in the minds of the public. In these long-term strategies, the cause-related campaign offers a corporate sponsor the opportunity to make the connection with the nonprofit a fundamental part of the brand's personality. In either situation, tactical or strategic, both the nonprofit and potential corporate sponsor should be careful to research and concept-test their target market's reactions to various product tie-ins with the social or environmental issue before proceeding with the campaign (Till and Nowak 2000).

The purpose of this article is to discuss what we do know about creating successful cause-related marketing campaigns. However, there is still much to learn about creating successful campaigns, from both the nonprofit's perspective and the corporate sponsor's. The article will conclude with a discussion on cognitive moral development and its implications for building a greater understanding of consumer decision making during these campaigns.

ANTECEDENTS TO SUCCESSFUL CAMPAIGNS

Applying Associative Learning Principles

Most businesses understand that the associations consumers make about their corporate responsibility influence the overall reputation of the company, which in turn can affect how consumers evaluate products and services from the company (Brown and Dacin 1997). Maignan, Ferrell, and Lukas (1998) have found a positive relationship between proactive citizenship and customer loyalty. Nonprofits must understand that the same principles apply to them. Associative learning is the mechanism by which consumers generate thoughts and feelings towards an object, in this case a cause or nonprofit organization, brought about through the linkage or fusion of two concepts (Shimp, Stuart, and Engle 1991; Murdock 1985). An alliance between a nonprofit organization and a corporate sponsor builds an associative link between the two. An association with a cause that is perceived positively by the consumer can build positive associations for the nonprofit and the business. Pairings with sponsors that consumers find inappropriate could potentially damage a nonprofit's positive image (Aaker 1991).

Associations between two objects or events in an individual's memory are developed and reinforced through repetition (Martindale 1991). The impact of cause-related marketing activities will be more effective as the target audience is exposed to an increasing number of pairings between nonprofit and corporate sponsor over time. Therefore, occasional or one-time promotions are likely to be less effective (Till and Nowak 2000). In other words, nonprofit managers should attempt to find corporate sponsors that are willing to commit to a long-term relationship that is more strategic in nature. As long as both the cause and the corporate sponsor continue to maintain positive public images, both parties should benefit from the consistent and repeated pairings in the minds of the consumer.

Seeking Corporate Sponsors with Quality Products

Spending on cause-related marketing has increased more than 300 percent since 1990, reaching $360 million in 1999 (Belch and Belch 2001). Visa's "Reading is Fundamental" campaign led to a 17 percent increase in sales. Wendy's International in Denver saw sales increase by more than 33 percent when a portion of purchases was contributed to Denver's Mercy Medical Center (Meyer 1999). However, consumers must be willing to purchase the products or services associated with the cause-related marketing campaign before the nonprofit benefits from any revenues. Recently measured consumer behavioral intentions towards a company that was donating 10 percent of its profits to the World Wildlife Federation found that while personal norms may be a strong predictor of intentions to purchase the company's products, the strongest predictor is often product quality (Nowak 2001).

These findings are consistent with an earlier study conducted by Barone, Miyazaki, and Taylor (2000). They found that in the case of homogeneous products between Company A and Company B, the extent to which cause-related marketing affects relative purchase intentions depends on product performance and price trade-offs. Cause-related marketing appeared to be most effective when the consumer was not required to trade-off anything in exchange for selecting the brand undertaking the cause-related marketing activity. However, many people were still willing to accept lower performance or higher price in return for perceived corporate social responsibility if the consumers trusted the underlying motivations regarding the company's cause-related marketing efforts.

Finding Corporate Sponsors with Positive Reputations

It is critical that the nonprofit organization choose its corporate sponsor wisely. Studies have found that the public's attitudes and intentions to support a cause appear to be significantly increased by association with a sponsor with a strong reputation and are not significantly affected by sponsorship from a company with a weak reputation. Trust for the nonprofit organization, intentions to support through volunteerism or donations, perceptions of importance to society, feelings of responsibility to help, and feelings that personal support can make an overall difference for society, were all significantly increased through associations with a strong corporate sponsor (Nowak and Washburn 2000).

A nonprofit's name is its most valuable asset. It is the nonprofit's name and good reputation that a potential corporate sponsor is trying to buy with its cause-related marketing offer (Gifford 1999). What would it cost a nonprofit organization to earn back its reputation once it had been damaged through a corporate sponsorship with a company with a negative image? A nonprofit should research any potential corporate sponsors carefully by reading recent news articles and talking to members of the target audience as well as other nonprofits with which the firm has been involved. The nonprofit should continue to monitor the corporate sponsor's reputation throughout the life of the venture.

Committing to Corporate Sponsors
Who Share the Nonprofit's Values

Shared values are described as "the extent to which partners have beliefs in common about what behaviors, goals, and policies are important or unimportant, appropriate or inappropriate, and right or wrong" (Morgan and Hunt 1994, p. 25). Morgan and Hunt (1994) found that shared values were important antecedents to both relationship commitment and trust. Sponsors that share similar values with their nonprofit partner will be less likely to engage in behaviors that could damage the relationship and the reputation of the nonprofit.

Organizational commitment may lead to such important outcomes as higher motivation (Farrell and Rusbult 1981) and increased organizational citizenship behaviors (Williams and Anderson 1991). When two parties are committed to a relationship, in this case a cause-related marketing campaign, they are more apt to ensure that the relationship endures (Morgan and Hunt 1994; Moorman, Zaltman, and Deshpande 1992). Commitment on the part of the corporate sponsor may insure that the cause-related marketing campaign gets the resources and proper planning it requires for success.

A nonprofit should find a corporate sponsor who will give the campaign the attention it needs for success. If the sponsor really believes the cause is important, the right thing to do, then the sponsor is less apt to bail out of the project if progress is hampered in some way. Checking the company's track record regarding environmental issues, human rights issues, and employee hiring and benefits should be an eye-opening research project for the nonprofit.

Approaching Potential Corporate Sponsors

Businesses receive numerous proposals every month from nonprofits asking for their support (Adkins 1999). Most businesses willing to consider a cause-related marketing campaign are motivated by one or more of the following: (1) creating a positive image for the firm, (2) communicating the organization's views on social, business, and environmental issues (Belch and Belch 2001), and/or increasing sales. The nonprofit should try to find a potential sponsor with the reputation, corporate values, and product quality that fits its campaign needs, and then approach this company with a well-organized presentation that addresses the following topics.

Benefit to the Company. Few corporate sponsors will respond negatively to proposals that will benefit the firm. Part of the work for any nonprofit is to convince the potential sponsor that it could improve company sales, reputation, and goodwill. The nonprofit should explain how employees, stockholders, and consumers will "feel good" about being involved in the endeavor. Examples of successful cause-related campaigns should be cited.

Benefit to the Community. People want to believe that what they do will really affect social or environmental change (Roberts 1996). The nonprofit should make sure it clearly describes to the potential corporate sponsor how its participation will make a difference in the form of increased awareness and support for the cause. It would be a mistake for the nonprofit to assume that the long-term benefits of an alliance, whether it be for society or the environment, are clearly understood by the corporation.

Benefit to the Nonprofit. The nonprofit's representative should be specific about what the nonprofit needs from the relationship. Sponsors may be hesitant about getting involved if they do not understand what level of resources and company commitment is required. The nonprofit should clearly define what it expects to accomplish from the campaign. Does the nonprofit need to raise awareness about its cause, educate the public about health or social issues, or increase donations and volunteerism?

Time Commitment. As stated earlier, long-term relationships tend to be more beneficial for both nonprofit and sponsor. In associative learning, repetition is the key. A long-term, well-publicized, and consistent relationship strengthens associative links in the minds of the consumers. Both sponsors and nonprofits benefit from these positive associations in the form of increased awareness and trust. The nonprofit should explain to the potential sponsor that an on-going relationship also has the advantage of eliminating down-time and start up costs for each partner. If either party is apprehensive about a long-term commitment, a shorter term, "trial" campaign could be considered.

Protecting the Nonprofit's Assets

For most businesses, the purpose of a cause-related marketing campaign is to use the goodwill from the nonprofit's name to generate more sales for the business and improve its image. Therefore, the nonprofit should make certain the negotiated terms of the relationship represent the full value the business will derive from the use of the nonprofit's good name.

Gifford (1999) has presented several points that any nonprofit would be wise to follow in their dealings with a corporate sponsor. First, if the nonprofit is to get a sum of money from the sponsor, it should receive it at the outset. After all, the sponsor benefits from the use of the nonprofit's name as soon as it lends it to the campaign. Second, the nonprofit should make sure it approves all uses of its name. This means prior approval is required for all copy, photos, and media placements. Finally, the nonprofit should make sure the "proceeds to benefit" language meets the guidelines of the Philanthropic Advisory Service of the Better Business Bureau and the National Charities Information Bureau. In all its dealings with a corporate sponsor, the nonprofit should be sure the terms of the alliance are specific and in writing.

Managing the Relationship

Effective communication between the nonprofit and the corporate sponsor is essential for a successful cause-related marketing campaign. Communication refers to "the formal as well as informal sharing of meaningful and timely information between firms" (Anderson and Narus 1990, p. 44). It creates an environment in which goal adjustment, task coordination, and interfirm learning can take place (Sivadas and Dwyer 2000). Successful partnerships exhibit better communication quality and information gathering. Both parties must be mindful of their communication accuracy and timeliness.

Trust is another important component of a successful relationship. According to Morgan and Hunt (1994, p.23), trust exists when "one party has confidence in an exchange partner's reliability and integrity." Andaleeb (1992) describes trust as possessing three parts: predictability, dependability, and faith. Mohr and Spekman (1994) and Kanter (1994) found trust to be a key element in alliance success, and lack of trust to be a major cause of alliance failure (Sherman 1992). If either party in the cause-related marketing campaign abuses the relationship, or seeks benefits at the expense of the other partner, the relationship will most likely not survive.

A cause-related marketing campaign will have difficulty succeeding if the nonprofit and the corporate sponsor cannot coordinate their activities competently. Coordination refers to the extent that the different players function according to the requirements of the other parties and the overall system (Mohr and Spekman 1994). Successful coordination of a cause-related marketing campaign requires that both parties be competent, reliable, professional, and focused on the mission and goals of the campaign. Both parties must be willing to stay involved, stick to a time schedule, and give the project the attention and resources it needs.

Understanding the Corporate Sponsor's Customers

Nonprofits and corporate sponsors need to better understand how individual consumer characteristics influence responses to cause-related marketing campaigns. Osterhus (1997) found that personal norms translated into pro-environmental behavior when those norms were strengthened through the awareness of the consequences of the individual's action or inaction regarding the behavior. Consumers realize that benefits accrue for a social or environmental cause when a large segment of the population supports it (Nowak and Washburn 2000) and when the corporate donations are larger (Dahl and Lavak 1995).

Additional insights may be gained by studying the relationship between an individual's level of cognitive moral development (CMD) and the manner in which that individual processes information about a cause-related marketing campaign. Past research on organizational ethics has shown that an individual's evaluation of an ethical problem is influenced by CMD level (Ferrell, Gresham, and Fraedrich 1989; Trevino 1986). Social and environmental issues could be deemed ethical issues in many instances. An individual's cognitive ability to integrate the legitimate interests of many distinct and diverse publics, in part, determines CMD level. Individuals high in CMD could be expected to recognize the importance of multiple stakeholders and business' socially responsible behavior. Goolsby and Hunt (1992) found that marketing professionals scoring high on CMD possessed socially responsible attitudes and behaviors. These findings suggest that, as consumers move to higher CMD levels, they are increasingly able to define the appropriate role of business in society. Would consumers with higher CMD levels be more likely to respond positively toward the cause-related marketing campaign when the issues around the cause are made known to them? This question brings us to a discussion on future research opportunities.

DIRECTIONS FOR FURTHER RESEARCH

Lawrence Kohlberg (1969) proposed that advanced moral reasoning requires a highly developed capacity for advanced logical reasoning and hypothesized that moral development should follow a cognitive developmental process. In a decision possessing a moral dimension, individuals with poorly developed logical reasoning abilities would be unable to recognize and analyze the complex relationships among all of the interacting elements. Therefore, such individuals would neither be capable of recognizing all the possible contingencies and consequences that might result from a particular course of action nor able to assimilate the rightful needs of all stakeholders into a judgment satisfying a moral ideal. Kohlberg's research, as extended by James Rest and others, provides the central core of the CMD literature (e.g., Kohlberg 1984; Rest 1986). The CMD approach to moral reasoning centers on the progressive way in which, through time, individuals acquire an increasingly accurate understanding of the nature of moral obligations in complex social systems (Rest 1979). The emphasis is on the cognitive decision-making process as it becomes more complex and sophisticated with development.

Kohlberg describes moral development in six stages (1969). At stages one and two (the preconventional level), an individual is concerned with concrete consequences, particularly external rewards and punishments, and his or her own immediate interests. At stages three and four (conventional level), "right" is that which conforms to the expectations of good behavior of the larger society or some segment like a family or peer group. In other words, in stages three and four, the motivation of ethical decisions is fulfilling the expectations of significant others. A society's laws become an important determinant of the individual's decision. Kohlberg places most adults in our society in stages three or four. At stages five and six (principled or postconventional level), "right" is determined by universal values or principles. According to Kohlberg, less than 20 percent of American adults reach the principled level of development.

Previous studies have shown age, education, ethics education, and gender to be related to level of CMD. Age and formal education have been found to be significant predictors of CMD level (Rest 1986); with education being far more predictive than chronological age. Gender differences in CMD have been hotly debated (Rest 1986); however, Goolsby and Hunt (1992) found that marketing professionals high in CMD tended to be female and highly educated. Formal training in moral philosophy has also been found to have a positive effect on CMD level (Rest 1986).

Future research should examine how consumers at the various stages of cognitive moral development react to cause-related marketing campaigns. Is the consumer at the "conventional" level of moral development more influenced by economic trade-offs than the individual at the "principled" level? At the "conventional" level, individuals look outside themselves for cues about what is right (appropriate) behavior and what is wrong (inappropriate) behavior. If the products being offered during the campaign are targeted at consumers who are primarily at the conventional level of moral development, perhaps the popularity of the corporate sponsor or testimonials by professional athletes and movie stars would increase the success of the campaign. Perhaps an individual at the "principled" level would be more influenced by the potential benefits to society and personal trust in the corporate sponsor.

Much of what has been reported in the literature on cause-related marketing is based on self-reported consumer behavior, consumer attitudes, and consumer behavioral intentions. It would be helpful to track actual consumer behavioral changes, customer by customer, from corporate sales data, before, during, and after the campaign. With the excellent customer databases most corporations maintain, this purchase data, in conjunction with the customer's demographics, should enable marketers to develop a deeper understanding of the psychological, social, and situational variables which interact in the consumer's decision making process.

Another research direction should be into the effects that cause-related marketing has on the long-term sustainability of the nonprofit organization. Do volunteerism and donations increase as a result of the greater awareness created during the cause-related marketing campaign? Or as soon as the campaign is over, are consumers pulled in another direction by a different nonprofit's cause?

CONCLUSION

Businesses and consumers are pulled in all directions by good causes soliciting their support. As the popularity of cause-related marketing increases, more information about critical success factors, costs versus benefits, and consumer reactions is necessary for continued success. Employees, retailers, corporate sponsors, and nonprofits, must believe in the cause, be well-informed, and committed to doing what it takes to make the campaign a success.

The corporate sponsor's product quality, pricing, reputation, and customers all are factors that contribute to the success of a campaign. Shared values, mutual respect, excellent communication, commitment, a well-planned and executed campaign, and specific contracts that protect the nonprofit's assets and clearly outline each partner's responsibilities are essential to a successful and on-going relationship between corporate sponsor and nonprofit.

Understanding what appeals to the consumer targeted in the campaign is critical. Successful campaigns require careful monitoring, problem solving, and sometimes, major alterations. A carefully researched, structured, and implemented cause-related marketing campaign can be a win-win alliance for both the nonprofit and the business.

REFERENCES

Aaker, David A. 1991. *Managing Brand Equity*. New York: The Free Press.

Adkins, Sue. 1999. *Cause Related Marketing: Who Cares Wins*. Oxford: Butterworth-Heinemann.

Andaleeb, Syed Saab. 1992. "The Trust Concept: Research Issues for Channels of Distribution." In *Research in Marketing*, Vol. 11, Ed. Jagdish N. Sheth. Greenwich, CT: JAI Press, 1-34.

Anderson, James C. and James A. Narus. 1990. "A Model of Distributor Firm and Manufacturer Firm Working Partnerships." *Journal of Marketing* 54 (January): 42-58.

Barone, Michael J., Anthony D. Miyazaki, and Kimberly A. Taylor. 2000. "The Influence of Cause-related Marketing on Consumer Choice: Does One Good Turn Deserve Another?" *Journal of the Academy of Marketing Science* 28 (2): 248-62.

Belch, George E. and Michael A. Belch. 2001. *Advertising and Promotion*. New York: Irwin/McGraw-Hill.

Brown, Tom J. and Peter A. Dacin. 1997. "The Company and the Product: Corporate Associations and Consumer Product Responses." *Journal of Marketing* 61 (January): 68-84.

Dahl, Darren W. and Anne M. Lavack. 1995. "Cause-Related Marketing: Impact of Size of Corporate Donation and Size of Cause-Related Promotion on Consumer Perceptions and Participation." In *Proceedings of the American Marketing Association Winter Educators' Conference*, Vol. 6, 476-81.

Farrell, D. and C. Rusbult. 1981. "Exchange Variables as Predictors of Job Satisfaction, Job Commitment, and Turnover: The Impact of Rewards, Costs, Alternatives, and Investments." *Organizational Behavior and Human Performance* 28: 78-95.

Ferrell, O.C., Larry G. Gresham, and John Fraedrich. 1989. "A Synthesis of Ethical Decision Models for Marketing." *Journal of Macromarketing* (Fall): 55-64.

Gifford, Gayle. 1999. "Cause-related Marketing: Ten Rules to Protect Your Nonprofit Assets." *Nonprofit World* 17 (6): 11-13.

Goolsby, Jerry R. and Shelby D. Hunt. 1992. "Cognitive Moral Development and Marketing." *Journal of Marketing* 56 (January): 55-68.

Kanter, Rosabeth Moss. 1994. "Collaborative Advantage." *Harvard Business Review* 72 (July/August): 96-108.

Kohlberg, Lawrence. 1969. "Stage and Sequence: The Cognitive Developmental Approach to Socialization." In *Handbook of Socialization Theory and Research*, Ed. D. Goslin. Chicago: Rand McNally, 347-480.

_____ 1984. *Essays on Moral Development: Vol II. The Psychology of Moral Development*. New York: Harper & Row Publishers, Inc.

Maignan, Isabelle, O.C. Ferrell, and Bryuan Lukas. 1998. "Corporate Citizenship: Cultural Antecedents and Business Benefits." In *Proceedings of the American Marketing Association Summer Educators' Conference*, Vol. 9, 64.

Martindale, C. 1991. *Cognitive Psychology: A Neural-Network Approach*. Pacific Grove, CA: Brooks/Cole.

Meyer, Harvey. 1999. "When the Cause Is Just." *Journal of Business Strategy* (November/December): 27-31.

Mohr, Jakki and Robert Spekman. 1994. "Characteristics of Partnership Success: Partnership Attributes, Communication Behavior, and Conflict Resolution Techniques." *Strategic Management Journal* 15 (2): 135-49.

Moorman, Christine, Gerald Zaltman and Rohit Deshpande. 1992. "Relationships Between Providers and Users of Marketing Research." *Journal of Marketing Research* 29 (August): 314-29.

Morgan, Robert M. and Shelby D. Hunt. 1994. "The Commitment-Trust Theory of Relationship Marketing." *Journal of Marketing* 58 (July): 20-38.

Murdock, Bennett B., Jr. 1985. "The Contributions of Hermann Ebbinhaus." *Journal of Experimental Psychology: Learning, Memory, and Cognition* 11 (3): 469-71.

Nowak, Linda I. 2001. "Consumer Reactions to Pro-Environmental Business Policies." In *Proceedings of the American Marketing Association Winter Educators' Conference*, Vol. 12, p. 366

Nowak, Linda I. and Judith H. Washburn. 2000. "Marketing Alliances Between Non-Profits and Businesses: Changing the Public's Attitudes and Intentions Towards the Cause." *Journal of Nonprofit & Public Sector Marketing* 7 (4): 33-44.

Osterhus, Thomas L. 1997. "Pro-Social Consumer Influence Strategies: When and How Do They Work?" *Journal of Marketing* 61 (October): 16-29.

Rest, James R. 1979. *Revised Manual for the Defining Issues Test: An Objective Test of Moral Judgment Development*. Minneapolis: Minnesota Moral Research Projects.

_____ 1986. *Moral Development: Advances in Research and Theory*. New York: Praeger Publishers.

Roberts, James A. 1996. "Green Consumers in the 1990s: Profile and Implications for Advertising." *Journal of Business Research* 36: 217-231.

Sherman, Stratford. 1992. "Are Strategic Alliances Working?" *Fortune* 126 (September 21): 77-78.

Shimp, Terence A., Elnora W. Stuart, and Randall W. Engle. 1991. "A Program Of Classical Conditioning Experiments Testing Variations in the Conditioned Stimulus and Context." *Journal of Consumer Research* 18 (June): 1-12.

Sivadas, Eugene and F. Robert Dwyer. 2000. "An Examination of Organizational Factors Influencing New Product Success in Internal and Alliance-Based Processes." *Journal of Marketing* 64 (January): 31-49.

Till, Brian D. and Linda I. Nowak. 2000. "Toward Effective Use of Cause-Related Marketing Alliances." *Journal of Product & Brand Management* 9 (7): 472-484.

Trevino, Linda Klebe. 1986. "Ethical Decision Making Organizations: A Person-Situation Interactions Model." *Academy of Management Review* 11 (3): 601-617.

Varadarajan, P. Rajan and Anil Menon. 1988. "Cause-Related Marketing: A Coalignment of Marketing Strategy and Corporate Philanthropy." *Journal of Marketing* 52 (July): 58-74.

Williams, Larry J. and Stella E. Anderson. 1991. "Job Satisfaction and Organizational Commitment as Predictors of Organizational Citizenship Behaviors and In-Role Behaviors." *Journal of Management* 17 (3): 601-17.

Revisiting Business and the Arts

Derrick Chong

SUMMARY. From a critical perspective, this paper examines the development of closer relationships between business and the arts. There has been a concerted effort to expand "exchange transitions," a fundamental marketing concept, so that marketing is now viewed as a pervasive social activity. As such, marketers like corporate sponsors are the possessors and disseminators of a new and powerful language. Three strands of investigation are pursued: the conceptualization of the consumer in relationship to the arts organization; the significance of the (American-based) Business Committee for the Arts, since its founding in the late 1960s, in championing stronger relationships between commercial enterprises and arts organizations; and interventions by visual artist Hans Haacke, as an example of culture jamming, against what he perceives to be the corporate takeover of the arts. These cases are points of contact representing the complex and contested managerial imperatives faced by arts organizations. *[Article copies available for a fee from The Haworth Document Delivery Service: 1-800-HAWORTH. E-mail address: <getinfo@haworthpressinc.com> Website: <http://www.HaworthPress.com> © 2003 by The Haworth Press, Inc. All rights reserved.]*

KEYWORDS. Corporate sponsorship, Business Committee for the Arts, Hans Haacke, arts consumer, critical marketing

---

Derrick Chong, PhD, is Lecturer in Management, Royal Holloway, University of London, Egham, Surrey TW20 0EX, United Kingdom (E-mail: d.chong@rhul.ac.uk).

[Haworth co-indexing entry note]: "Revisiting Business and the Arts." Chong, Derrick. Co-published simultaneously in *Journal of Nonprofit & Public Sector Marketing* (Best Business Books, an imprint of The Haworth Press, Inc.) Vol. 11, No. 1, 2003, pp. 151-165; and: *Nonprofit and Business Sector Collaboration: Social Enterprises, Cause-Related Marketing, Sponsorships, and Other Corporate-Nonprofit Dealings* (ed: Walter W. Wymer, Jr. and Sridhar Samu) Best Business Books, an imprint of The Haworth Press, Inc., 2003, pp. 151- 165. Single or multiple copies of this article are available for a fee from The Haworth Document Delivery Service [1-800-HAWORTH, 9:00 a.m. - 5:00 p.m. (EST). E-mail address: getinfo@haworthpressinc. com].

151

The marketing landscape is littered with texts geared to budding visual and performing arts marketers. Even non-marketers are apt to accept that "marketing [is] now widely held to be the most important of industrial and commercial disciplines" (cited in Bullock and Trombley 1999: 504). What seems to be missed in such overtly managerialist assumptions is that marketing is predicated on social and cultural constructs. With a critical marketing perspective in mind (e.g., Morgan 1992; Brown 1995; Holbrook 1999), this paper examines the complex issues underpinning relationships between business and the arts since the 1960s. Particular reference is made to art museums: they are viewed as among the most complex, powerful, and successful of modern socio-political institutions. As one of the most broadly resonant metaphors of our time, public perceptions concerning the meaning and role of art are shaped by art museums.

We view marketers such as corporate sponsors as the possessors and disseminators of a new and powerful language. The dominant language of marketing, which has a positivistic orientation, carries assumptions and tendencies. Absences and omissions in marketing orthodoxy remain worthy of examination. Three linked points of contact are examined: much has been done in the name of marketing to define the role of the (arts) consumer in relationship to the organization; the Business Committee for the Arts was founded in the late 1960s as a lead organization to champion stronger links between commercial enterprises and arts organizations; and interventions by contemporary visual artists like Hans Haacke serve as acts of resistance against the overt managerialist orientation associated with business-arts relationships. These cases illustrate imperatives of management encroaching on decisions that, conventionally and historically, have been made without such explicit reference to extra-artistic (i.e., financial) considerations. It is fair to accept that arts and cultural organizations cannot be immune from these pressures, yet the full implications have yet to be examined.

MARKETING ORTHODOXY

Central to marketing thought and philosophy is the concept of exchange transaction. "Law the Second: The man of marketing and the consumer form a couple: the man of marketing is the male; the consumer the female," according to marketing consultants Jack and Jenny, who offer seven laws:

Law the First: The number of man's needs is limited but his desires and fears know no number. Through marketing they may grow . . .

Law the Seventh: The man of marketing is a priest and a soldier, a man of faith and of steel doubting nothing and defying all created of both fire and ice. (Vinaver 1997: 81)

The man of marketing is everything all at once: a lover, a creator, a destroyer, etc. This list from Michel Vinaver's play *Overboard* (translated from the original French *Pardessus bord,* which was completed in 1969) gives an exaggerated importance to the subject under discussion (e.g., how a traditional family-owned French toilet manufacturer can compete against a larger and more aggressive competitor from the United States). In many respects Vinaver, who was a senior executive with Gillette in Europe at the time, was commenting on marketing orthodoxy, as articulated from the mid-1950s to the early 1970s (e.g., Drucker 1954; Levitt 1960; Kotler and Levy 1969; Kotler 1972; also see Enis, Cox and Mokwa 1992: especially Part I).

By the early 1970s attention was being directed to marketing as a pervasive social activity: could marketing be integral to understanding the management of human exchange? If Philip Kotler was over-excited in the prospects of marketing–it is "a category of human action indistinguishable from other categories of human action such as voting, loving, consuming, or fighting" (Kotler 1972: 52)–he was merely the first to adopt such a rhetorical tenor. Jack and Jenny's "Laws of Marketing" are even more apposite today. Marketers stress "relationships" (e.g., relationship marketing and customer relationship management) often without recognizing its potential as parody: the "marketer as hunter" (i.e., going after the immediate sale or kill) is giving way to the "marketer as gardener" (i.e., cultivating longer term relationships as a means in recognition of the benefits from the supposed lifetime value of customers). For example, even a *Financial Times* columnist has noted that the language of marketing has let rip: "There are no words too inflated to describe just how highly a company values its consumers" (Kellaway 2000: 120). Yet, in practice, according to humorist Dave Barry, writing in *Fortune* magazine, "I think customer service is a really brilliant system designed to keep customers from ever getting service. My theory is that the most hated group in any company is the customers" (Barry 1997: 199).

CONCEPTUALIZING THE (ARTS) CONSUMER

Much has been done in the name of marketing to define the role of the consumer in relationship to the organization. Is marketing *itself* the cultural phenomenon of our time? Some cultural critics have contested the conceptualization of the consumer as a homogeneous entity. John Tusa, director of the Barbican Centre in London, offers an instructive interpretation of the contemporary arts landscape: "Gone are the days when viewers went to galleries, audiences attended concerts or the theatre; they are all consumers" (Tusa 1997: 38). What Tusa appears to be suggesting is that consumerism washes out the diversity of genuine choice, with an accent on the lowest common denominator. Raymond Williams's bone of contention was that the term consumer, during the latter half of the twentieth century, gained widespread and overwhelming extension into traditionally non-commercial fields, including politics, education, health, and the arts (Williams 1976). There is a realignment of relationships between patients and doctors, students and teachers, and voters and politicians, for example. Distinctions in relationships are negated; moreover, according to Williams, social human needs "are not covered by the consumer ideal: they may even be denied because consumption tends always to be materialist as an individual activity" (Williams [1960] 1980: 188). Similar sentiments are expressed at present by Naomi Klein (2000), a leader of the anti-capitalist movement, who believes that branding initiatives by multinational enterprises are marked by an undemocratic shift from citizens to consumers.

It is recognized by respected commentators that relationships between works of art and spectators exist. Georges Bataille acknowledged to the importance of museum visitors:

> We must realize that the halls and art objects are but the container, whose content is formed by visitors. It is the content that distinguishes a museum from a private collection. A museum is like a lung in a great city; each Sunday the crowd flows like blood into the museum and emerges purified and fresh. (Bataille [1930] 1986: 25)

The quasi-spiritual sensation intimated by Bataille is not far removed from the role of the spectator, according to Marcel Duchamp:

> In the last analysis, the artist may shout from all the rooftops that he is a genius; he will have to wait for the verdict of the spectator in order that his declarations take a social value and that finally, pos-

terity includes him in the primers of art history. (Duchamp [1957] 1973: 47)

What seems to have changed post-Duchamp, to the ire of Williams and Tusa, is the ascendancy of so-called blockbuster exhibitions. "Blockbusters presuppose corporate sponsorship," according to the (late) Rodin scholar Albert Elsen, who described this spectacle as "a large-scale loan exhibition which people who normally don't go to museums will stand in line hours to see" (Elsen 1986: 24). In the main, Elsen contended that political benefits accrue from blockbusters: there is an attempt at a public goods argument that "although museums are always vulnerable to charges of cultural elitism, a successful blockbuster is one of the best pieces of evidence for the argument of tax-supported benefit to the public at large"; and, "like champion baseball teams, blockbusters help put cities on the cultural map" and "blockbusters means crowds, and crowds mean business" (Elsen 1986: 24).

Yet blockbusters are not unproblematic when viewed alongside a commitment to artistic excellence and integrity. For example, Germain Bazin concluded his important book, *The Museum Age* (1969), criticizing the queue of visitors at the 1966 Picasso exhibition at the Grand Palais: "Mass culture poses a very grave problem for museums and increases the impending danger of making works of art inaccessible to the very public for whom they are so widely offered" (Bazin 1969: photo caption 141). Furthermore, it has been posited that blockbusters have merely fuelled "the mechanization of exhibition attendance (Ticketron, Acoustiguide, etc.) and the crowded viewing conditions threaten to dehumanize the entire experience" (Anonymous 1986: 358). Does marketing contribute to genuine audience development, which goes beyond more of the same (socio-economic category of spectator), to widening participation?

BUSINESS COMMITTEE FOR THE ARTS

Arts patronage during the latter half of the twentieth century was marked by the emergence of business corporations. The American-based Business Committee for the Arts (BCA)–the first national, business-supported, not-for-profit organization that encourages business to support the arts and provides them with the services and resources necessary to develop and advance partnerships–was founded in 1967 as an initiative of David Rockefeller, chairman of Chase

Manhattan Bank, who advocated business understanding and involvement in the arts:

> The modern corporate has evolved into a social as well as an economic institution. Without losing sight of the need to make a profit, it has developed ideals and responsibilities going far beyond the profit motive . . .
>
> The public has come to expect corporations to live up to certain standards of good citizenship. (cited in Gringrich 1970: xi; see also *www.bcainc.org*)

The BCA was answering calls put forward in the Rockefeller Panel Report (1965) that collective corporate action was needed to stimulate support in the arts. *Business and the Arts* (1970), essentially a publicity document, provided a means for the BCA to communicate its message. From the outset, the general gist of the BCA has provoked criticism. Thomas Guback interpreted corporate sloganeering as "the good community-minded citizens hides the ultimate nature of its policies" namely that profits can be counted "in dollars as well as goodwill"; furthermore, he voiced concern over the formalization of a nexus in which "the same men are running both spheres":

> While no sphere in society can remain entirely insulated from or insensitive to others, there is a difference between independently-activated response and the kind of cooperation bred and initiated by power and control. Especially now it is untenable that one institution should further extend its influence in monolithic fashion. (Guback 1970: 132, 134)

The BCA provided the model for like-minded organization in other countries: the Council for Business and the Arts in Canada (CBAC) was established in 1974; and, in the United Kingdom, the Association for Business Sponsorship in the Arts (ABSA)–now called Arts & Business (A&B)–was established 1976. Both the Canadian and British organizations have missions and membership requirements that are similar to those espoused by the BCA. The most significant impact of these organizations in promoting business alliances has been to inculcate the current "arts industry" environment: big business feels comfortable supporting the arts, arts organizations deem support by big business as an essential ingredient for financial success; and target audiences are made aware of the corporate contribution to cultural life. For example, the BCA estimated total American business sponsorship of the arts in 1967 at $22 million; thirty years later the figure was $1.2 billion.

At its inception, the BCA articulated to Fortune 500 firms the advantages of closer business dealings with the arts: improving corporate image, increasing sales, aiding recruitment, and attracting industry to an area were cited as direct benefits; at the same time, indirect business benefits to employees, the community, and society as a whole were also perceived. Social benefits came under the broad banner of corporate responsibility (e.g., helping to alleviate the problems of the under-privileged and the plight of the inner city). The seemingly diverse range of benefits reflected concerns being voiced during the 1960s in the U.S. Business corporations, like many established institutions, were criticized for being removed from the economic and social crises plaguing larger urban cities. Equally, there was a conspicuous wane in the confidence in American business. Arts sponsorship was presented as one relatively inexpensive way of regaining public support. Furthermore there are the often undisclosed personal benefits to the senior executives who make decisions about business support to the arts such as accumulating social prestige and displaying "good taste" (e.g., Bourdieu and Haacke 1995).

Altruism and enlightened self-interest are two general positions that can be discerned in statements made by the BCA. The altruistic stance addresses social benefits by recognizing that corporations have "assumed a central role in industrial society that the military organization or the religious community has occupied at other times and in other places" (Strum 1985: 158). Corporate power must be used to pursue profits to ensure economic viability. However, corporations do not exist by divine right: "The corporation like the Sabbath, was not made for its own survival. Its legitimacy depends on whether its meaning is truly representative of the meaning of life itself" (Strum 1985: 158). With an enlightened self-interest perspective the firm garners more tangible benefits without necessarily forfeiting broader societal concerns since "increasing sales and spreading goodwill will no longer be mutually exclusive objectives but can be goals which complement each other" (Mescon and Tilson 1987: 59). For example, "museum-goers tend to be affluent, well educated, upscale consumers . . . the very audience that corporations want to target" (Glennon 1988: 39). According to Arnold Edinborough, founder of CBAC, the link between corporate sponsorship and marketing is strong:

It is the marketing aspect of sponsorship which has brought business to the fore again in the arts. It is, in fact, the success of sponsorship which makes people believe business is involved as never before. (Edinborough 1987: 9)

The links between corporations and large, metropolitan-based art museums are well-established. For example, the inaugural meeting of the BCA, in January 1968, under the chairmanship of C. Dillon Douglas was convened at the Metropolitan Museum of Art (Met), where Dillon was a trustee. Given the Met's stature, it attracted the most socially prominent and financially powerful individuals in New York. It is not surprising that the Met established the first Corporate Patrons Program, in the mid-1970s, a most visible venture under the auspices of its Business Committee. "The business behind the art knows the art of good business" was the pitch for the Corporate Patrons Program which served to promote the benefits of membership:

Many public relations opportunities are available at The Metropolitan Museum of Art through sponsorship of programs, special exhibitions and services. These can often provide a creative and cost effective answer to a specific marketing objective, particularly where international, governmental or consumer relations may be a fundamental concern. (Metropolitan Museum of Art n.d.)

Whereas art museums in the U.S. have been hustling to attract corporate money, the sponsorship of temporary exhibitions is a relatively recent activity at most British arts institutions. For example, the Tate Gallery's first example of exhibition sponsorship did not occur until 1982 (with support from S. Pearson and Son for an exhibition by the popular Victorian-era painter Sir Edwin Landseer). Prominent sponsors of the Tate–like British Petroleum (for New Displays, the annual rehang of the permanent collection, started in 1990) and British Nuclear (for the Turner Scholarships)–represent the accepted pattern of museum-corporation relations as they have developed in the U.S. since the 1960s:

In an era of heightened consciousness of public relations, image building is the most powerful incentive behind corporate museum patronage. Since sponsorship of temporary exhibitions provides the most exposure, it's not accidental that, historically, the biggest funders have been those with image problems. (Glennon 1988: 39)

In practice, arts organizations seldom refuse corporate sponsors based on the corporation's business activities. The director of the Tate during the ascendancy of corporate sponsorship, Alan Bowness (1980-88), remarked: "We have only discriminated against sponsorship by tobacco companies partly because the government itself takes a different attitude to this form of advertising" (cited in Coombs 1986: 3).

HANS HAACKE ON CORPORATE PATRONAGE

The advocacy group Adbusters is dedicated to making us resist "those who pollute our minds" by engaging in "culture jamming" (see *www.adbusters.org*). An example of proactive resistance is expressed by the contemporary visual artist Hans Haacke, who has criticized the closer links between the interests of large business enterprises and art museums. Haacke's critique complements Erik Barnouw's *The Sponsor* (1978), and has much in common with what sociologist Herbert Schiller describes as "the corporate takeover of public expression" (Schiller 1989). Haacke's work adopts a media-savvy orientation, as he readily acknowledges in a public dialogue with sociologist Pierre Bourdieu:

> One can learn a lot from advertising. Among the mercenaries of the advertising world are very smart people, real experts in communication. It takes practical sense to learn techniques and strategies of communication. Without them, it is impossible to subvert them. (Haacke in Bourdieu and Haacke 1995: 107)

Since the cancellation of a proposed solo exhibition at the Guggenheim Museum in 1971–viewed by many as an act of censorship by the Guggenheim–Haacke has devoted himself to exposing what he feels to be an unhealthy alliance between the arts and multinational enterprises:

> In the '60s the more sophisticated among business executives of large corporations began to understand that the association of their company's name–and business in general–with the arts could have considerable and long-term benefits, far in excess of the capital invested in such an effort. (Haacke 1981: 56)

Haacke discusses patronage as "a tool for the seduction of public opinion":

I think it is important to distinguish between the traditional notion of patronage and the public relations maneuvers parading as patronage today. Invoking the name of Maecenas, corporations give themselves an aura of altruism. The American term *sponsorship* more accurately reflects that what we have here is really an exchange of capital: financial capital on the part of the sponsors and symbolic capital on the part of the sponsored. Most business people are quite open about this when they speak to their peers. Alain-Dominique Perrin, for example, says quite bluntly that he spends Cartier's money for purposes that have nothing to do with the love of art. (Haacke in Bourdieu and Haacke 1995: 17-18, 17; italics in the original)

Of course, one is able to discern in Haacke's sentiments a thesis articulated in *Ways of Seeing* (1972) on the relationships between oil painting and publicity:

Any work of art 'quoted' by publicity serves two purposes. Art is a sign of affluence; it belongs to the good life; it is part of the furnishing which the world gives to the rich and the beautiful.

But a work of art also suggests a cultural authority, a form of dignity, even of wisdom, which is superior to any vulgar material interest; an oil painting belongs to the cultural heritage; it is a reminder of what it means to be a cultivated European. (Berger 1972: 135)

Haacke seeks to highlight the contradictions inherent in the business-arts nexus, issues those most involved in forming alliances and collaborations feel are unimportant, or are quick to gloss over. According to Bourdieu, Haacke has "a truly remarkable 'eye' for seeing the particular forms of domination that are exerted on the art world to which, paradoxically, writers and artists are not normally very sensitive" (Bourdieu in Bourdieu and Haacke 1995: 1). Two works are highlighted which seek to offer an intervention, as Haacke puts it:

The more the interests of cultural institutions and business become intertwined the less culture can play an emancipatory, cognitive, and critical role. Such a link will eventually lead to the public to believe that business and culture are natural allies and that a questioning of corporate interest and conduct undermines arts as well.

Art is reduced to serving as a social pacifier. (Haacke cited in Heartney 1990: 53)

On Social Grease (1975) was Haacke's attempt to emphasize the extent to which initiatives by corporations in the arts originate "from the public relations department of a company that wants to project an image of modernity, optimism, efficiency, and reliability" (Sheffield 1976: 122). Integral to the work, and framed as a plaque on an august corporate edifice, was a pronouncement attributed to Robert Kingsley, an Exxon executive: "Exxon's support of the arts serves as a social lubricant. And if business is to continue in big cities, it needs a more lubricated environment." Haacke used *MetroMobiltan* (1985) to draw attention to unease he felt with a specific relationship, namely that between the Mobil Corporation and the Met. Nuanced references were made to the brochure distributed by the Met's Corporate Patron Program and Mobil's activity in supporting recent exhibitions at the museum, including a show of ancient Nigerian art (1980) and works by New Zealand tribal artists (1984). At the same time, Haacke included as part of the piece the justification proffered by Mobil to opposition demands to terminate petroleum supplies to the South African police and military:

> Mobil's management in New York believes that its South African subsidiaries' sales to the police and military are but a small part of its total sales . . . Total denial of supplies to the police and military forces of a host country is hardly consistent with an image of responsible citizenship in that country. (text from *MetroMobiltan* 1985)

From Haacke's perspective, there is the sense that multinational enterprises use the arts as a qualifier of character, hoping that symbolic associations with well-known arts institutions will be more important than the pragmatic description of what the firm produces, and its commercial relationships.

MANAGERIAL IMPERATIVES

The increasing naturalization of commercial practices has taken place such that the new breed of arts managers know no other world apart from entrepreneurial norms of performance. Given the pressures to secure plural sources of funding and the ascendancy of marketing precepts to all types of organizations, business-arts relationships would seem to be straightforward and uncontroversial, characterized as "win-win." But below the immediate surface, most relationships are complex. The arts spectator may receive less attention than is ideal when corporate sponsorship deals, for example, are being negotiated. What compromises to artistic excellence and integrity have to be made given the managerial imperatives faced by arts organizations?

The selected cases have attempted to accentuate matters that are often overlooked if the adopted marketing focus emphasizes *practice* (i.e., how to do it better, as opposed to asking whether it should be done). First, what does using the term consumer add to the arts experience? Is there a changed relationship between the spectator and the arts organization? Is there some loss of trust? Widening participation by making the arts more accessible is viewed as good. But is there a cost? Do artistic tastes that need to satisfy corporate sponsors necessitate flamboyant programming? Is success measured against buoyant attendance figures? Second, as a cultural critic Haacke is wary of corporate clout. He casts a cynical eye over the practical consequences of the position championed by the BCA for business involvement in the arts. Social responsibility and ethical behaviour positions promoted by the BCA are viewed against a model of "corporate productivity" (see, for example, O'Hagan and Harvey 2000) in which business get involved in the arts as a means to enhance the commercial bottom line (as measured by profit) or to preserve corporate power (by seeking to influence political and regulatory decision makers).

One cannot avoid corporate sponsors. Indeed one might argue that arts institutions like the Guggenheim Foundation, with its current "one museum, five locations" banner, are now in the driving seat as global brands on the rise. Globalization in art can be seen to have certain parallels with what is going on in economics. In the post-Cold War environment, art museums, like fast-food and entertainment conglomerates, need satellites and franchises to make a profit, hence the need to invade "empty" cultural spaces (for reasons of cultural tourism and economic regeneration). For example, the Guggenheim's first new site for the twenty-first century is in Las Vegas. Central to the Guggenheim project–the Guggenheim Las Vegas (focusing on travelling exhibitions) and the Guggenheim Hermitage Museum (in partnership with Russia's State Hermitage Museum)–is "The Venetian Resort-Hotel-Casino" complex, in which the chairman, Sheldon Adelson, seeks to establish as the world's largest resort and convention centre under one roof. It represents the only significant collaboration of an art museum and a casino-hotel chain in the U.S. Assumed European connotations of "good taste" and "distinction" are explicit: as suggested by its name, the resort-hotel-casino complex positions itself as "Las Venice" by reproducing some of the 'cultural' features (e.g., Campanile di San Marco and the Rialto Bridge over the Grand Canal–including gondola rides) found in the Italian city-state. According to a spokesman for the Venetian:

> Culture is here to stay. People are finding that as Las Vegas reinvents itself–in dining and in shopping and retail–it's now gaining a worldwide reputation as a place where you can actually seek culture, away from the typical stereotypes that have plagued Las Vegas for a long time. (cited in Ouroussoff 2000)

Of course, this type of context raises problems about the treatment of art and culture in which it becomes another theme for brand values to be exploited.

CONCLUDING REMARKS

By revisiting business and the arts from key contact points, a central implication concerns cultural hegemony and the homogenization of taste. There is a case that institutions trust institutions. Large corporations and metropolitan-based "high" arts organizations (e.g., art museums and opera companies) form alliances, partnerships, or sponsorship arrangements. Does this lead to a greater convergence of what is made available for public consumption? Are some forms of expression and representation squeezed out of the arts marketplace?

At the same time, there are indications that business dealings with the arts are entering new arenas of activity. For example, broadening the reach of the business-arts relationship has started to include an examination of creativity and innovation issues (as part of staff and organizational development). What can business learn from the arts? This, of course, raises issues about the transformative value of the arts and the institutionalization of culture. In the U.K., the first Arts & Business Week, in 2001, focused on the "idea that the creators of wealth and the creators of culture share ideas and experiences with the aim of precipitating more joint projects" (Thorncroft 2001: 20). Will the first decade of the twenty-first century be marked by more significant changes to the cultural landscape than the last forty years of the twentieth century?

REFERENCES

Anonymous. (1986) "Editorial: art history and the 'blockbuster' exhibition," *Art Bulletin* (September): 358.

Barnouw, Erik. (1978) *The Sponsor: notes on a modern potentate*. New York: Oxford University Press.

Barry, Dave. (1997) "Business is weird," *Fortune* (7 July): 199-200.

Bataille, Georges. (1986) "Museums" (1930). Trans. Annette Michelson in *October* 36 (Spring): 25.

Bazin, Germain. (1969) *The Museum Age*. Trans. Jan van Nuis Cahill. New York: Universe Books.

Berger, John. (1972) *Ways of Seeing*. London: BBC and Harmondsworth: Penguin Books.

Bourdieu, Pierre and Haacke, Hans. (1995) *Free Exchange*. Trans. Randal Johnson. Oxford: Polity Press.

Bullock, Alan and Trombley, Stephen., eds. (1999) *The New Fontana Dictionary of Modern Thought*. Third edition. London: HarperCollins.

Brown, Stephen. (1995) *Postmodern Marketing*. London and New York: Routledge.

Coombs, David, ed. (1986) "What price arts sponsorship?" Transcript of debate at the Tate Gallery. London.

Drucker, Peter. (1954) *The Practice of Management*. New York: Harper and Row.

Duchamp, Marcel. (1973) "The creative art," paper presented to the American Federation of Arts (1957). In Gregory Battcock, ed., *The New Art*. New York: Dutton.

Edinborough, Arnold. (1987) "The role that business plays in Canada," *Canadian Speeches* (December): 8-10.

Elsen, Albert. (1986) "Museum blockbusters: assessing the pros and cons," *Art in America* (June): 24-7.

Enis, Ben, Cox, Keith and Mokwa, Michael, eds. (1991) *Marketing Classics: a selection of influential articles*. Eighth edition. Upper Saddle River, NJ: Prentice Hall.

Glennon, Lorraine. (1988) "The museum and the corporation: new realities," *Museum News* (January/February): 37-42.

Gringrich, Arnold. (1970) *Business and the Arts: an answer for tomorrow*. New York: Paul S. Eriksson.

Guback, Thomas. (1970) "Review essay: *Business and the Arts*," *Journal of Aesthetic Education* (July): 131-7.

Haacke, Hans. (1981) "Working conditions," *Artforum* (September): 56-61.

Heartney, Eleanor. (1990) "Haacke's Helmsboro," *Art in America* (May): 53.

Holbrook, Morris. (1999) "Higher than the bottom line: reflections on some recent macromarketing literature," *Journal of Macromarketing* (June): 48-74.

Kellaway, Lucy. (2000) *Sense and Nonsense in the Office*. London: Financial Times.

Klein, Naomi. (2000) *No Logo: taking aim at the brand bullies*. New York: Picador.

Kotler, Philip. (1972) "The generic concept of marketing," *Journal of Marketing* (April): 46-54.

Kotler, Philip and Levy, Sidney. (1969) "Broadening the concept of marketing," *Journal of Marketing* (January): 10-15.

Levitt, Theodore. (1960) "Marketing myopia," *Harvard Business Review* (July/August): 45-60.

Mescon, Timothy and Tilson, Donn. (1987) "Corporate philanthropy: a strategic approach to the bottom-line," *California Management Review* (Winter): 49-61.

Metropolitan Museum of Art. (nd) "The business behind art knows the art of good business." Pamphlet. New York.

Morgan, Glenn. (1992) "Marketing discourse and practice: towards a critical analysis." In Mats Alvesson and Hugh Willmott, eds., *Critical Management Studies*. London: Sage.

O'Hagan, John and Harvey, Denice. (2000) "Why do companies sponsor arts events," *Journal of Cultural Economics* 24/3 (August): 205-24.

Ouroussoff, Nicolai. (2000) "Venetian Hotel, Guggenheim in talks for museum brand," *Reno Gazette-Journal* (14 July) online at *www.rgj.com*

Rockefeller Panel Report. (1965) *The Performing Arts: problems and prospects*. New York: McGraw Hill.

Schiller, Herbert. (1989) *Culture Inc.: the corporate takeover of public expression*. New York and Oxford: Oxford University Press.

Sheffield, Margaret. (1976) "Hans Haacke," *Studio International* (March/April): 117-23.

Strum, Douglas. (1985) "Corporate culture and the common good: the need for thick description and critical interpretation," *Thought* (June): 141-60.

Thorncroft, Antony. (2001) "Looking beyond the cheque," *Financial Times* (5 March): 20.

Tusa, John. (1997) "For art's sake," *Prospect* (January): 36-40.

Vinaver, Michel. (1997) *Plays I (Overboard; Situation Vacant; Dissent, Goes Without Saying; Nina, That's Something Else; A Smile on the End of the Line)*. Ed. David Bradby. London: Methuen Drama.

Wallis, Brian, ed. (1986) *Hans Haacke: unfinished business*. New York: New Museum of Contemporary Art and Cambridge, MA: MIT Press.

Williams, Raymond. (1976) *Keywords: a vocabulary of culture and society*. London: Fontana.

_____. (1980) "Advertising: the magic system," *New Left Review* (1960). Reprinted in Williams, *Problems in Materialism and Culture*. London: Verso.

www.adbusters.org [Adbusters]

www.aandb.org.uk [Arts & Business]

www.bacinc.org [Business Committee for the Arts, Inc.]

When Soloists Form a Choir: Communication Requirements of Sustainability Networks

Christiane E. Pfeiffer

SUMMARY. In this paper sustainability-oriented intersectoral collaboration is studied with a focus on communication aspects. In contrast to earlier contributions in literature, the major perspective here is not how the marketers involved can use such a partnership as an effective communications tool. Rather the sustainability network itself is seen as pluralistic actor who strives for optimizing its comunication both to internal and external target audiences. Drawing on results from a qualitative case study of a sustainability network, requirements of intersectoral communication are determined. These sets of demands comprise the basis for the elaboration of a network communication design in the future. *[Article copies available for a fee from The Haworth Document Delivery Service: 1-800-HAWORTH. E-mail address: <getinfo@ haworthpressinc.com> Website: <http://www.HaworthPress.com> © 2003 by The Haworth Press, Inc. All rights reserved.]*

KEYWORDS. Sustainability networks, intersectoral collaboration, sustainability communication, integrated network communications

Christiane E. Pfeiffer, MA, is Doctoral Candidate, University of Hannover/Department of Marketing I, Hintergasse 3, D-69469 Weinheim, Germany (E-mail: Christiane.Pfeiffer@t-online.de).

[Haworth co-indexing entry note]: "When Soloists Form a Choir: Communication Requirements of Sustainability Networks." Pfeiffer, Christiane E. Co-published simultaneously in *Journal of Nonprofit & Public Sector Marketing* (Best Business Books, an imprint of The Haworth Press, Inc.) Vol. 11, No. 1, 2003, pp. 167-193; and: *Nonprofit and Business Sector Collaboration: Social Enterprises, Cause-Related Marketing, Sponsorships, and Other Corporate-Nonprofit Dealings* (ed: Walter W. Wymer, Jr. and Sridhar Samu) Best Business Books, an imprint of The Haworth Press, Inc., 2003, pp. 167-193. Single or multiple copies of this article are available for a fee from The Haworth Document Delivery Service [1-800-HAWORTH, 9:00 a.m. - 5:00 p.m. (EST). E-mail address: getinfo@haworthpressinc.com].

167

INTRODUCTION

Cooperation between multiple actors has steadily gained relevance around the turn of the century. Economic globalization and an increasing pressure on companies as well as on regions competing as business locations have led to a higher interest in collaborating. Also more and more complex social and ecological issues have fostered joint action of different societal groups which employ their various resources, competencies, and expertise for solving the common problem (Hartman, Stafford and Polonsky 1999, p. 168). Collaboration on such sustainability topics has grown dynamically in recent years–a development that has been given a strong impetus by the Earth Summit in Rio in 1992 where the political call for intersectoral collaboration as a step towards the solution of global development problems entered the public debate.

The increasing interest of practitioners and the emerging empirical evidence of sustainability-related intersectoral cooperation are reflected in the growing body of literature in the recent decade. Various terms have been coined addressing the empirical phenomenon for instance as "collaborative alliances" (Gray and Wood 1991), "environmental partnerships" (Long and Arnold 1995), societally oriented cooperations ("Gesellschaftsorientierte Kooperationen," Brockhaus, 1996), "green alliances" (Hartman and Stafford 1997), "intersectoral partnering" (Charles, McNulty and Pennell 1998), and "new social partnerships" (Copenhagen Centre 2000).

However, in numerous cases the focus of related studies remains limited to dyadic relationships thus neglecting more complex forms of collaboration. In contrast, authors like Rowley or Gemünden and Ritter underline the importance of the network perspective for matching the empirically present interconnectedness of one organization's various relationships with external partners (Rowley 1997, p. 894; Gemünden and Ritter 1997, p. 294).

As a consequence, the study that forms the basis for this paper takes a network perspective when examining intersectoral partnerships in the field of sustainable development. Therefore, the term *sustainability networks* is used comprising:

> voluntary, mid- to long-term oriented cooperations with a polycentric organizational structure in which different actor groups combine their expertise and specific organizational resources try-

ing to jointly solve societal problems that are related to a sustainable development.

The rather new concept of sustainability networks (Halme and Fadeeva 1998, pp. 2, 4; Pfeiffer 2001, pp. 2, 6) not only meets the demand for a network perspective. It also allows one to take a macro perspective; thus exceeding the still-prevailing preferential treatment of a single member's viewpoint be it a corporate actor or a non-governmental organization. Instead, the concept distinguishes the macro perspective of the network as an organizational entity from the micro perspective of its various member organizations. This differentiation is important, since a network acts as such within the environment in which it is embedded. However, its member organizations' interests, goals, and behavior may deviate to a greater or lesser degree. Therefore, this level must also be considered in order to draw a comprehensive picture of the factors that are acting within the network.

The interaction of the actors in sustainability networks is examined here with a special focus on the communication aspect. While marketing literature offers various approaches of how to design a single organizational entity's communications, communication recommendations for intersectoral collaborations like sustainability networks are still underdeveloped. A network communication design that is to fill this gap has to meet specific requirements. These requirements ensue, firstly, from the distinctive background of the actors who collaborate, secondly, the structure of the network, and thirdly, the general features of sustainability-related communication of organizations.

It is the aim of this paper to determine these various requirements as a vital step towards a communication design for sustainability networks. In other words, the question to be answered is, which specific demands arise when soloists join their voices and form a choir in order to perform the song of Rio.

METHOD OF THE STUDY– GROUNDED IN EMPIRICAL DATA AND CASE STUDY ORIENTED

As literature so far provides little knowledge of the subject, a qualitative-explorative approach was chosen. An iterative methodology was viewed as most appropriate, taking up a basic idea from grounded theory developed by Glaser and Strauss (1967). In contrast to the rather linear logic of deduction and induction, grounded theory is based on a cyclic research process–following a categorization by Norman Blaikie–i.e., an abductive research strategy (Blaikie 1993, p. 176). The "[. . .] back-and-forth interplay with data [. . .]" (Strauss and Corbin 1994, p. 282; Pidgeon and Henwood 1997, p. 87) is typical for the methodology and fosters the practical relevance of the research. Consequently, grounded theory constitutes one of the two pillars of the research design of this study.

Case studies are seen as useful instrument for the identification of relevant determinants and the interpretation of factor interdependencies (Mayring 1996, p. 28). Especially relevant here is the strength of case study research when it comes to considering context conditions (Yin 1994, pp. 8-9, 13). Thus, it was chosen to constitute the second pillar of the research design.

The combination of both pillars had been put in concrete terms for instance by Kathleen M. Eisenhardt (1989) whose description of a case study research process was taken as basis. Figure 1 visualizes this approach in form of a hermeneutical spiral (e.g., Danner 1998, p. 57; Mayring 1996, p. 18).

Multiple data collection methods were employed in order to enable triangulation (Yin 1994, pp. 91-94; Eisenhardt 1989, p. 538). The key sources were the following:

- Network documents and archives such as press releases, brochures, reports, homepages, and member lists (unless otherwise noted all translations of originally German documents are the author's).
- Tape-recorded and subsequently transcribed semi-structured interviews with network actors who were identified on the basis of theoretical considerations, i.e., theoretical sampling (Strauss and Corbin 1994, p. 275). (The interviews were conducted in German language; the author's subsequent translation into English was validated by the focal network coordinator of Living Lakes.)
- Observations of network events like member meetings and press conferences.

Theoretical coding laid the foundation for the interpretation of the data in the ongoing iterative research process (Strauss and Corbin 1994, p. 280).

THE CASE LIVING LAKES–
A GLOBAL NETWORK
FOR THE PROTECTION OF FRESHWATER RESOURCES

The case selected to discuss the central research question and to provide relevant insights was *Living Lakes,* an ongoing worldwide partnership between

- international and national environmental non-governmental organizations (ENGOs),
- companies, both global players and small and medium-sized enterprises (SMEs),
- and administrative actors.

Living Lakes was initiated by the two ENGOs German Environmental Fund ("Deutsche Umwelthilfe," abbreviated to DUH) and the international Global Nature Fund (GNF) as follow-up and expansion of a regional partnership around Lake Constance, Central Europe's second largest freshwater lake on the borders of Austria, Switzerland, and Germany (Living Lakes 1999b). Living Lakes is still GNF's most important project, and the organization serves as the focal coordinator of the network (GNF 2000, p. 5). In June 1998 Living Lakes was publicly launched at a press conference in Los Angeles (GNF n.d., p. 2).

The network's mission is to promote "voluntary international collaboration among organizations that carry out projects benefiting lakes, wildlife, and people [. . . and thus to support the] conservation and restoration of lakes by moving Agenda 21 from paper to practice" (Living Lakes 1999a). The goals towards which support is directed include all dimensions of sustainability with the environmental one at the center. The principal objectives are described as follows (Living Lakes 1999a):

- Permanent protection of natural resources and lake watersheds.
- Environmentally friendly economic activities and structures.
- Cooperation among multiple actors, i.e., citizens, non-governmental organizations, government authorities, and businesses.

In the three years of its existence the network has grown from initially four member lakes, among these the Californian Mono Lake, to currently 19 partner regions around lakes on four continents.

FIGURE 1. The Iterative Case Study Research Process

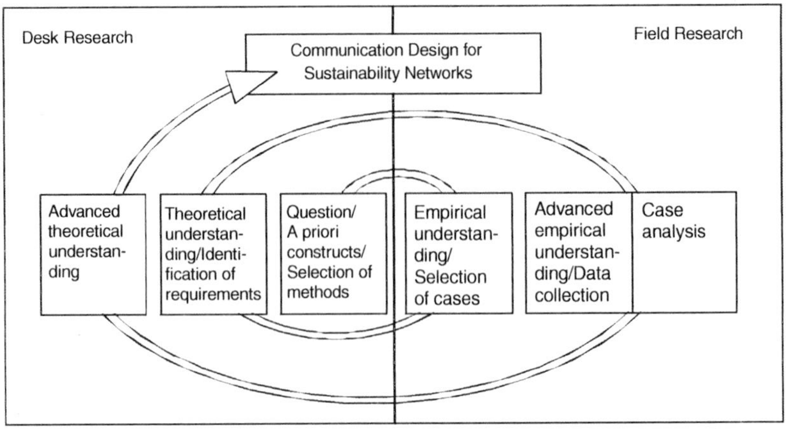

SUSTAINABILITY NETWORKS–
WHEN DIFFERENT CULTURES COLLABORATE

There are a number of theoretical approaches that are helpful for understanding the dynamics that lie beneath the structure and process of sustainability networks, such as collaboration theory (e.g., Gray 1989), stakeholder theory (e.g., Freeman 1984; Polonsky 1996), relationship marketing with its focus on lateral relationships (e.g., Morgan and Hunt 1994), resource dependence theory (e.g., Pfeffer and Salancik 1978), network theory (e.g., Håkansson and Snehota 1995; Nohria and Eccles 1992; Sydow 1992), and the organizational culture approach (e.g., Martin 1992; Crane 2000). For this paper, desk research was primarily concentrated on collaboration theory, the commitment-trust theory of relationship marketing, and the organizational culture approach. With regard to its relevance for communication-related aspects, the latter guided the investigation of the different actors in the network.

Collaboration theorists emphasize that the actors to be involved are those who have a legitimate stake in the issue that forms the core of the network (Gray 1989, pp. 64, 121). In the case of Living Lakes these were communities, NGOs, and companies that are active on and around one lake, with the latter two being the key actors. Subsequently, both societal groups shall be depicted in more detail.

Among the ENGOs the DUH and the GNF play the most prominent roles since they initiated and respectively coordinate the network. Both are based in Southern Germany and have strong personal links. Interestingly, GNF was co-founded by the DUH in order to serve the global expansion of the Living Lakes network better than a nationally operating organization like DUH had been able to–a clear sign that the internationalization process has reached the NGO sector.

The DUH itself was one of the first NGOs that cooperated with businesses in Germany, i.e., it paved the way for a market-based environmentalism in the German context (for a discussion of market-based environmentalism versus the command and control model see, e.g., Livesey 1999). While other organizations had been hesitant to collaborate with "the enemy," the DUH established close working relations with industry, e.g., by consulting Lever Germany during the product development process of an environmentally friendlier detergent ("Skip"; GNF 1998c, p. 4).

> I'm convinced that the truly successful way is to go for compromises in specific cases and to try to co-design something rather than stay in a distance and criticize it altogether. It is better to move a little step forward–but to move–than only theoretically demand that somebody else should do it. That is too simplistic and from my point of view also too convenient. (DUH, director; the names of the interviewees are kept anonymous for confidentiality reasons)

This early partnership proves that one of the most important assets of NGOs is their expertise in a specific field alongside with their sensibility for public issues. As Steve Waddell (1999) of the United States Agency for International Development points out: "NGOs more often have the deepest understanding about specific communities–both geographic and interest-based–because NGOs are particularly focused upon community values, structures and relationships."

A second competitive advantage of NGOs is their high public credibility (Mendleson and Polonsky 1995, p. 10; Meffert and Kirchgeorg 1998, pp. 99, 102). Their ability for "trust generation" (Waddell 1999) is a key to attract companies to partner with ENGOs. It is the basis for NGOs' societal legitimacy which in turn is decisive for public support, the commitment of volunteers, and of donors. Thus, it is existentially relevant for NGOs. For the GNF, for instance, in 1999 more than

€435,000 (approx. $370,000) of its €500,000 (approx. $425,000) income was from donations (GNF 2000, p. 20).

Furthermore, as long as journalists accept NGOs as a trustworthy source of information the high credibility can guarantee NGOs access to the media–an aspect that is central to the communication side of sustainability networks.

> Media representatives are very sensitive, they don't want to be abused as a public relations agency. This is why NGOs have an advantage, because journalists say: "What they do is for a good purpose, they don't want to sell us a product." This credibility is essential–and so is its fostering. Therefore it is extremely important how the organization works and what it gets involved in. (GNF, project coordinator)

These last remarks emphasize that in order to maintain credibility and thus also influence, NGOs must carefully avoid any impression of sell-out for non-altruistic motives (Handelman and Arnold 1999, p. 35; Heap 2000, p. 67). The risk of being perceived as giving up goals and values is inherent in most intersectoral partnerships (Stern and Hicks 2000, pp. 18-19; Hartman and Stafford 1997, p. 190). NGOs that aim at preserving their public watchdog image have to keep an arm's length relationship to other actor groups. Such a distant position enables them to take more radical, "truly environmentalist" positions. As Simon Heap (2000, p. 17) underlines in his study of NGO engagement with business, "[i]t is easier for NGOs to maintain coherency of approach in attacking a problem than to get consensus on the best way to solve it."

This is a main argument for NGOs that prefer conflictual strategies to cooperative ones (Hey and Brendle 1994, p. 169). For such organizations John Elkington and his colleagues from SustainAbility coined the term "polarisers" dichotomically differentiating them from "integrators" (Elkington and Fennell 2000, p. 158). Those NGOs that follow the integrator strategy face the described dilemma of having to balance independence and compromising their position. In the Living Lakes case, GNF attempted to solve this problem through a limitation of formal membership to NGOs and public authorities: In the language of the network the companies involved are not "members." They are rather referred to as "global partner" in the case of Unilever and as "supporters" in the cases of Compaq, Conica Technik, DaimlerChrysler, Gruner +

Jahr, Lufthansa, natur & kosmos, Ökobank, Rohner, and Saeco (Living Lakes 2000).

> We have limited our business partners' status to the one of a global partner and of supporters respectively mainly for credibility reasons: Environmental projects are our core competence and in turn, we respect that our business partners have a high competence in their fields. We listen to them and we want to achieve improvements with them. However, the overall control over the environmental projects remains with us, as they have the overall control when it comes to their core competencies. (GNF, member of presidency)

The sponsorship explicitly excludes options of product endorsements. This is because that could mean "skating on thin ice since the environmental organization then publicly holds a position on a specific product" as the Living Lakes project coordinator with GNF emphasized in the interview. Furthermore, as non-members the Living Lakes business actors are not entitled to vote in network elections, e.g., on the admission of new member regions. However, their voice is heard during the proposal and application process. This is especially evident for Unilever.

> Canada and Turkey were concrete suggestions by Lever. They said: "We are active in these countries, from our point of view it would be desirable if there was a Living Lakes project established. We would be willing to support it if you like." (GNF, project coordinator)

> It is fascinating when national Lever companies approach us and propose a lake for membership. We start to check it according to our criteria. And then for instance the chairman of Lever Turkey personally hosts the application team and starts to keep his fingers crossed for them being accepted as new Living Lake. (GNF, member of presidency)

Firstly, this impingement on the network is based on the financial power of the economic partners and their societal impact: They are important contributors to the network's monetary resources and help the NGOs to exert pressure on political decisions in the lake areas. In the

Appendix an example is given for how these assets of the business partners have a share in synergistically achieving the network's goals.

Secondly, the openness of the member NGOs to let companies like Unilever influence network affairs is the result of a long-lasting partnership in which the business partners have already proved their trustworthiness, commitment, and win-win-orientation, i.e., a cooperative attitude. This is not easy to achieve since the economic community is still considered to take the market logic as its fundamental guideline (Waddell 1999): "Businesses' primary playing field is with economic systems where owners are given pre-eminent power and the principle [*sic*] mechanism to induce people to do what an organization desires is through monetary (remunerative) rewards."

Recent years, however, have seen the rise of environmental and social responsibility and a shift towards a more proactive approach which is not only driven by positive economic incentives but also by less measurable factors like the improvement of the company's image and the relationships with its stakeholders (Hastings 1999, p. 2; KPMG 1998, p. 5).

Unilever can be seen as pursuing such a market based environmentalist approach. An ecological or sustainable orientation is chosen following strategic considerations as it becomes obvious in the statement of Anne Weir, manager of community and non-governmental affairs at Unilever:

> [. . .] we are determined to find solutions because we recognise that the prospects for our business are intimately linked with society's ability to build a more sustainable future. (Weir 2000, p. 118)

If the core goal of the sustainability network is congruent with the company's image and behavior, credibility can be transferred from the NGO to the business partner (for a detailed discussion see Stafford and Hartman 2000). This is a major incentive for companies to commit to such intersectoral collaborations as the following quotation illustrates; it is taken from a speech given by Sabine Tandela, director of the environmental division of Lever Fabergé Germany, on a Living Lakes meeting:

> What do we at Unilever understand as the project's success? By supporting such projects Unilever gains credibility in the environmental community, it proves that the company exceeds its core field of activities and takes on social responsibility. (Tandela, 1999, pp. 18-19)

Following the new impetus that movements like the World Business Council for Sustainable Development and the Global Reporting Initiative have given, the economic actors' understanding of sustainability is being widened beyond the environmental dimension. The triple bottom line is set as a more comprehensive orientation for business activities in the field (European Communications Consultants n.d.).

Still the entrepreneurial time horizon is dominated by short- to medium-term investment and amortization cycles. This leads to discrepancies with the requirements of sustainability-related activities. In contrast, NGOs typically have to be long-term oriented: Their goals–like the protection of natural resources–are only achievable in the long run and thus need strategic, continuous activity. This also affects the collaboration of the actor groups in sustainability networks.

> One of the most serious problems in the cooperation is long-term orientation. Companies consider a time span of one or two years in their planning, sometimes with an option for a third year. For such projects, however, we need certainty for five years. Business partners find it very difficult to tie themselves down for such a long period. (GNF, member of presidency)

In recent years, the relationship marketing debate has helped to shed some light on long-term orientated bonds between organizations and their environment. Ties to socio-political forces like NGOs are understood as relevant for economic success. Thus, looking at public policy as a new dimension of management Rogene Buchholz (1992, p. 13) demands from future business managers that "[t]hey must be concerned about the long-range survival and performance of the organization and be aware that this long-range outlook involves thinking about public policy issues that may affect the corporation in the future."

At the end of this overview of some of the core organizational characteristics and differences, it must be pointed out that this description had been based on the assumption that each of the actors forms a distinct culture. In her study of organizational culture Joanne Martin has labeled such an approach as "*Integration* perspective" (Martin 1992, p. 12; italics in original). Its emphasis on the actors' diversity that is rooted in sector affiliation and the specific organizational culture raises the question of whether such heterogeneous partners can cooperate successfully (Crane 2000, p. 169). The discussion of the issue of cultural clash versus cultural fit in literature leads to two core, yet paradoxical insights

(Child and Faulkner 1998, pp. 233, 242; Long and Arnold 1995, p. 54; Ibarra 1992, pp. 180-181):

1. *Opposites attract*: The variance between the distinct sets of organizational backgrounds and hence, e.g., competencies makes partnering attractive (e.g., Waddell 2000). It gives access to complementary resources as set forth in detail in resource dependence theory (Pfeffer and Salancik 1978, p. 43).
2. *Birds of a feather flock together*: Like-mindedness makes collaborating easier. It shortens time consuming processes like finding common ground and reduces the probability of tension that stems from contradictory principles or misunderstandings.

On the basis of the study of sustainability networks in six European tourism regions Minna Halme formulates the rule of thumb that "members should be *as diverse as necessary and as similar as possible*" (Halme 2001, p. 112). Diversity should be prevalent with regard to access to resources while goals and personal characteristics should resemble one another (Ibarra 1992, p. 180). Also the commitment-trust theory describes access to attractive resources and similarity of values as a fundamental part of organizational culture as important conditions for the development of relationship commitment and trust which are according to Morgan and Hunt key factors for successful networks (Morgan and Hunt 1994, pp. 25, 34).

John Child and David Faulkner (1998, p. 244) argue in their work on networks and alliances in general that "[t]he more that the cultures of cooperative partners diverge, the more of a challenge it becomes to achieve a 'fit' between them." To optimize this fit is a central task of network management (Hartman and Stafford 1997, p. 192). In the Living Lakes case the focal coordinator lays special emphasis on the phase of bringing both partners together and providing a platform for getting to know each other:

> The first contact should never take place without a facilitator. That doesn't work out. They must get to know each other. This is just like if Martians and terrestrials met–they wouldn't understand each other and would start to beat each other to death. (GNF, member of presidency)

Bridging the perceived cultural diversity hence calls for "cultural mediators" (Crane 2000, p. 174) also referred to as "strategic bridger[s]"

(Stafford, Polonsky and Hartman 2000, p. 125), "linking pins" or "liason[s]" (Tichy, Tushman and Fombrun 1979, p. 508). The cultural mediators should be supported in this role by means of internal network communications. According to Child and Faulkner there are three strategies for a successful coordination of clashing organizational cultures in cooperations (Child and Faulkner 1998, pp. 244-248):

- Synergy, i.e., the attempt of forming a new network culture which equally integrates the diverse member cultures.
- Domination, i.e., dominance of one partner in the area of its key competence which coins the network culture while still considering–yet not fully integrating–the other cultures.
- Segregation, i.e., balancing the different cultural inputs without integrating them but rather pursuing a policy of avoiding potentially conflictual issues.

Concluding from the statement of the GNF member of presidency above, the Living Lakes coordinators have adopted the second strategy. This becomes evident for instance in the mottoes of the so-called Living Lakes Conferences on which network actors meet at least on an annual basis. So in 1999 the conference was headed "Restoring Streams and Lakes–Revitalizing Communities" (Living Lakes 1999c), a title that clearly speaks the language of a nature conservancy NGO. Whereas the motto of the conference in summer 2000, "From Confrontation to Co-operation" (Living Lakes 2000), can be seen as attempt to also consider business culture. The domination strategy is tantamount to steering a middle course in balancing the allocation of scarce (time) resources for the task of cultural coordination on the one hand and potential synergetic advantages that successful bridging can bring about on the other hand.

However, the question of achieving cultural fit between the collaborative partners gains another facet when addressing the issue from Martin's second view on organizational culture, the *"Differentiation perspective"* (Martin 1992, p. 12; italics in original). It assumes that within one organization various subcultures are formed. As Andrew Crane (2000, pp. 171-172) showed in his investigation of the WWF 1995 Plus Group, the identification of such groupings can successfully elucidate collaborative dynamics. In the Living Lakes case it can be proved that within sustainability networks subcultural affiliations can be formed even across organizational sectors:

Mostly I have to deal with the environmentally oriented persons in the partner companies. This is why it [the cross-sectoral collaboration] is so unproblematic. They are the environmental consultants, in many respects they are as committed as we are, they have a similar background and far-reaching goals for the ecological orientation of their company. They are so to speak the outpost of the ecological feasibilities. Therefore, we often have the same ideas and opinions and it is they who say: "Well, probably we won't get that through." (GNF, project coordinator)

Thus, from a differentiation perspective such subcultural similarities concerning goals and personal characteristics can considerably facilitate the internal communication task of cultural mediation. However, the focus of bridging then shifts from the interface between the various actor organizations to intraorganizational interfaces such as between the environmental division of a company and the procurement department.

THE NETWORK STRUCTURE–
JOINT ACTION ON DIFFERENT LEVELS

This last consideration moves the attention on to the network's structure. The sets of dimensions that authors use to describe the structure of a network are quite heterogeneous (Balling 1997, p. 152). However, the constellation of the actors is concurrently discussed as characteristic feature. With regard to the communication situation of a network three aspects are of prior interest:

1. The spatial distance between the various knots of the net,
2. the formation of clusters and different levels, and
3. polycentrism and/or centrality of the network's coordination.

For Living Lakes the first issue means handling a globe-spanning network. This is mainly managed via e-mail and fax contacts, the exchange on the Living Lakes homepage, and at least annual meetings on the Living Lakes Conferences that are hosted in turn by the member regions. The network's international scope raises again the topic of culture, here with an emphasis on national differences.

The second and the third aspect are intertwined: Three levels can be identified in the structure of Living Lakes. On the first two levels, based on both explicit ground rules of the network and implicit interaction structures certain actors gained a hub position. That results in a certain degree of centrality, but on different levels of the network.

First, there is a *macro level* referring to the international umbrella network. On this level there are two main actors: GNF as focal coordinator and Unilever as global partner of the network. This hub position also affects the power structure of the network (Brass and Burkhardt 1992):

> It goes without saying that the one who coordinates has an actual power position. And we also raise the money. But this means that we have to keep in the background when it comes to decisions. If you give rise to the feeling that we don't care about the opinion of the others because it is us who pay the money, then you immediately have dissociation. I would always take the risk that the others reject a proposal we make–the possibility of co-decision must be given! (GNF, member of presidency)

Regional networks around the member lakes form the second or *meso level*. In the case of the initiating region around Lake Constance–like for most lakes–the focal coordinator on the meso level is again an NGO, the Lake Constance Foundation ("Bodensee-Stiftung"). It brings together representatives of companies like Lever Fabergé Germany, and SMEs in the neighborhood of the lake as well as NGOs and administrative authorities from municipalities around the lake. These actors have for instance jointly established eco-camping and solar ferryboats on Lake Constance. The meso level mainly constitutes the network's polycentric character that goes hand in hand with a hub or focal coordinating structure (Sydow 1992, p. 82; Renz 1998, pp. 185-186; Winkler 1999, p. 39).

On the third or *micro level* the single organizational actor becomes the focus of attention. As mentioned, the dissemination of network-related information is not only dependent on bridging interorganizational barriers, but it has also to be managed within each organization. Here the organization's representative in the network has a coordinating function. In the case of Lufthansa for instance the representative of the company in the network is head of the public relations department. This facilitates the dissemination of information on the network through Lufthansa media, e.g., in its board magazines or environmental reports (e.g., Deutsche Lufthansa AG 2000, pp. 20-25). Above all, relationship commitment and thus allocation of organizational resources are dependent on the actor considering the cooperation as important (Morgan and Hunt 1994, p. 23).

Thus, for the support of network activities and of intraorganizational dissemination of network-related information on the micro level persons are needed who are convinced of the network's "core relevance," i.e., of a high overlap of its goals with the organization's own mission (Long and Arnold 1995, p. 59). These "relationship promoters" (Gemünden and Walter 1997, pp. 180-184) simultaneously need access to personal and structural sources of power in order to guarantee the organization's commitment. (In the on-going collaboration the initial conviction that commitment to the network will be worthwhile for the organization must be reinforced by early visible progress to ensure continuity in resource allocation for intra- and interorganizational network activities (Charles and McNulty 1999, p. 14).

With regard to its structure the Living Lakes network has set up a detailed three-step procedure for the admission of new members–from the applicant status via the official candidacy to full membership–that is also explicitly described in network documents (Living Lakes 1999d). In contrast, the structure of the network as such has been formalized to a far lesser degree.

> We have deliberately avoided to define a structure which for instance could suggest a hierarchy and would restrict the development of the network to a certain direction. The network is still very flexible; it is still in its initial phase, still growing. You must be very cautious: Something that is recorded in words is fixed once and for all. This is why we decided to take our time. (GNF, project coordinator)

This experience is backed up in literature. For instance, Jörg Sydow in his work on strategic networks maintains that evolutionary processes are at least as important for the structural development of networks as intentional managerial activities (Sydow 1992, p. 154).

In this sense driven by the personal background and interests of individuals involved in the network, in the Living Lakes case, an informal structure for various tasks has been developed, among these the communication task. Again on the macro level the focal coordinator at GNF plays a central role in coordinating for instance press contacts, or the publication of reports on the Living Lakes Conferences. Actors on the meso level support this work, e.g., by contributions to the joint homepage.

COMMUNICATING ON SUSTAINABILITY TOPICS–
THE POST-RIO CHALLENGE

The content of the messages that are communicated by these means to external target audiences is related to the core goals of the network, i.e. sustainable approaches to the development of life in and around lakes. The topic of sustainability communication, however, is complex. Each of the three dimensions of the sustainability concept–the environmental, the social, and the economic–includes a wide range of issues and has specific difficulties associated with communicating it. Taking the environmental dimension as an example (Hansen and Bode 1999, p. 192; Fuller 1999, p. 224) the following aspects have to be taken into account in the external communication of sustainability networks:

- *Perceptibility:*

  Environmental problems often have a latent character or are not tangible to the lay public, e.g., the decrease of the biodiversity of lakes. In this aspect they differ significantly from many of the environmental problems in the '70s where whitecaps on the rivers, for example, were a very evident sign for pollution. This feature can be transferred as well to the social dimension. For instance, for the majority of Western consumers unjust labor conditions in the Southern hemisphere remain hidden or at least not directly ascertainable.

- *Longevity:*

  Cause and effect of environmentally relevant behavior are often far apart making their immediate relationships hard to perceive and to communicate. For instance, the continuous growth of the demand for drinking water in the area of Los Angeles in the last century and the dropping of the water level of the Mono Lake 300 miles south of the city (GNF 1998b, p. 1).

- *Complexity:*

  The reasons for ecological problems–and this applies equally to the social dimension–are numerous; many actors are involved.

Isolated measures of single companies, institutions, or consumers are not sufficient.

- *Free-Rider:*

  The natural environment is mainly a public good and can also be used by those who do not assist in contributing to the maintenance of the resource (i.e., the free-riders). Thus, personal investment in environmental protection is often not only for individual but also for common benefit which might reduce the willingness to invest. This dilemma also occurs for issues of social or inter-generational justice.

The rules according to which journalists act as gatekeepers and decide on the news value of an event are prone to clash with several of these features of environmental communication, especially with longevity and perceptibility. In one of the interviews a member of the GNF presidency alluded to information on Living Lakes lacking such news value:

There is the principal problem: If we always came up with new horror stories–Madonna suffers incurably from poisoned water–we would be in all gazettes. However, this positive topic is much harder to bring across. It is because if you don't watch carefully, you don't see anything at all. (GNF, member of presidency)

Besides these specific conditions for sustainability-related topics, there are also requirements of external communication in general which must be considered by all organizational entities regardless of their structure being mono- or polycentric as in the case of sustainability networks. These aspects include (Kotler 2000; Bruhn 1997):

- *Strategic planning* with the formulation of the organization's mission, a situation analysis, the definition of short-, mid-, and long-term communication objectives and of strategies for achieving these goals.
- Using a *mix of communications tools* in order to reach the various previously identified target audiences.
- *Making oneself heard* in spite of the information overload in today's society (Kotler 2000, p. 551; Hopfenbeck and Roth 1994, p. 29).
- A *dialogue-orientation* of the communicator, i.e., not an unidirectional but a multi-way interaction with the target audiences.

DISCUSSION–
IMPLICATIONS FOR THE COMMUNICATION
OF SUSTAINABILITY NETWORKS

Complex structures and dynamics are characteristic of networks. As was shown, this is particularly true for intersectoral networks. Thus, "[t]o realize the full benefits of an alliance, the partners need to have means of communicating effectively, efficiently, and frequently" (Austin 2000, p. 86). As the results of the study of cultural differences within sustainability networks suggest, internal communication plays a vital role. It should be directed towards building trust among the partners so that openness and commitment can be fostered. Internal communication can support the understanding of the partners, their way of thinking, basic values and interests, and so paves the way for finding common ground. Subcultural similarities should be identified and emphasized to promote this process.

Particularly, during the "Initiation Phase" (Long and Arnold 1995, p. 11) of a sustainability network face-to-face communication is needed both in formal and informal settings to provide a platform for personal contact. However, especially in dispersed networks like the one presented here, in many occasions electronic media have to replace more direct forms of interaction. On the one hand, this helps saving time and in this way increases the probability of participation. On the other hand, it demands extremely communicative partners that can balance out the higher degree of anonymity of these means of communications. In general, face-to-face communication should be complemented by means of internal communications such as network newsletters.

With regard to the multi-level structure of sustainability networks, relay stations for network messages are needed in order to guarantee dissemination. For this task integrative and committed persons on the macro, meso, and micro levels are required who again are interlinked. Thus, the polycentric structure of the network is mirrored in the structure of its internal communications channels. However, as was shown a distinct structure is the result of many evolutionary processes during the network development. A top down planning would therefore be inappropriate. Rather, an interactive structuring and decision process must be allowed that integrates the opinions and interests of the various partners, i.e., a "down up planning" (Bruhn 1995, p. 118).

Saying this, it becomes evident that within sustainability networks the demand for systematic planning, implementation, and evaluation of organizational communications can only be partially met. The younger the partnership the harder it will be to manage such joint professional communication activities (Austin 2000, pp. 91-92). Sustainability networks that successfully collaborate over a longer period of time may be able to establish the relay stations mentioned above. Besides their important role in internal network communications, they can also take on the responsibility for external network communications–at least as long as their partners legitimize them.

In order to maintain credibility both of the network itself and its members, the independence of all partners needs to be emphasized (Stafford and Hartman 2000, p. 185). The arm's length character of their relationship should be transported to the target audiences in order to prevent any doubts about the NGO's non-venality from arising. Thus, the actor groups involved should strive for being perceived as–though partnering and compromising–still behaving coherently with their particular organizational goals and cultural background. That also includes questions of wording in external communications (see the example of Livesey's (1999) comparison of EDF's and McDonald's way of communicating their partnership to external target audiences), and choice of specific communications channels. Still, on the macro level the network as such gains from this variety on the micro level because in this way its messages can be disseminated more effectively.

With regard to the sustainability-related contents of the communication it became obvious that the perceptibility of the environmentally or socio-economically relevant problem in question must be increased. Slow changes over long periods of time have to be communicated so that they can be grasped more easily. Classical public relations tools can be useful here, for instance the creation of events in order to bundle up long-term developments into a single incident that is more likely to meet the selection criteria of the journalistic gatekeepers (Rossmann 1993, p. 91). Complexity has to be broken down, and in spite of the risk of free-riders, willingness to take individual responsibility must be promoted. Here, it can be helpful to stress the significance of individual action, i.e., sending a well baby appeal in contrast to a sick or starving baby appeal which lays emphasis on the severity of the problem (Obermiller 1995, p. 55; Wiener and Doescher 1995). Stressing added values for the target audiences as well as giving unambiguous orientation can help to increase motivation.

OUTLOOK

In this paper sustainability-oriented collaboration between actors from different societal groups has been studied with a focus on communication aspects. However, in contrast to contributions from sustainable marketing and green alliance literature, the major perspective here was not how the marketers involved can use such a partnership as an effective communications tool. Instead of focusing on a single organization's perspective the sustainability network itself is seen as (pluralistic) actor who strives for optimizing its communication both to internal and external target audiences. This research perspective matches the approach of network management in practice. (The various members of Living Lakes for instance explicitly agreed that the media work of the network has to be improved as an important tool for achieving the collaboration's general lake protection goals (Living Lakes 2000, p. 26.)

Based on grounded case study research various communication requirements could be determined. These demands arise from the characteristics of the actors, the structure of their collaboration and the peculiarities of sustainability-related communication itself. Some of these requirements are not unique to sustainability networks; for instance, multinational companies also have to manage communications within a very dispersed organizational setting, and other innovations also face the problem of intraorganizational dissemination. This offers the chance to learn from other fields. However, such transfer must be carefully handled since it is the combination of requirements that is unique to sustainability networks. In particular the aspect that some of these demands stand in contradiction to one another needs special attention when taking the next step in the research process: finding ways of how sustainability networks can successfully fulfil these requirements, i.e., formulating recommendations for network communications.

The identified sets of requirements suggest that a potential solution lies in the coordinating integration of communication means and activities while still allowing each network actor a certain degree of autonomy. In the ongoing research on internal and external communications of sustainability networks these considerations will be elaborated into a framework of *Integrated Network Communications*. This design will be tailored for sustainability-oriented intersectoral networks. However, it is a secondary goal of future research in the field to examine the design's applicability to non-sustainability topics–so that the choir that is formed can enhance its repertoire beyond the song of Rio.

AUTHOR NOTE

Christiane E. Pfeiffer has studied communication sciences at universities in Germany and Ireland. Having graduated in 1995 she started to work as an environmental journalist for print media in Germany and South America. In 1998, Christiane joined the Department of Marketing I at the University of Hannover leading one of the teams of an EU sustainability research project. In mid-2000 she took up her Ph.D. research project on "Integrated Communications of Sustainability Networks" supported on a scholarship by the German Industrial Research Foundation ("Stiftung Industrieforschung").

The author would like to thank the anonymous reviewers as well as my colleagues and friends who provided valuable feedback on earlier drafts, particularly, Dr. Peter Hayhurst, and Marc H. Pfeiffer. She also wants to express my gratitude for the fruitful exchange with Prof. Dr. Edwin R. Stafford and Prof. Dr. Minna Halme and for the insightful discussions with her supervisor at the University of Hannover/Germany, Prof. Dr. Dr. H. C. Ursula Hansen. Last but not least, her thanks go to the German Industrial Research Foundation ("Stiftung Industrieforschung") for supporting this research project, and the organizations which generously shared their experiences.

REFERENCES

Austin, James E. (2000), "Strategic Collaboration between Nonprofits and Businesses," *Nonprofit and Voluntary Sector Quarterly*, 1 (Supplement), 69-97.

Balling, Richard (1997), *Kooperation. Strategische Allianzen, Netzwerke, Joint Ventures und andere Organisationsformen zwischenbetrieblicher Zusammenarbeit in Theorie und Praxis* [Cooperation. Strategic Alliances, Networks, Joint Ventures, and Other Organizational Forms of Interfirm Collaboration in Theory and Practice], Frankfurt am Main: Peter Lang.

Blaikie, Norman (1993), *Approaches to Social Enquiry*, Cambridge: Polity Press.

Brass, Daniel J., and Marlene E. Burkhardt (1992), "Centrality and Power in Organizations," in *Networks and Organizations: Structure, Form, and Action*, ed. Nitin Nohria, and Robert G. Eccles, Boston: Harvard Business School Press, 191-215.

Brockhaus, Michael (1996), *Gesellschaftsorientierte Kooperationen im ökologischen Kontext: Perspektiven für ein dynamisches Umweltmanagement* [Societally Oriented Cooperations in the Ecological Context. Perspectives for a Dynamic Environmental Management], Wiesbaden: Gabler.

Bruhn, Manfred (1995), *Integrierte Unternehmenskommunikation. Ansatzpunkte für eine strategische und operative Umsetzung integrierter Kommunikationsarbeit* [Integrated Corporate Communications. Starting-points for a Strategic and Operative Application of Integrated Communication Activities], 2nd ed., Stuttgart: Schäffer-Poeschel.

_____ (1997), *Kommunikationpolitik. Bedeutung–Strategien–Instrumente* [Organizational Communications. Relevance–Strategies–Tools], Munich: Verlag Vahlen.

Buchholz, Rogene A. (1992), *Business Environment and Public Policy. Implications for Management and Strategy*, 4th ed., Englewood Cliffs: Prentice Hall.

Charles, Chanya L., Stephanie McNulty, and John A. Pennell (1998), *Partnering for Results. A User's Guide for Intersectoral Partnering. Prepared for the U.S. Agency for International Development for Mission Directors' Conference, November 1998* [online, cited 18 October 2000], available from World Wide Web: ⟨http://www.usaid.gov/pubs/isp/guide.htm⟩.

_____, and Stephanie McNulty (1999), *Partnering for Results. Assessing the Impact of Inter-sectoral Partnering. October 1999* [online, cited 18 October 2000], available from World Wide Web: ⟨http://www.usaid.gov/pubs/isp/handbook/isp2toc.html⟩.

Child, John, and David Faulkner (1998), *Strategies of Co-operation. Managing Alliances, Networks, and Joint Ventures*, Oxford: Oxford University Press.

Copenhagen Centre (2000), *Definition of NSP's* [online, cited 13 May, 2000], available from World Wide Web: ⟨http://www.copenhagencentre.org⟩.

Crane, Andrew (2000), "Culture Clash and Mediation. Exploring the Cultural Dynamics of Business-NGO Collaboration," in *Terms for Endearment. Business, NGOs and Sustainable Development*, ed. Jem Bendell, Sheffield: Greenleaf Publishing, 163-177.

Deutsche Lufthansa AG (2000), *Umweltbericht Balance 1999/2000* [Environmental Report Balance 1999/2000], Frankfurt am Main: Deutsche Lufthansa AG.

Deutsche Umwelthilfe (DUH), Director (2000), Interview by the author, tape recording, Hannover, 31 July.

Eisenhardt, Kathleen M. (1989), "Building Theories from Case Study Research," *Academy of Management Review*, 14, 532-550.

Elkington, John, and Shelly Fennell (2000), "Partners for Sustainability," in *Terms for Endearment. Business, NGOs and Sustainable Development*, ed. Jem Bendell, Sheffield: Greenleaf Publishing, 150-162.

European Communications Consultants (n.d.), *Die "Triple Bottom Line" für ein vollständigeres Unternehmensbild* [The "Triple Bottom Line" for a More Comprehensive Corporate Picture] [online, cited 6 April, 2001], available from World Wide Web: ⟨http://www.agenturcafe.de/_sustainability/index_9673.htm⟩.

Freeman, R. Edward (1984), *Strategic Management: A Stakeholder Approach*, Boston: Pitman Publishing Company.

Fuller, Donald A. (1999), *Sustainable Marketing. Managerial-Ecological Issues*, Thousand Oaks: Sage Publications.

Gemünden, Hans G., and Thomas Ritter (1997), "Managing Technological Networks: The Concept of Network Competence," in *Relationships and Networks in International Markets*, ed. Hans G. Gemünden, Thomas Ritter, and Achim Walter, Oxford: Elsevier Science, 294-304.

_____, and Achim Walter (1997), "The Relationship Promoter-Motivator and Co-ordinator for Inter-organisational Innovation Co-operation," in *Relationships and Networks in International Markets*, ed. Hans G. Gemünden, Thomas Ritter, and Achim Walter, Oxford: Elsevier Science, 180-197.

Glaser, Barney G., and Anselm L. Strauss (1967), *The Discovery of Grounded Theory. Strategies for Qualitative Research*, Chicago: Aldine.

Global Nature Fund (GNF) (n.d.), *Living Lakes-Lebendige Seen*, brochure, Radolfzell: Global Nature Fund.

_____ (1998a), *Ausstellung GNF DaimlerChrysler* [GNF Exhibition DaimlerChrysler], exhibition, Radolfzell: Global Nature Fund.

_____ (1998b), *Ausstellung GNF Mono Lake* [GNF Exhibition Mono Lake], exhibition, Radolfzell: Global Nature Fund.

_____ (1998c), *Ausstellung GNF Unilever* [GNF Exhibition Unilever], exhibition, Radolfzell: Global Nature Fund.

_____ (2000), *Jahresbericht 1999* [Annual Report 1999], Radolfzell: Global Nature Fund.

_____, Member of Presidency (2000), Interview by the author, tape recording, Hannover, 31 July.

_____, Project Coordinator (2000), Interview by the author, tape recording, Hannover, 31 July.

Gray, Barbara (1989), *Collaborating. Finding Common Ground for Multiparty Problems*, San Francisco: Jossey-Bass.

_____, and Donna J. Wood (1991), "Collaborative Alliances: Moving from Practice to Theory," *Journal of Applied Behavioral Science*, 27, 3-22.

Håkansson, Håkan, and Ivan Snehota, eds. (1995), *Developing Relationships in Business Networks*, London: International Thomson Business Press.

Halme, Minna, and Zinaida Fadeeva (1998), "Sustainability Networks–Value Added? Preliminary Findings of a Project on Sustainable Tourism," in *Partnership and Leadership. Building Alliances for a Sustainable Future*, CD-ROM, ed. The Greening of Industry Network, n.p.: Legambiente/Fondazione Eni Enrico Mattei/ European Partners for the Environment.

_____ (2001), "Learning for Sustainable Development in Tourism Networks," *Business Strategy and the Environment*, 10, 100-114.

Handelman, Jay M., and Stephen J. Arnold (1999), "The Role of Marketing Actions with a Social Dimension: Appeals to the Institutional Environment," *Journal of Marketing*, 3, 33-48.

Hansen, Ursula, and Matthias Bode (1999), *Marketing & Konsum. Theorie und Praxis von der Industrialisierung bis ins 21. Jahrhundert* [Marketing and Consumption. Theory and Practice from Industrialization to the 21st Century], Munich: Verlag Vahlen.

Hartman, Cathy L., and Edwin R. Stafford (1997), "Green Alliances: Building new Business with Environmental Groups," *Long Range Planning*, 30, 184-196.

_____, Edwin R. Stafford, and Michael Jay Polonsky (1999), "Green Alliances: Environmental Groups as Strategic Bridges to other Stakeholders," in *Greener Marketing. A Global Perspective on Greener Marketing Practice*, ed. Martin Charter, and Michael Jay Polonsky, Sheffield: Greenleaf Publishing, 164-180.

Hastings, Marilu, ed. (1999), *Corporate Incentives and Environmental Decision Making. A Case Studies and Workshop Report* [online], Houston: Houston Advanced Research Center [cited 6 June, 2001], available from World Wide Web: (http://www.harc.edu/mitchellcenter/corporations/index.html).

Heap, Simon (2000), *NGOs Engaging with Business. A World of Difference and a Difference to the World*, Oxford: INTRAC.

Hey, Christian, and Uwe Brendle (1994), *Umweltverbände und EG. Strategien, politische Kulturen und Organisationsformen* [Environmental Organizations and the European Community. Strategies, Political Cultures, and Organizational Forms], Opladen: Westdeutscher Verlag.

Hopfenbeck, Waldemar, and Peter Roth (1994), *Öko-Kommunikation. Wege zu einer neuen Kommunikationskultur* [Eco-Communications. Ways to a New Communication Culture], Landsberg/Lech: verlag moderne industrie.

Ibarra, Herminia (1992), "Structural Alignments, Individual Strategies, and Managerial Action: Elements Toward a Network Theory of Getting Things Done," in *Networks and Organizations: Structure, Form, and Action*, ed. Nitin Nohria, and Robert G. Eccles, Boston: Harvard Business School Press, 165-188.

Kotler, Philip (2000), *Marketing Management. The Millennium Edition*, Upper Saddle River: Prentice Hall.

KPMG (1998), *Qualitäts- und Umweltmanagementsysteme bei Dienstleistern und in der Industrie* [Quality and Environmental Management Systems in the Service and the Industrial Sector], Berlin: KPMG.

Livesey, Sharon M. (1999), "McDonald's and the Environmental Defense Fund: A Case Study of a Green Alliance," *The Journal of Business Communication*, 36, 5-39.

Living Lakes (1999a), *About the Living Lakes Partnership* [online], Radolfzell: Living Lakes Partnership [cited 7 December 1999], available from World Wide Web: (http://www.livinglakes.org/partnership.htm).

———— (1999b), *Lake Constance (Bodensee): Austria, Germany, and Switzerland* [online], Radolfzell: Living Lakes Partnership [cited 7 December 1999], available from World Wide Web: (http://www.livinglkaes.org/bodensee/index.htm).

———— (1999c), *Restoring Streams and Lakes-Revitalizing Communities. 3rd "Living Lakes" Conference, Mono Lake, Lee Vining, California, USA, 1-4 October 1999, documentation*, [Radolfzell]: Living Lakes/Global Nature Fund.

———— (1999d), Wie wird man Mitglied im Netzwerk Living Lakes? [How to Become a Member of the Living Lakes Network?] [online], Radolfzell: Living Lakes Partnership [cited 12 June, 2001], available from World Wide Web: (http://www. globalnature.org/livlakes/kandidaten/index.htm).

———— (2000), *From Confrontation to Cooperation. 4th "Living Lakes" Conference, EXPO 2000, Hannover, Germany, 16-17 June 2000*, documentation, [Radolfzell]: Living Lakes/Global Nature Fund.

Long, Frederick J., and Matthew B. Arnold (1995), *The Power of Environmental Partnerships*, Fort Worth: The Dryden Press.

Martin, Joanne (1992), *Cultures in Organizations. Three Perspectives*, New York: Oxford University Press.

Mayring, Philipp (1996), *Einführung in die qualitative Sozialforschung. Eine Anleitung zu qualitativem Denken* [Introduction to Qualitatively Social Research. An Instruction for Qualitative Thinking], 3rd ed., Weinheim: Psychologie-Verlags-Union.

Meffert, Heribert, and Manfred Kirchgeorg (1998), *Marktorientiertes Umweltmanagement. Konzeption–Strategie–Implementierung* [Market-Oriented Environmental Management. Concept–Strategy–Implementation], 3rd ed., Stuttgart: Schäffer-Poeschel Verlag.

Mendleson, Nicola, and Michael J. Polonsky (1995), "Using Strategic Alliances to Develop Credible Green Marketing," *Journal of Consumer Marketing*, 2, 4-18.

Morgan, Robert M., and Shelby D. Hunt (1994), "The Commitment-Trust Theory of Relationship Marketing," *Journal of Marketing*, 3, 20-38.

Nohria, Nitin, and Robert G. Eccles, eds. (1992), *Networks and Organizations: Structure, Form, and Action*, Boston: Harvard Business School Press.

Obermiller, Carl (1995), "The Baby is Sick/The Baby is Well: A Test of Environmental Communication Appeals," *Journal of Advertising*, 2, 55-70.

Pfeffer, Jeffrey, and Gerald R. Salancik (1978), *The External Control of Organizations. A Resource Dependence Perspective*, New York: Harper and Row.

Pfeiffer, Christiane (2001), "Joining Forces, Joining Voices. Insights into the New Concept of Integrated Communications of Sustainability Networks," in *Sustainability at the Millennium. Globalization, Competitiveness & the Public Trust*, CD-ROM, ed. GIN-Asia, Bangkok: Chulalongkorn University.

Pidgeon, Nick, and Karen Henwood (1997), "Grounded Theory: Practical Implementation," in *Handbook of Qualitative Research Methods for Psychology and the Social Sciences*, ed. John T. E. Richardson, reprint, Leicester: BPS Books, 86-101.

Polonsky, Michael Jay (1996), "Stakeholder Management and the Stakeholder Matrix: Potential Strategic Marketing Tools," *Journal of Market Focused Management*, 1, 209-229.

Renz, Timo (1998), *Management in internationalen Unternehmensnetzwerken* [Management in International Interfirm Networks], Wiesbaden: Gabler.

Rossmann, Torsten (1993), "Das Beispiel Greenpeace. Öffentlichkeitsarbeit und ihr Einfluß auf die Medien" [The Example of Greenpeace. Public Relations and Their Influence on the Media], *Media Perspektiven*, 2, 85-95.

Rowley, Timothy J. (1997), "Moving Beyond Dyadic Ties: A Network Theory of Stakeholder Influences," *Academy of Management Review*, 22, 887-910.

Stafford, Edwin R., and Cathy L. Hartman (2000), "Environmentalist-Business Collaborations: Social Responsibility, Green Alliances, and Beyond," in *Advertising Research: The Internet, Consumer Behavior and Strategy*, ed. George Zinkhan, Chicago: American Marketing Association, 170-192.

_____, Michael Jay Polonsky, and Cathy L. Hartman (2000), "Environmental NGO-Business Collaboration and Strategic Bridging: A Case Analysis of the Greenpeace-Foron Alliance," *Business Strategy and the Environment*, 9, 122-135.

Stern, Alissa J., and Tim Hicks (2000), *The Process of Business/Environmental Collaborations: Partnering for Sustainability*, Westport: Quorum Books.

Strauss, Anselm L, and Juliet Corbin (1994), "Grounded Theory Methodology. An Overview," in *Handbook of Qualitative Research*, ed. N. K. Denzin and Y. S. Lincoln, Thousand Oaks: Sage Publications, 273-283.

Sydow, Jörg (1992), *Strategische Netzwerke. Evolution und Organisation* [Strategic Networks. Evolution and Organization], Wiesbaden: Gabler 1992.

Tandela, Sabine (1999), Grußworte [Welcome Statements], in *Recreation and Restoration Erholung und Renaturierung. 2nd "Living Lakes" Conference, Langenargen, Lake Constance, Germany, 5-8 May 1999*, documentation, [Radolfzell]: Living Lakes/Global Nature Fund, 17-19.

Tichy, Noel, Michael L. Tushman, and Charles Fombrun (1979), "Social Network Analysis for Organizations," *Academy of Management Review*, 4, 507-519.

Waddell, Steve (1999), *The Evolving Strategic Benefits for Business in Collaboration with Nonprofits in Civil Society. A Strategic Resources, Capabilities and Competencies Perspective* [online], Providence: The United States Agency for International Development (USAID) [cited 19 April 2001], available from World Wide Web: (http://www.usaid.gov/pubs/isp/resource/evolve.html).

Weir, Anne (2000), "Meeting Social and Environmental Objectives through Partnership. The Experience of Unilever," in *Terms for Endearment. Business, NGOs and Sustainable Development*, ed. Jem Bendell, Sheffield: Greenleaf Publishing, 118-124.

Wiener, Joshua L., and Tabitha A. Doescher (1995), "Green Marketing and Selling Brotherhood," in *Environmental Marketing. Strategies, Practice, Theory, and Research*, ed. Michael Jay Polonsky, and Alma T. Mintu-Wimsatt, New York: The Haworth Press, 343-360.

Winkler, Gabriele (1999) *Koordination in strategischen Netzwerken* [Coordination in Strategic Networks], Wiesbaden: Gabler.

Yin, Robert K. (1994), *Case Study Research: Design and Methods*, 2nd ed., Thousand Oaks: Sage Publications.

APPENDIX

The following incident gives an example for how the business partners support the NGOs in the exertion of political pressure:

In the '90s, Living Lakes member St. Lucia in South Africa was threatened by a planned mining project on its shores. In the environmental report 1999/2000 of the German airline Lufthansa a member of GNF recounts how the company's support of Living Lakes affected political decisions in the South African member region (Deutsche Lufthansa AG 2000, p. 25): "In mid-1995 Lufthansa organized a press trip to St. Lucia. By this means, the case was internationally revealed to the public. And consequently, leading South African politicians and Prime Minister Kwa-Zulu-Natal came to the lake for the first time: When a project is paid attention to on an international level, then it is also taken seriously on a national level." As a result the mining project was stopped.

Index